Chuck Tanner's positivity acted as the perfect tonic to the world's cynicism, toxicity and disruptions. His life inspired all who knew him.
—*Sean Kanan, actor, writer and Emmy Award–winning producer*

—⟆⟆—

Dale Perelman has captured the essence of Chuck Tanner as a player, manager and, most importantly, as a fine human being.
—*Jack Zduriencik, retired general manager of the Seattle Mariners*

—⟆⟆—

The story brought back many pleasant memories—a job well done.
—*Joe Friendly, public relations director for the 1979 Pittsburgh Pirates*

—⟆⟆—

The book clearly divulges the way Chuck Tanner focused on looking for an opportunity to give and not to take.
—*Kent Tekulve, all-time Pittsburgh Pirates save leader*

CHUCK TANNER

AND THE

PITTSBURGH PIRATES

DALE PERELMAN

THE
History
PRESS

Published by The History Press
Charleston, SC
www.historypress.com

Copyright © 2023 by Dale Richard Perelman
All rights reserved

Cover images: Chuck Tanner photograph courtesy of the Pittsburgh Pirates.

First published 2023

Manufactured in the United States

ISBN 9781467154864

Library of Congress Control Number: 2023934783

CONTENTS

Never give in. Never give in. Never, never, never, never—in nothing, great or small, large or petty—never give in, except to convictions of honor and good sense.

—WINSTON CHURCHILL

ACKNOWLEDGEMENTS

Thank you to the dozens of helpers who allowed me to assemble the stories for this Chuck Tanner biography, including his friends, the children of friends, relatives, neighbors and former Major League Baseball managers, executives and players. In alphabetical order, they include Joe Abraham, outfielder and Wampum native Harold "Hank" Allen, Frank Augustine, high school classmates Jack Benninghoff and Sarah Klingensmith Brest, Bill Brown, Judge Francis and Roselee Caizza, Pirates pitcher John Candelaria, Tom Colschen, barber Arsenio "Sammy" Coiro, Pittsburgh minor-league head of scouting Murray Cook, accountant Tom DeLorenzo Jr., NFL football lineman Darrell Dess, neighbor Dan DiFerio, Chuck Dombeck, New Castle Public Library researcher Chris Fabian, friend Chuck Farris, neighbor David "Fuzzy" Fazzone, Bill Fitz, Hank Forney, Pittsburgh second baseman and Houston Astros baseball manager Phil Garner, Dr. Lew Grell, Jeff Grossman, Josh Haims, Director of Pirates Media Relations Dan Hart, University of Pittsburgh basketball All-American Dr. Don Hennon, Jesse Horton, Bob Jackson, Jamie Jones and Andrew Henley of the Lawrence County Historical Society, CPA David Kennaday, attorney Carmen Lamencusa, former Pirates manager Jim Leyland, Dewey Lutz, Craig MacCullough, Cathedral stage manager Bob McKibben, barbershop quartet member Jim McKim, *New Castle News* sportswriter Robert Melder, childhood neighbor Charles Morrone, Bob Naugle, Kirk Olescyski, basketball coach Connie Palumbo, Tanner's Restaurant owner "Gus" Papazekos, Jeff Pitzer, Greg Reynolds, Norm Rigotti, Pittsburgh

Pirates pitchers Don Robinson and Jim Rooker, 1979 Pirates media relations director Joe Safety, Alan and Adam Saginak, Pirates All-Star catcher Manny Sanguillén, Rich Shaffer, Chuck Shira, Dr. Gary Snow, Paul and Victor Stefano, Detroit Tigers scout and youngest son Bruce Tanner, grandson Mat Tanner, All-Star Pirates relief pitcher Kent Tekulve, professional golfer Harry Toscano, Baltimore Orioles manager Dave Trembley, Carol and Ron Valentine, restauranteur Egidio James Vascetti, Pirates pitcher Bob Walk, orthopedic surgeon Dr. Gerald Weiner, Reverend John Yergan, Seattle Mariners general manager Jack Zduriencik and Dr. Lou and Mrs. Pat Zona. I hope I have not forgotten anyone.

This book never could have been completed without the support of my wonderful wife, Michele, who is my number one fan, as well as my two talented children, Sean Kanan and Robyn Bernstein, who both happen to be excellent authors.

I must give a special commendation to my readers, starting with my wife, Michele Perelman; pitcher Kent Tekulve, who spent days with me on the phone reviewing his wonderful relationship with Chuck; 1979 Pirates public relations director Joe Friendly; former general manager of the Seattle Mariners and New Castle native Jack Zduriencik; and Bruce Tanner. I also wish to add the name of J. Banks Smither, my acquisitions editor, who has provided great assistance to this story and my previous four books with The History Press, and my project editor for this book, Ryan Finn.

Some of the stories have been sourced through the internet, newspaper articles, books and official baseball records, but most came through interviews of those who knew Chuck the best. The author may have taken minor license with specific words used, but hopefully the feelings and intentions prove accurate. Most of all, I must thank Chuck Tanner, "Mr. Sunshine," a local New Castle hero whose positive attitude, loyalty to his hometown and wonderful career have made New Castle and all Western Pennsylvania proud.

INTRODUCTION

Whoever wants to know the heart and mind of America had better learn baseball.
—*Jacques Barzun*

A crowd of 21,235 Detroit fans at Tiger Stadium cheered wildly as the home team pounded hit after hit against the visiting Los Angeles Angels on Friday evening, April 27, 1962. The Angels had lost 6–4 to the Cleveland Indians the previous day, leaving them with a 6-7 losing record early in the season. Now in a mound duel, Angels fastball pitcher Ken McBride faced Detroit ace Jim Bunning, the only baseball player ever elected to both the Hall of Fame and the U.S. Senate to date. This would not be McBride's night.

After a scoreless first inning, outfielder Leon Wagner led off the second with a home run to deep right field for the visiting Angels to provide a short-lived lead. The Tigers roared back with a vengeance in their half of the inning. Light-hitting shortstop Dick McAuliffe walked. Catcher Dick Brown, a .244 lifetime batter, followed with a solid single to left. Bunning laid down a perfect bunt to reach first and scratch out a hit, sending Brown to second and landing McAuliffe on third. With the bases loaded and no outs, second baseman Jake Wood grounded out on a fielder's choice, but McAuliffe dashed home to create a 1–1 tie. Brown advanced to third. Center fielder Billy Bruton hit into a fielder's choice, forcing Bunning at second but bringing Brown home for run number two and a second out. Future Hall of Fame right fielder Al Kaline came to the plate and promptly rapped a single to left field, landing the speedy Bruton on second.

Slugging first baseman Norm Cash followed Kaline with a single to center, bringing home Bruton for a third run. Angels manager Bill Rigney had seen all he wanted of McBride. He called in reliever Red Witt to stem the bleeding. The ploy failed.

Detroit's power-hitting left fielder Rocky Colavito greeted reliever Witt with a long double to center, scoring Kaline from third and Cash all the way from first for two of the 112 RBIs he would amass during that season. With two outs and Colavito on second, third baseman Steve Boros reached first on an error, allowing runner Colavito to advance to third. Dick McAuliffe, who had begun the rally with a walk, drove Colavito home with a single to left. Mercifully, Dick Brown popped out to left to end the inning with Detroit holding a commanding 7–1 lead. The Angels' only hit off Jim Bunning had been Wagner's lead-off homer. A walk, an error, five singles and a double in the second proved the prelude to another losing Angels effort.

Manager Rigney, in a foul mood after watching his team getting clobbered, opted to replace Witt, who had given up two hits in just a third of an inning. He yelled down the bench, "Donahue, warm up. You're going in for Witt. Tanner, get ready! You're batting for Witt."

Pinch hitting proved a tough task. Few possessed the skill and calmness to perform this job competitively, but Tanner, an eight-year veteran, thrived on pressure. Baseball DNA surged through his veins, and he spent most of his major-league life as a pinch-hitting specialist. The job required the batter to get off the bench cold, often in a tight situation, and face tough competition. Nonetheless, Chuck retained confidence in his ability to hit, even against top-notch pitchers like Jim Bunning, a star who would put up 19 victories during that 1962 season and 224 over his seventeen-year career.

Chuck had failed to hit in his last four pinch-hit appearances. Although a torn Achilles tendon he suffered from a fall had mended after successful surgery at the hands of Dr. Gerald Weiner, his career had stalled. Age and the lingering results of the injury militated against him. He had lost a step, but his tenacity and willingness made him push his body to its limits and kept him going. He always had given his best, and he intended to continue during this at bat as well.

At the top of the third inning with no outs, down 7 to 1, Chuck faced a formidable opponent, a competitor who would lead the league in strikeouts during three separate years and who had won twenty games in 1957. The odds seemed stacked against an Angels victory, but Chuck intended to do his job and get a hit. He never doubted his ability to bat against major-league talent.

Chuck Tanner. *Pittsburgh Pirates.*

Tanner had performed as a journeyman major leaguer who rarely started. He had played with the Milwaukee Braves, the Chicago Cubs, the Cleveland Indians and now the Los Angeles Angels over the years. He loved every minute of his baseball career and thanked the stars for providing him with the grit, skill and luck to stick it out and play at baseball's highest level. He considered himself a pro, who once led the league in pinch-hitting appearances and also hit a home run on the first pitch of his first at bat. Recently, he had qualified for a major-league pension by the skin of his teeth after appearing in the required number of games. With his future playing time limited by age and injuries, he knew that his days with the Angels soon would end. The team would cut him loose to make room for younger and fresher talent.

Management, the fans and his teammates liked Chuck. He had a great attitude, worked hard and did everything asked of him without complaint. Now at the end of his playing days in a profession he truly loved, he questioned what the future would bring, but at this moment, he concentrated 100 percent on the job at hand. "I've got this," he told himself. "Done this before, I can do it again." He intended to get a hit. He eyed the ball as it approached the plate—a fastball, and Bunning had a great one, one of the best in the majors. With only a millisecond to react, he guessed correctly and swung hard and level, driving a single to right. He chugged to first base as fast as his old legs would take him, smiling to himself—a hit. "Yep, I still have it."

Right fielder Allie Pearson and second baseman Billy Moran followed with routine fly outs. When center fielder Lee Thomas walked, Chuck jogged to second. A Bunning wild pitch moved Tanner to third and put Thomas on second. A walk to Leon Wagner loaded the bases. Chuck sat in prime position to score a run. A homer would put the Angels back into the game, but fate decreed a different ending. The comeback victory was not meant to happen. First baseman Tom Burgess in his second and last year in big-league baseball struck out, stranding Chuck at third. The game ended in a 13–4 Angels drubbing. Chuck had recorded his 231st and last hit in

Chuck Tanner's bat. *Mat Tanner.*

his major-league career. He had experienced a great ride and loved every moment he had spent in the major leagues. Tanner held few regrets.

Even while spending most of his time on the Los Angeles bench, Chuck told everyone who would listen that he was the luckiest man on earth. He had played major-league ball with and against many of the best players in the world—Hall of Famers Hank Aaron, Ernie Banks, Warren Spahn, Eddie Mathews and Minnie Miñoso, to name a few. "I even got paid for it," Tanner joked. He possessed the unique ability to find something positive in even the most negative event. He drank from a half-full glass—rarely a half-empty one. That in a nutshell summed up "Mr. Sunshine."

The end of Tanner's career in the bigs came quickly. He played his last major-league game on May 8, 1962, less than two weeks after his pinch-hit single. He fouled out to third while pinch hitting for right-handed reliever Bob Botz in the fifth inning. After that game, the team sent him to the AAA Dallas–Fort Worth Rangers for the balance of the season, where he led the team with a .315 batting average. Rather than mope about his demotion, he recognized it as part of the game. Without a hint of despondency, Chuck accepted this turn of events as part of baseball. He now envisioned a new and even better future for himself, one that would bring him more fame and fortune and just as much happiness as he had enjoyed as a player. He intended to return to the majors—not as a player, but as a manager.

CHAPTER 1

1928

In good times and bad times, never sacrifice who you are.
—*Cynthia Bailey*

On Wednesday, July 4, 1928, unseasonably wet weather cramped Western Pennsylvania's holiday festivities. Rainstorms pelted New Castle and forced family celebrations to move inside the home. On a brighter note, that same day, Anna Baka Tanner delivered the first of her three sons: Charles William Tanner Jr., a youngster who brought a ray of sunshine to their Stanton Avenue home.

Baby Chuck arrived in a town filled with prosperity during an exciting time. The *New Castle News* reported a cascade of headlines on his birth date. Thirty-six-year-old Canadian American daredevil Joseph Lussier of Concord, New Hampshire, successfully plunged over the Niagara Horseshoe Falls in a 1,026-pound, nine-foot rubber ball. Rescuers fished him from the swirling waters unharmed. He would earn a living during the rest of his seventy-nine-year lifespan signing autographs and selling rubber scraps from his protective device.

Fifty-one-year-old Belgian financier Alfred Lowenstein, supposedly the world's third-richest man, "mysteriously" fell from an airplane and died. The sports page, a local favorite, detailed the results of the previous day's baseball games. The Pittsburgh Pirates—a decent club whose roster included future Hall of Fame players Burleigh Grimes, Paul Waner, Lloyd Waner and Pie Traynor—dropped a double-header to the Cincinnati Reds by lopsided 6–0 and 11–3 scores.

The Roaring Twenties had delivered prosperity throughout the entire country. In Lawrence County, the New Castle Works of Carnegie Steel, Shenango China, Blair Strip Steel and Elliott Steel provided thousands of good paying jobs for one of the state's faster-growing areas. The population ballooned to forty-eight thousand inhabitants. Locals believed that the economy would continue to expand and that this prosperity was a God-given right. The press dubbed the city "Little Pittsburgh" due to the importance of its iron, steel and tin industries.

Impressive buildings dotted the city's landscape. The post office on North Street, the stately First Presbyterian Church on North Jefferson and the Greek Revival courthouse on Court Street testified to the growing stature of New Castle. The recently constructed Scottish Rite Cathedral on Lincoln Avenue, built at a cost of more than $1 million, towered above the downtown and served as a symbol for the euphoria of the times.

The imposing Gothic Revival St. Mary's Church, built in 1925 at the corner of North and Beaver Streets, welcomed the Catholic immigrant population brought to New Castle to furnish labor for the area's plants and limestone quarries. At the top end of the economic scale, upper-crust mansions built for the barons of industry like the Hoyts, the Reis family and the Johnsons lay scattered like mini-castles along the North Hill's better streets.

The community offered much to see and do. The 138-acre Cascade Park on the outskirts of the city included seventeen rides, a lake and a penny arcade. Folks came from nearby towns to sample the park's cotton candy, hot dogs, French fries topped with vinegar and a ride in the rental rowboats.

New Castle's citizens flocked to the movies, especially on weekends. With the advent of *The Jazz Singer*, talkie films became all the rage through the larger cities, but New Castle still showed the silents. Norma Shearer starred in *The Actress* at the Penn Theater, and Douglas Fairbanks headlined *The Gaucho* at the Cathedral to the accompaniment of the auditorium's famous Moller pipe organ.

In the '20s, times proved simpler compared with today. Children spent their free time outside playing baseball, football or basketball in warm weather or skating and sled riding in winter. There were no big-box outlets, televisions, electronic video games, online shopping or internet to keep families in the house. The radio, newspaper and magazines presented all the music, news and stories folks required.

People did not travel to shop like today. They stayed in town. The downtown retail mix in 1928 provided a strong enough selection to satisfy the whims and needs of most, and shoppers remained on a first-name basis with the sales personnel at the local stores.

The July 5 *New Castle News* presented dozens of enticing advertisements. Crowl-Weldon Motors promoted the spiffy Hudson 65 automobile for $1,250, a hefty sum when one considered that a 1924 Ford Tudor sold for just $495. The Durant's starting price of $830 presented an "upscale but economical" touring sedan for the most discerning customer.

My grandfather Jacob F. Perelman promoted the availability of $25 to $300 loans with easy terms to assist those in temporary need of cash. Perelman's Jewelry pictured a diamond-solitaire engagement ring for a mere $29.95. The dollar went far in the '20s.

Pedestrians and cars packed the downtown streets, especially on Monday nights and Saturdays. More and more people drove to shop in their recently purchased automobiles, although for just five cents the trolley would take them to Washington Street, Mahoningtown or the Southside, each providing a substantial selection of retail stores and services.

People generally dressed to the nines to shop downtown. Many men wore a jacket and tie, and women vied with one another for attention by donning the latest in headwear—the cloche, the slouch, the mad cap, beret, wide brim or picture hat to match their fancy outfits. Best of all, for the store owners, the economy soared to a fever pitch. The citizenry had plenty of spare money jingling in their pockets.

Life appeared rich and easy in 1928. New Castle proved quite the place, a developing metropolis, full of fun, theaters, shopping and jobs—a great place for Chuck Tanner to grow up and live. Most of the city's populace danced to the beat of the Charleston, certain that the good times and fast dollars of the '20s would last forever.

CHAPTER 2

THE EARLY YEARS

Children are not things to be molded, but are people to be unfolded.
—*Jess Lair*

Not everyone proved lucky or rich in the '20s. Charles Tanner Sr., Chuck's father, worked as a brakeman and conductor for the Pennsylvania Railroad. He eked out a living, and the Tanner family lived frugally in the area known as the "Fall Track" on Stanton Avenue in Shenango Township, just two hundred yards from the New Castle city line.[1] One neighbor called their tiny two-bedroom house "not much better than a shack." The Tanner household lacked both electricity and indoor plumbing. A single potbellied stove heated the entire house in winter. After dark, oil lamps provided the home's only light.

"There were days I would wake up with snow in my pockets," Chuck Tanner told a reporter for Florida's *Sun Sentinel*. He and his two younger brothers, Bill and Bob, shared a room. Ever the optimist, Chuck recalled, "We were better than some, because we owned a two-holer out back. Some only had one."

By the time Chuck reached ninth grade, his folks had installed running water, although the family still used the outhouse. The Tanners eventually splurged for electricity when Chuck entered tenth grade.

The Tanners' neighbors included his mother's parents, Grandpa and Grandma Baka, and the Morrones on Wilson Avenue in Shenango Township. The Farris family lived across the street in New Castle. Chuck's grandparents owned a cow for milk, like many other immigrant families, and a huge barking dog that terrified the younger kids in the neighborhood. A large apple tree supplied fruit during the fall and preserves for the winter months. Grandma Baka shooed away any kid who dared to sneak an apple from her tree.

Even in the Roaring Twenties, life presented financial difficulties for the German-Slovak Baka-Tanner clan, but they made do without complaint. Dad and Granddad worked hard to stay ahead of the bills, a lesson Chuck would take to heart.

The Great Depression of 1929 crushed the euphoria of the Roaring Twenties and delivered a stark dose of cod liver oil to a community used to stuffing itself on candy and cake. A wave of misery struck the country with a vengeance, toppling businesses and families like a bowling ball flung down the center of the lane, knocking down and scattering all ten pins. Unemployment levels reached 25 percent by 1932. Those lucky enough to keep their jobs often worked under the stagger system—five or six people splitting three jobs. Many lost their spot entirely.

The Depression certainly tightened the Tanner family's already strained finances, but they had been used to living on a tight budget. Grandpa's cow and Grandma's apple and cherry trees helped with food supplies, and they

"Lefty" Chuck Tanner as a youngster. *Chuck Morrone's 1946* Tomahawk *yearbook.*

watched every penny to make ends meet. On the other hand, Chuck appreciated his loving and supportive parents and enjoyed his home life.

In grade school, a teacher asked the children in her class to raise a hand if they liked school. The hands of all the girls went up, but none of the boys raised theirs—that is, none except for Chuck Tanner. He proved positive even as a child. He intended to enjoy himself regardless of the circumstances.

Whenever possible, grade schooler Chuck took the short walk to the field at Gaston Park for pickup games of softball or baseball with the older neighborhood kids. Dreams of doubles and triples danced through his head. He loved the game right from the start, and he developed a knack for it. "We didn't have gloves as kids on the playground so all of us became pretty good at catching the ball," friend Chuck Farris mentioned. Lots of the boys wanted to play, so Chuck made sure he arrived early to get a spot on a team. Often the youngest on the field, he played far better than the other boys his age.

His mother's peanut butter sandwiches allowed him to remain on the field, but his stern and practical grandfather warned him that he would turn into a "bum" if all he did was play ball. But that is exactly what he wanted to do. When not playing baseball, throwing horseshoes or doing chores, Chuck tossed around the football or shot hoops into the basketball net nailed to the side of the Morrones' barn.

"My mother and father didn't have many rules for my two brothers and me. We just had to do what was right when we were kids, that's all."[2] Chuck tended to his chores, although he might rush through the dish washing. Sports always came first.

Anna Tanner supported her son's love of athletics and eventually became an ardent sports fan as well. "Junior," as mom called him, had been a good boy in almost everything he did, although like most youngsters he skipped some of his cleanup tasks to play ball with his friends whenever possible. Mom would just laugh it off and watch him race toward Gaston Park.

Chuck wore a Mooney Brothers uniform in 1941 at the age of twelve to play his first game in Junior American Legion baseball. Although the youngest boy on the team, he batted cleanup and led off the season with four doubles. His coach, Frank Coen, remembered him as a strong line-drive hitter and a potential star from the start.

Even as a preteen, Chuck dreamed about becoming a major leaguer, and he worked hard to achieve his goal. One afternoon, rain canceled his game. His coach watched him stay on the field and practice sliding into the base head first over and over again to perfect his skill.

Younger neighbor Bob Melder watched Chuck smack a home run out of Gaston Park and into the Cunningham Woods during a pickup game. "After batting the ball out of the field, Chuck joined the opposing team in hunting for the ball so play could continue."

As Chuck grew into his teens, he baled hay for his grandfather and stowed it in the loft. A part-time job at the Fenati brickyard while in high school added bulk to his growing body and provided him with a lifelong viselike grip. Anyone shaking hands with young Tanner remembered the power of that handshake. Hard work along with sports and exercise strengthened his upper torso.

During his secondary school years, sports dominated his attention. At Shenango High, he starred in football, basketball and track, earning ten letters. Former New Castle High basketball coach Connie Palumbo considered him one of the finest athletes to ever graduate from Shenango, or from any school in the county for that matter.

Football quarterback-halfback "Lefty" Tanner, as his teammates called him, lettered as a sophomore and contributed in his junior year as a key offensive player on a team that tied for a three-way district championship. Shenango's football fortunes rose even higher during his senior year in the 1945 season. Co-captain Tanner, big number "25," lifted the team to the top of its division as the team's leading runner and passer. The squad took home the Class B, Section 20 conference title.

On Friday night, September 28, against an outmanned George Junior Republic squad, Lefty scored four touchdowns, including an eighty-yard kickoff return. His three other scores came from sixty-five, fifteen and twenty-yard runs through powerful and skillful broken-field running. In addition, he completed a long spiral pass to teammate Don Mayberry at the opponent's ten-yard line. The crowd marveled that anyone could throw the ball that long and with so much accuracy.

Battling rival Evans City, Tanner plunged four yards over the goal line to seal a tight 6–0 victory. Against Hopewell, Chuck completed a forty-five-

Chuck Tanner, no. 45, junior year. *Chuck Morrone's 1945* Tomahawk *yearbook.*

yard pass to receiver Paul Tanner to the fifteen. On a subsequent play, Chuck ran off tackle through the opposing line to complete the score. In the third period, he broke into another long run but failed to reach the end zone. Later in the game, Chuck uncorked a pass from his own twenty to his neighbor Anthony Morrone that traveled eighty yards in the air to the end zone, but his usually sure-handed receiver dropped the ball. Had Morrone held on to the pass, this would have been the longest throw in the air in high school history. As it was, Shenango dropped a tight 9–7 decision.

Coach Eddie Nahas's Wildcats slogged out a 12–0 away victory over Union High as Tanner spearheaded the offense with a perfectly thrown spiral to Jack Cochran during the second half to set up an insurance touchdown. Cheered on by at least half the two thousand fans, Chuck led the Shenango Wildcats to a final 19–12 victory over Bessemer to seal the conference title. Lefty received an honorable mention citation on the All-State football team for the year 1945. His coach, Ed Nahas, called him "the best I ever coached by far."

When football season ended, Lefty pivoted into basketball, where he starred as a forward and co-captain of the team. Chuck led the squad to a regular-season 11-3 record. Overall, Shenango finished 1946 at 19-5, counting preseason and postseason games. Number 5, Chuck Tanner put up strong numbers in a low-scoring era, prior to the advent of the modern three-point shot.

In December 1945, Lefty Tanner led the team to victory with fourteen points against an overmatched Mars five in a 43–21 game. Against Eastbrook High School, he scored sixteen for Coach Nahas's Wildcats in a 45–17 rout. Tanner netted twenty-three points on January 11, including the winning shot in overtime against New Wilmington in a tight 31–29 victory.

Chuck drained another 23 points on February 5 in a win against New Wilmington, giving him a team-high 146 points for the year with several games to go. Shenango dropped a 40–39 heartbreaker away game against Coach Butler Hennon's powerhouse Wampum team on February 8. During Chuck's junior year, Wampum had eked out a win against Shenango at the Tri-County Tournament by a 3-point margin. In his senior year, Wampum beat them again. Chuck played brilliantly and scored 15 in the losing cause.

Battling Mount Jackson in a thriller, Tanner sunk a free throw with thirty seconds left in the game to squeak out a 35–34 win. On the nineteenth, the Wildcats dumped Princeton in a 51–31 lapper. Chuck played well but only scored eight. In the season's final game, Shenango walloped Mars 71–23 for a second time during the year, with Chuck sinking fifteen points.

In the 1946 Tri-County Tournament, Shenango dumped Union, Zelionople and Bessemer, with co-captain and guard Lefty Tanner leading the way to the championship. As winners, the team received a gold cup and each member a gold basketball trophy.

On March 8, with the formal high school basketball season completed, Chuck played for the County All Stars at Mount Jackson High School against the Croton AC in an exhibition.

CHARLES TANNER
FORWARD
"Ah! Another one!"

Chuck Tanner, no. 5 on the Shenango High basketball team. *Chuck Morrone's 1946 Tomahawk yearbook.*

Opposite page: Chuck Tanner, no. 5, Shenango High School. *Charles Morrone's* Tomahawk *yearbook.*

He scored ten points in a 63–36 win. He continued to play recreationally at the YMCA when time allowed, as well as on the New Castle Lions and Morella teams.

In the spring, Chuck turned his attention to track and field. He ran the 100-yard dash, the 220 and the 440, in addition to throwing the shot put and discus. On May 6, he won the 100-yard dash, the shot put and the discus in a triangular meet against Union and Bessemer. On the eighteenth, he earned the WPIAL Class B gold medal for the shot with a heave of 50 feet, 11.5 inches. He missed winning the Class B state discus championship by inches but took home a silver medal at the Mount Lebanon tournament with a toss of 134 feet, 10 inches, at that time a Shenango record.

Besides his participation on the Shenango football, basketball and track teams, Chuck served as the president of the Varsity Club and took part in the Latin Club, the school newspaper, the yearbook and the Tract Club. The senior class elected him as its treasurer.

Shenango aficionados considered Chuck's senior year as the epitome of sports excellence. *The Tomahawk*, the high school yearbook, praised his achievements: "To a renowned athlete, a mighty cheer, our Lefty Tanner, the star of the Year."

Chuck enjoyed all sports—football, basketball and track—but baseball remained his first love. He had played baseball and softball as a preteen at Gaston Park and excelled on the diamond. During the spring and summer, when not involved in school sports, he could be found on the ball field.

On May 10, he played shortstop for the South Hill Athletic Association ball club, where he shined as a power hitter. Chuck also pitched on occasion. He threw a two-hitter for the Elks, fanning eleven. Dr. Jim Snow, a talented amateur player, recalled a game at Progressive Field where he tossed a one-hitter only to lose 1–0 to Chuck's no-hitter.

Although Tanner displayed skills as a left-handed fastball pitcher, a speedy runner and a good fielder, his proficiency with the bat overshadowed his other strengths. He hit the ball consistently and with power. His teammates considered him an American Legion phenom.

Bill Brown recalled a game on the Cascade Street field behind the Blair Steel plant. "Chuck ripped a fastball out of the park. It smacked onto the wall of the adjoining building on a fly. I never before or after saw anyone hit a ball that far. It was an amazing feat."

Neither Shenango nor New Castle High School fielded a formal baseball team, possibly due to budgetary constraints and the expense of uniforms. Others pointed to the influence of Phillip "The Fox" Bridenbaugh of New Castle High, the legendary football coach who lived to the age of one hundred and put up a distinguished 265-65-25 lifetime record. He pushed his athletes to remain in shape by training on the track team during spring to prepare for the following year's football season rather than "wasting their time playing organized baseball" during the school year.

High school kids possessed a natural affinity for the national pastime. As soon as the school year ended, they appeared in droves in the Lawrence County summer leagues, which fielded highly competitive squads. Chuck joined the American Legion Post 343 team, where he became a star player.

In a major brouhaha, a rules violation disqualified Tanner from playing for the state playoffs. The Tanner family lived on Stanton Avenue in Shenango Township, just two hundred yards outside the New Castle city line. However, Chuck played in the city league along with his pal Fred Shaffer. Soon-to-be-sheriff Frank Coen managed the team. When the opposition balked at a non-city resident on the squad, the league authorities disqualified the star player from competing for a championship.

Years later, Jim Canan, a former American Legion second baseman and author of the books *Super Warriors* and *War in Space*, returned to New Castle for a lunch at Tanner's Restaurant with his cousin Bill Brown. Chuck greeted Jim like a long-lost brother. The two reminisced about the local guys who had played American Legion ball with them many years ago. With an uncanny memory, Chuck related each player's idiosyncrasies, skills and weaknesses for nearly an hour. Chuck could talk baseball with the best of them. He also spoke of his time with the Lawrence Indies.

Throughout his high school years, Chuck Tanner and Barbara "Babs" Weiss had become "an item." In fact, the two had known each other as classmates since first grade. The 1946 *Tomahawk* Shenango yearbook rhymed, "Babs and Lefty, a favorite pair, are seen together everywhere." In a section of the yearbook entitled "Isn't Love Grand," a couplet read, "In whatever corner you see Babs and Dolly, Chuck and Ernie are there, attentive and jolly." Like Chuck, Babs participated in a variety of activities. She took part in chorus, the school newspaper, the yearbook, basketball and Girl Reserves. She served as treasurer of the Cabinet and secretary of the Gigi Club.

During games, Babs sat in the stands as Chuck's number one fan. She watched him play football, basketball, track and baseball, cheering his every move. Chuck's friend Mike Saginak, who lived in the city, dated Barbara's neighbor, Phyllis, and the two often double-dated. Chuck joked that his "rich" pal Mike drove home after their dates. "I walked one hundred yards, then ran one hundred yards putting me in great shape—so much so that I became a 'man' among 'boys' when I played football. If I couldn't get a ride to see Babs, I walked to Butler Avenue and hitchhiked to her house. If that didn't work, I turned to Plan B: walk and jog."

With Chuck's part-time job at Fenati Brick, his farm chores for his grandparents and the years of sports, his body had hardened by graduation. He stood six feet tall and weighed a solid 185 pounds. A steel grip enabled him to heave a shot put or discus, complete a deep football pass, grab a basketball rebound and pound a baseball out of the park. Those who played with or against him testified to his amazing physical strength.

Classmates remembered Chuck as Mr. Friendly, one of the nicest guys in the school. Shenango High was small, not even fifty in the graduating class, and everyone knew one another. "Chuck never put on airs," classmate Sarah Klingensmith Brest remembered. "Babs had a funny streak, and everyone in school liked her as well, but she wasn't as outgoing as Chuck. She and her older sister lived next to Smith's Dairy."

As the county's leading athlete, Chuck received numerous football and basketball scholarship offers during his senior year from large and small colleges, including Youngstown and Westminster. He even received a feeler from the National Basketball League's Chicago American Gears, where six-

Chuck with sisters Babs and
Thelma Weiss. *Bruce Tanner.*

foot-ten star center George Mikan played, but Chuck had planned his own
agenda. He held on to a special dream. He intended to follow the road
less traveled, one with plenty of bumps along the way. He aimed to play
professional baseball and work his way to the major leagues.

"Babs, I don't think I want to go to college. I talked it over with my parents,
and I want to play baseball. I think I'm good at it."

"You know you could play in college," Babs countered.

"Yes, but I want to play professional baseball, and the best way for me to
do it is to work my way up through the minors."

"Chuck, if that is your dream, you should go for it. I'll support it in any
way I can," Babs replied. "And I will wait for you."

That was the answer Chuck hoped Babs would give him. While Lefty
intended to make his way into the minor leagues, Babs worked as a cashier
at the A&P on Mill Street and waited for her man, just like she promised.

CHAPTER 3

THE MINOR LEAGUES

Until the final out is made, anything can happen. "It ain't over until it's over."
—*Yogi Berra*

German-born minor-league outfielder and scout Jack G. Reider of the Boston Braves had watched Chuck play American Legion ball, and he liked what he saw. The kid had power, bat speed and coordination, but most of all, he possessed the right attitude. Reider recommended him to the Braves, who drafted Lefty in June 1946. Chuck's $6,000 signing bonus gave him more money than he or anyone in his family had ever seen. The seventeen-year-old high school graduate jumped at the opportunity.

The Braves listed Chuck's birthday as July 4, 1929, instead of 1928 to make their Class D team appear even younger. The rookie outfielder never had spent a night away from New Castle, but the adventure of baseball drew him like iron to a magnet. With Babs and his parents supporting his goal, the decision became even easier. He intended to become a professional baseball player.

Chuck would spend nine long years slogging his way through the swampland of the minors. Facing some of the top competition in the country, most of his teammates quit along the way. Bad luck, an injury and wrong timing could sabotage even the most skillful of players, but not Chuck. He intended to make baseball his career, and he resolved not to quit until he reached the major leagues.

Injuries reduced his playing time to twenty-three games in the Class D level Kitty (Kentucky-Illinois-Tennessee) League with the Owensboro Oilers during his first season. Playing manager Earl Browne, an ex–major leaguer who batted .292 with the 1937 Philadelphia Phillies, led the team with a hefty .429 batting average.

Although the Oilers topped the league with eighty-three victories, Chuck met up with a tough first year. He batted just .250 with twenty hits in eighty at bats and only three doubles, one triple and no home runs. Nonetheless, his manager recognized Chuck's potential and never-quit mindset and the strong contact he made with the ball.

Aches and pains racked Chuck's body during that frustrating first season in Kentucky. Baseball can be a dangerous game. A wild pitch broke his jaw, slicing his time on the field. Then a bleeding ulcer landed him in the hospital. His parents drove the 510 miles from New Castle to be with him. He recalled that visit and one in Denver as being the only times his mom and dad came to see him as a minor-league ball player. "You don't have to see someone every day to know they love you," Tanner later told a *Washington Post* reporter. He also admitted to missing Babs, his family and his hometown friends.

In 1947, Chuck upped his performance significantly. He batted .337 with nine doubles and three triples in twenty-five games, earning him a promotion to the Class C Eau Claire Bears in the Northern League under Hugh Wise, a former catcher who spent a short time with the 1930 Detroit Tigers.

Chuck batted a solid .325 in forty games at Eau Claire with six doubles, three triples and seven home runs. The following year, Chuck pounded out a booming .361 average in sixty-seven games, his highest average ever, with twenty-two doubles, five triples and seven home runs for his new manager, former New York Giants second baseman Andy Cohen. The Braves took notice, moving him up to the B-level Pawtucket Slaters in the New England League under manager Hugh Wise, his former manager at Eau Claire. In forty-six games, his average dropped to .275. However, as Chuck moved up to the B level, he found himself in the company of future major leaguers, including a Milwaukee Braves four-time All-Star shortstop named Johnny Logan.

Jim Snow and Chuck Tanner had played ball together in New Castle and developed a lifetime friendship. Jim traveled to Pawtucket, Rhode Island, to watch his pal play at McCoy Stadium in the International League. Chuck treated him like a long-lost brother, providing him with a free front-row seat at the ballpark and access to the locker room.

A few years earlier, the Philadelphia Athletics had offered Snow, an excellent pitcher in his own right and the winner of the Outstanding Athlete of the Year Award at Westminster College, a $2,000 signing bonus to enter their minor-league system as a pitching prospect. When Jim sought Chuck's opinion, his buddy suggested, "You should ask for more money. If they really want you, they'll up the ante." Jim listened to Chuck's advice and asked for an increase. The Athletics balked and told the recruit that he was an unproven entity. The scout held firm to $2,000 as a take-it-or-leave-it offer. Snow, a recent college graduate, already had received an acceptance to the University of Pittsburgh Dental School, and he declined. Years later, after he completed his degree and became a highly respected New Castle dentist, he read Yogi Berra's biography, *Yogi: Life Behind the Mask*. The catcher had signed for just $1,500 but earned a spot in the Hall of Fame. Dr. Snow always wondered what would have happened had he taken that $2,000 and pursued a career in baseball.

In 1949, the Braves promoted Tanner to the Class A Denver Bears in the Western League. He played under three managers, the last one being Earl Browne, his first boss from the Kitty League. Playing 124 games, Chuck showed star potential. He batted .313 with ninety-two runs scored and forty-two extra base hits. He led the team with thirty-two doubles and demonstrated the patience at the plate to get seventy walks, tied for the second highest on the squad.

Chuck played for Denver in the days before manufacturers like Nike and Adidas provided free cleats for upcoming athletes. New shoes proved a luxury Chuck could ill afford on his tight minor-league salary. Chuck owned two pairs of cleats, neither in great shape. Following a heavy rain, mud covered the base paths, so he picked the older and looser of his two pairs. "Well, I got a long hit and was rounding third base, trying to make an inside-the-park home run when one of my shoes got stuck in the mud. I slid across home plate safely, but with only one shoe."

Luckily for the young ball player, he had selected an understanding and loving girlfriend. Barbara "Babs" Weiss, his high school sweetheart, partnered with her boyfriend's quest to reach the majors. Everyone who knew Babs had wonderful things to say about her good heart, temperament and loyalty. Babs and Chuck married on February 12, 1950, in a small ceremony during his fourth year as a professional. Their good friend Mike Saginak served as Chuck's best man.

Although Chuck had developed into a solid .300 minor-league hitter and a competent fielder and worked his way up to the A level with Denver, promotions had come slower than he hoped. Money worries continued as a prime concern for the Tanner household. Skimpy baseball wages made economics a struggle, just as it did for the other married men on the team.

In the early months, Babs joined Chuck in Denver, but life away from New Castle proved difficult. The couple lived on hamburgers, and the time away from her parents tattooed the young wife with loneliness. She missed her family and friends. Once she became pregnant with her first son, she moved back to her hometown to be close to her parents.

The Tanners recognized that minor-league baseball demanded sacrifices, and both faced them stoically and with a smile. No one got rich playing Class A, and Chuck certainly would not be the exception. While the single guys went out on the town, he worked out in his room to keep his body in tip-top physical shape, and he watched every penny of his salary. He had given his all to baseball and refused to waste his hard-earned money on a night out with the guys.

In the off season, Chuck worked with his father-in-law at Clark's Plumbing or took what odd jobs he could get. Babs's parents, Fritz and Mae Weiss, who lived near Smith's Dairy off Old Butler Road, converted an old chicken coop behind their house into a small home for the young newlyweds. Chuck and Babs guarded their limited earnings. Luxuries proved out of the question. Babs knew that Chuck loved baseball and his time on the playing field, and she continued to support her husband's dream by living frugally and without complaint.

When not working, Chuck and his pals frequented Valentine's Restaurant on Washington Street in downtown New Castle for a morning cup of coffee and some baseball talk. Even the waitresses joined in the chatter along with the Valentine brothers. As the years passed and Chuck became a regular, he developed a close relationship with the Valentine brothers and his restaurant cohorts.

With Chuck away much of the time, Babs bore the brunt of raising four active boys. Mark, the oldest, arrived on October 30, 1950; Gary in 1953; Brent in 1957; and Bruce in 1961. The two youngest brothers were born while Chuck played in the major leagues. Everyone who knew Babs described her as a terrific mother and a saint who raised four active and athletic sons pretty much on her own.

During 1950, Chuck continued his progress as a Denver player. He batted .315 with thirty-four doubles in 154 games. He led the team with 195 hits, and his 268 total bases landed him second on the squad behind outfielder Pete Whisenant, another future major leaguer. Shortstop Steve Kuczek, second baseman Jack Dittmer, pitcher Virgil Jester and infielder Buddy Peterson from the team also would reach the big leagues along with Chuck and Pete Whisenant in the future.

During the winter months, in addition to helping his father-in-law at Clark's Plumbing, he signed up students and schools for class pictures for Regional Director Steve Kors of Hewlett-Packard Photographers in a broad territory encompassing the Kane–Corry northern area and the New Castle–Washington region of Western Pennsylvania. To this day, faculty members and students remember Chuck from this job.

In 1951, Chuck moved up to the AA Atlanta Crackers in the Southern Association under colorful manager Dixie Walker, a former Brooklyn Dodgers batting and RBI champion, a .306 lifetime hitter and a beloved son of Georgia. Walker tutored Chuck on old-time baseball, and Chuck responded with a very respectable .318 batting average combined with twenty-eight doubles and eighteen home runs. His stats made him the second leading hitter on the team behind second baseman Jack Dittmer as part of a talented squad that included sixteen future and past major leaguers, with All-Star third baseman Eddie Mathews certainly being the most famous.

In 1952, Chuck put together a .345 batting average, one of the best seasons in his career, just behind future major-league outfielder Junior Wooten for the team leadership. At the end of the season, the Braves management rewarded Tanner by moving him up for eleven games with the AAA Milwaukee Brewers in the American Association, a crew loaded with twenty-six members having past and future major league experience.

In March 1953, Boston Braves owner Lou Perini transferred his big-league franchise from Boston to Milwaukee, the first such change in half a century. Low attendance due to strong competition from the highly popular Boston Red Sox, the availability of a major league–ready Milwaukee County Stadium and strong Wisconsin support from local companies like Miller Brewing made the relocation a sound business decision. Chuck no longer played as property of the Boston Braves. He now played for the Milwaukee Braves organization.

In 1953, twenty-seven-year-old Gene Mauch replaced Dixie Walker, who left Atlanta for a coaching position with the St. Louis Cardinals. Tanner responded with another solid year for the new manager in 1953 by producing a .318 average, second on the team behind outfielder Dick Sinovik. He also hit twenty-nine doubles; eleven triples, which led the team; and six home runs. At the end of the season, management moved him up to the Toledo Sox of the AAA American Association for seventeen games, a team loaded with nineteen players who eventually would appear on big-league rosters. Chuck only batted .192 in fifty-two at bats but managed two homers.

The year 1954 meant another year with Atlanta as he patiently waited for his opportunity to move up to the big leagues. In 594 at bats, the most in his career, Chuck's overall performance and hustle culminated in his finest overall offensive year ever. The Atlanta locals considered him a true star.

Between 1947 and 1954, Chuck had batted above .300 almost every year as he advanced up the B, A, AA and AAA levels. In 1949, the writers elected him to the Western League All-Star team. The following year, he led the Southern Association in hits with 195. In 1951, he hit safely in twenty-nine consecutive games for the Atlanta Crackers. In 1953, Chuck again made the league All-Star squad. In '54, during his fourth year for the Crackers under Mauch's replacement, manager Whitlow Wyatt, a former twenty-two-game winner for the Brooklyn Dodgers in the early '40s, Chuck racked up 192 hits, 101 RBIs and 331 total bases, second best in the league. He also smacked 20 homers and carried a hot .323 batting average, the top on his team.

During one crazy game in May 1954, the Little Rock Travelers were crushing the Crackers by a 10–0 score. By the third inning, manager Whitlow Wyatt had used nearly every player on the team, and hundreds of fans had left Ponce de Leon Park early, certain that the home team would lose. However, that team refused to quit, and Chuck Tanner represented the very heart of the club. Somehow, the Crackers clawed back, and Chuck hit the winning home run to seal an amazing come-from-behind 11–10 victory.

Nine-year-old Joel Alterman and his father were among those leaving the park before the game had ended. During a previous game, Chuck had taken the time to spend twenty minutes speaking with the boy. That interaction impressed Joel, and Chuck immediately became his hero.

Imagine Joel's surprise when he awoke the next morning and discovered that Chuck Tanner had hit the winning home run. Alterman never forgot his hero's courtesy and the home run he had missed seeing.

Fifty years later, in 2004, Joel Alterman orchestrated a luncheon at Turner Field before the Cincinnati-Atlanta baseball game to celebrate the success of that 1954 team. Ten members of the Crackers attended, but a prior engagement prohibited Chuck from joining the festivities.

Chuck's top-notch performance throughout the season had pushed the team to a first-place divisional finish. The Crackers finished the year by taking the Dixie Series playoffs in five games against the Texas League sectional champs. Sixteen players from that squad would eventually play major-league ball, including Chuck.[3]

With all his success in the minor leagues, Chuck wondered what more he had to do in order to be called up by the Milwaukee Braves. Although he questioned the when, he had refused to quit and go home like so many other dejected minor leaguers.

A year or so earlier, Chuck had encouraged his younger friend and neighbor Chuck Farris to sign a contract with the Boston Braves Eau Claire Class C team following high school. New Castle sports fans still remember Chuck Farris as a power pitcher with a lively fastball. After a successful spring training session at Myrtle Beach, Farris received a $500 signing bonus and a salary of $250 per month as a pitcher/outfielder in the minors. Farris recalled breaking manager Bill Adair's ribs with a wild pitch, but the team liked his potential. The six-foot-three rookie possessed the ability to throw the ball.

Unfortunately, Farris learned that he was about to be drafted into the army, and he left the team to enlist. He found himself stationed as an honor guard at Arlington Cemetery. His brother Joe, later the New Castle chief of police, joined him in the military.

For excitement, the Farris brothers obtained a long-weekend pass and drove to Atlanta to surprise their old friend Chuck Tanner and watch him play with the Crackers. Growing up, the Farris boys lived on Arlington Avenue, directly across the street from the Tanner family's Stanton Avenue home. "We almost were neighbors," Chuck Farris recalled.

Tanner genuinely appeared shocked to see the Farris brothers. "Hey, you look like Chuck Farris," Tanner joked, pointing to Chuck. "Hi Joe." Tanner walked his buddies into the stadium for the Friday and Saturday games. No one stopped them, even though they didn't have tickets. After the games, the Farris brothers joined the team in the locker room. On Sunday, an usher came by and shooed the Farris brothers out of their seats. "Hey, these are reserved. You guys don't have tickets and can't stay here." Minus shoes and shirt, Chuck rushed over to intercede. As the Farris brothers and Tanner protested, Crackers team owner Earl Mann wandered by and asked, "What's this ruckus all about?"

The usher pointed out to his boss that the strangers had no tickets. Chuck explained, "These are my cousins, and they want to see the game." Mann smiled at his star outfielder and escorted the guys to the owner's box along the first base line as his guests. Farris remembered, "Atlanta won all three games to wrap up a division title over the Pittsburgh Pirates farm club, the New Orleans Pelicans, who ended the season just two games behind Atlanta. Chuck must have had three or four hits in our honor that day and eleven during the three-game series including a triple that could just as easily have been an inside-the-park homer."

Babs remained in New Castle with the boys after discovering that life on the road wasn't peaches and cream; rather, it consisted of greasy food and waiting for her husband to come home, all without the support of her parents and friends. While she tended the family, Chuck struggled to earn a spot with the Milwaukee Braves. He admired his wife for sucking up the difficulties of minor-league life and managing the growing family on a limited budget while he continued to chase his rainbow.

Tanner appreciated everything Babs had done for him. "You have to have a wife who is understanding especially after you have children, and she can't make trips with you. It means a ball player is away from his family a lot. The time goes slow for you. I'm glad I have a wife who understands."[4]

Fellow Pennsylvanian, pitcher Nellie King, a future Pittsburgh Pirate, faced Chuck in the Southern Association in 1954. "He played for Whitlow Wyatt, and I was with New Orleans when Joe E. Brown was the general manager and Danny Murtaugh was the manager. He was a competitive fellow. Yet I never saw him when he wasn't smiling. He's good people."[5]

Chuck later confessed to sportswriter David Condon, "You know, I didn't have it easy. They kept shoving me around the minors with no chance at the big leagues. Every time I was shifted from Evansville to Owensboro to Eau Claire to Pawtucket, I kept saying, 'The hell with them, I'm going to make it, and I will make it.'"[6] Dr. Don Hennon, the Wampum-born, All-American basketball phenom from the University of Pittsburgh, called Chuck the most enthusiastic man he ever met. "He never gave up." Against all odds, Chuck continued to play his best, waiting for the Braves to call.

Chuck relished the fun of playing baseball with some of the best, regardless of the frustration that ate at him. He felt like a kid with a lollipop every time he appeared on the field or batted. After a game, he might ingest the irritation of being stuck in the minors, but he kept the negative feelings to himself. He spit out an upbeat attitude that he shared with his teammates and carried throughout his entire life.

Chuck listened to the unfortunate tales of those mired in a downward spiral with faint hopes of making the majors, but he opted to be upbeat. He fed on the excitement of the up-and-coming hopefuls, guys like himself with big dreams and the ambition to do whatever it took to move forward. The young outfielder's offensive statistics excelled, and he looked like a prime candidate for future baseball stardom. The batting numbers he assembled with the Atlanta Crackers between the years of 1951 and 1954 put him in the top echelon of the entire Southern Association for that period.

Chuck had hustled his tail off in Kentucky, Rhode Island, Wisconsin, Colorado and Georgia. He worked hard, never complained, gave his all and strove to be a team player. He wondered why Milwaukee had not called him up to the bigs. He had prepared no Plan B for his life. He retained a single goal: to play major-league ball. A twinge of doubt quieted his inner positivity. Would he be mired in the minors forever? Tanner stewed about his future and actually thought about quitting.

While Chuck continued to star in the minors with the Crackers, Milwaukee Braves owner Louis Perini and General Manager John Quinn pondered whether to bring Chuck up to the bigs and, if so, where he would fit. The bosses had traded pitcher Johnny Antonelli, Don Liddell, Ebba St. Claire, Billy Krause and $50,000 for the Giants star outfielder Bobby Thompson, "the Flying Scotsman," on February 1, 1954.

That trade created a huge barrier for Chuck's potential advancement. He recognized the difficulty of cracking an outfield composed of Bill Bruton, Hank Aaron and Bobby Thompson with four-time All-Star Andy Pafko as a backup. "There was no place for me. I felt crushed." Chuck seriously considered leaving baseball and accepting a four-year scholarship to Youngstown University. "My wife talked me out of it, and I guess I was not yet ready to give up and quit."

CHAPTER 4

THE MAJOR LEAGUES

Crack! We hit the ball, and away we go. If we earn a run, we call it success.
We get back to home plate and sit on the bench. If we are thrown out,
we walk back to the bench—Win or lose baseball is special.
—O. Henry (William Sydney Porter)

It was good that Chuck listened to his wife and his own heart because the Milwaukee Braves needed another backup outfielder in 1955. Scottish-born, home run–hitting Bobby Thompson broke his ankle in 1954 during spring training. Although the Braves had brought up the incomparable Hank Aaron, a star who led Jacksonville of the Southwest League to a 93-44 record while batting .362 with 22 homers and 125 RBIs, they opted to bring up a pinch hitter and another substitute outfielder to play on the team.

Chuck had made quite a name for himself with the Atlanta Crackers during the past four years. His 1954 blockbuster statistics made him the ideal candidate to pinch-hit off the bench and share time as a substitute in the outfield with Andy Pafko. His thirty-five doubles, twelve triples and twenty homers, his best extra-base output ever, coupled with a solid .323 batting average, stood out against any other rookie potentials being considered. Tanner held the credentials to rest Thompson as necessary, and management recognized his ability to strengthen the team for the upcoming season.

"While others had more talent, I worked hard to get to the majors. While my teammates went out late, I stayed in the room doing sit-ups and push-ups and called Babs on the phone." His efforts at last paid off, and he approached the upcoming season with almost childlike glee.

"Imagine going up to the majors and being part of a lineup that included Hank Aaron, Bill Bruton, Warren Spahn, Del Crandall, Andy Pafko, Bobby Thompson, Johnny Logan and all of that bunch," Tanner told writer David Condon in an interview.

Chuck hired attorney Francis Caiazza, later a common pleas judge and federal magistrate judge, to help with the final negotiations. Francis's wife, Roselee Morrone Caiazza, joked, "The only reason Chuck hired my husband was because of me. I was Chuck's former neighbor when we lived on Wilson Avenue, and he lived on Stanton. I even remember the time Chuck and his teenage friends pushed one of my father's cars down the street to take it for a joy ride."

Lefty Tanner and Francis Caiazza caught the train to Milwaukee, arriving at Braves president Louis Perini's office in December 1954 to ink his major-league contract. Perini, who had made a fortune in the construction business, had purchased the Boston Braves for $500,000 from Bob Quinn in 1945 and had relocated the team to Milwaukee in 1953 to up attendance and improve finances.

Anticipation and excitement surged though Chuck's veins as he met with the team owner to finalize his lifelong dream. Here he stood in the office of the owner of the Milwaukee Braves about to sign a major-league contract.

Scuttlebutt in the minors hinted that a $5,000 bonus generally accompanied a promotion to the big leagues, and that would be more money than he had seen since receiving his initial signup bonus as a teenager.

After welcoming Chuck to the team with a warm handshake and a few introductory remarks, Mr. Perini got down to business. Chuck and his attorney drafted contract notes on a paper napkin. As the proceedings edged toward completion, Chuck said, "I always heard that a $5,000 bonus goes along with a promotion to the big leagues."

The remark genuinely surprised Perini. An uncomfortable silence followed for several seconds. Perini stared at the new addition and slowly explained, "Son, there's nothing in the contract along those lines."

The rookie's face dropped. A second moment of silence followed. Then Perini pushed back his chair and rose. "Chuck, just give me a second."

Perini walked to his safe and removed something. "Here you go," he said, handing his new outfielder $5,000 in cash. The day could not have gone better. Chuck had achieved his childhood goal. He had become a major leaguer, and one flush with cash as well.

A broad grin crossed Chuck's lips as he accepted the bonus. He reached out and shook Mr. Perini's hand and promised, "Sir, whatever happens, I intend to give my best. Thank you for this opportunity."

That night, Chuck returned to New Castle and Babs. He laid the bundle of cash on the kitchen table for his wife to see, presenting the Tanners with one of their best Christmases ever. In 1954, $5,000 proved a lot of money, especially when one considers that the country's average annual salary stood at $4,400. Milwaukee star third baseman Ed Mathews earned $50,000. Second-year right fielder Hank Aaron received $10,000 after batting a solid .280 during his rookie year. Chuck received about the same as Aaron but with a potential to earn even more. He could not have been happier.

Spring training in March at Braves Field in Bradenton, Florida, psyched Chuck Tanner to the gills. The workouts felt great. "I'm playing with the best of the best, and my manager is an old pro," he told Babs. Charlie "Jolly Cholly" Grimm, a former twenty-year major-league first baseman with a .290 lifetime batting average and a veteran manager since 1932, knew his stuff and certainly had been "around the Horn."

The flamingo-pink Manatee Hotel where the team stayed displayed a distinct upgrade from his minor-league housing. The food served to the players proved plentiful and tasty. Chuck's teammates welcomed him, and the coaches provided frank but useful advice. His body felt healthy, and he considered himself in excellent shape as he anxiously looked forward to his first day on a major-league ball field.

The Milwaukee team contained an amazing array of talent. The outfield included star right fielder Hank Aaron, sub Andy Pafko and left fielder Bobby Thomson, each one an All-Star at one time or another during their long and successful careers. Center fielder "Bullet Billy" Bruton led the majors three years in a row in stolen bases, twice in triples and once in runs scored.

The Braves pitching crew numbered among its staff future 203-game winner Lou Burdette and 166-game winner Bob Buhl. Gene Conley, a six-foot-eight three-time All-Star, both earned a World Series ring and played on a National Basketball Association championship team. Ray Crone would win ten games during the season as a valuable fill-in spot starter and long reliever. Most importantly, the team sported ace Warren Spahn. With the additional All-Star cast of Joe Adcock manning first, Del Crandall catching, Eddie Mathews at third and Johnny Logan at short, the Braves presented a strong contender. Chuck kept his mouth shut, listened to instructions and played his hardest to make certain the staff considered him an asset.

Manager Charlie Grimm knew that this team had a legitimate shot at the National League pennant. His squad finished second in 1953 with a 92-62 record and third in 1954 with an 89-65 tally. If his stars worked in tandem and met expectations, 1955 could be the Braves' year. Grimm had managed for sixteen years in the majors and had delivered pennants with the Chicago Cubs in 1932 and 1935. The current year provided the potential to deliver such outstanding results again.

With the season about to start, rookie Chuck Tanner understood the impossibility of breaking into the team's deep starting lineup. He had prepared himself to become a major leaguer. All he could do now was to try his best and be a team player ready to perform as needed.

During the home opener on Tuesday, April 12, 1955, the Braves faced a tough Cincinnati team. A crowd of 43,640 roared as the starting nine took the field at Milwaukee County Stadium. Rookie Chuck Tanner, no. 18, watched the game from the end of the bench in his new uniform. As expected, Hank Aaron, Bobby Thompson and Billy Bruton played the outfield.

Milwaukee's Warren Spahn, a lefty who would win 363 games in a Hall of Fame career, gave up a walk and a single in the first but escaped the inning unscathed. He faced Gerry Staley, a strong right-hander, who would rack up 134 wins in a highly successful fifteen-year career.

In the Braves half of the first, Billy Bruton scored on a Bobby Thompson double to give the home team a 1–0 lead. However, in the eighth, Cincinnati's Johnny Temple led off with a single, and big Ted Kluszewski drove him home with a towering home run to right. Spahn settled down and ended the inning with a Ray Jablonski pop-up to first base. Spahn now found himself on the losing side of a tight 2–1 game in the eighth inning against Staley.

Spahn had pitched well, scattering seven hits and two runs through eight innings, as much as a manager could ask, but Grimm thought that Warren might be tiring. He ordered Dave Jolly to warm up. Looking down the bench, he signaled Chuck, shouting loud enough for all to hear, "Hey rookie, this is your shot. You're batting second for Spahn." Chuck sucked in a deep breath of air to compose himself, picked up a bat and moved toward the on-deck circle.

"Hey, Tanner, hit one for me," Spahn urged as Chuck made his way out of the dugout.

Chuck Tanner had waited for this opportunity his entire life. This would be his moment to shine. Nerves jabbed him in the gut, but confidence in his ability to hit eased the pressure. He gulped another breath of air and kneeled in the on-deck circle after taking a practice swing or two.

On the bright side, regardless of what happened next, he had become a major leaguer, and that never could be taken away from him. He watched catcher Del Crandall open the inning by bouncing out, third to first on a routine play, an ominous start.

The loud speaker bellowed, "Now batting for Warren Spahn, pinch hitter, no. 18 Chuck Tanner." As he rose from the on-deck circle to the plate, a smattering of applause filled his ears. He thought he heard a fan yell, "Hit a big one."

Chuck swung the bat to loosen up before taking his stance. In pinch-hit situations, the batter arrived cold from the bench and had to guess at what pitch would come his way. Even if he made solid contact with the ball, the odds stood that it probably would be caught or fouled off, if he were lucky enough to make contact at all.

Chuck eliminated all negative thoughts from his mind. He concentrated on the pitch and the pitcher. Gerry Staley wound up and unleashed a fastball down the middle just like Chuck had hoped. Tanner swung smoothly with speed and power. *Crack!* The bat connected with the ball, and it traveled 325 feet through the air, high and strong as it cleared the right field fence. His teammates cheered wildly. The ecstatic fans at Memorial Stadium leaped to their feet and shouted their approval. The ball had flown above the outfielder's head and over the fence just like Chuck always had imagined as he trotted around the bases. He had dreamed of this moment since he was a child, but now this at bat became a reality. The home run really had happened.

As he rounded the bases, he looked into the crowd and took in the excitement of the moment. He heard the excited voice of the announcer but could not make out his words. A home run on the very first pitch of his first at bat proved a rare and unusual feat—the first in Milwaukee history and only the seventh time in baseball history a player had hit a home run on the first pitch of his initial at bat. Just as importantly, once he stepped on the home plate, his run had tied the score and had taken Spahn off the hook. He had contributed mightily in his very first game.

Back home in New Castle, Chuck's mom and dad, his youngest brother Bob (then a high school junior and a starter on the Shenango football, basketball and baseball teams) and his friend Jack Benninghoff, a senior year teammate, sat transfixed to the radio in the Tanners' tiny kitchen on the Old Butler Road, where the family now lived. When the announcer signaled the home run, the four listeners went crazy with excitement. "He did it! I can't believe he hit a home run in his first at bat," Bob screamed. "And on the first pitch!" The senior Tanners hugged in happiness, thrilled that their son's dream had come true. The announcer, recognizing the importance of that home run, told the crowd, "This is something Chuck Tanner one day can tell his grandchildren."

The home run had knocked Staley off stride. When the game continued, speedster Billy Bruton followed with a single. Then Hank Aaron unleashed a triple, scoring Bruton and shifting the lead. Reliever Jackie Collum replaced Staley and walked Eddie Mathews. Cincinnati brought in Jerry Laine to pitch to Bobby Thompson. The outfielder came through with a long sacrifice fly to score Aaron from third. The inning ended with Mathews caught stealing, but Lefty Tanner had led the charge. Reliever Dave Jolly wrapped up the ninth with two strikeouts and a groundout. Milwaukee's Warren Spahn had won the game, the 199th victory of his career, thanks in a large part to rookie Chuck Tanner's heroics.

This first at bat proved a highlight of Tanner's playing career. He would hit only twenty-one homers during his entire career in the majors. Pitcher Warren Spahn actually hit thirty-five during his time in the big leagues, fourteen more than Tanner.[7]

On the fourteenth of the month, in his second major-league at bat, Chuck pinch-hit for pitcher Charlie Gorin in the eleventh inning during a 7–7 tie game against the St. Louis Cardinals. He did not disappoint. He stroked a single. He had yet to make an out in the big leagues. Unfortunately, the team stranded him at first and lost the game on a Bill Virdon home run the next inning.

On April 17, Chuck ran for Bobby Thompson in the eighth inning,

reaching second on a walk to Joe Adcock and scoring on a Jack Dittmer single. Once the inning ended with catcher Del Crandall popping up to short, Tanner played left, his first major-league game on defense.

Chuck received his first start as a left fielder against the Philadelphia Phillies on May 15. In the fourth, he hit a single off future Hall of Fame member Robin Roberts, landing on second after an error, but he failed to score.

The season settled in with Chuck playing in ninety-seven games, primarily as a late-inning replacement or a pinch hitter. He produced some good moments and accepted his part-time role as the fifth outfielder behind Andy

Chuck Tanner. *Bruce Tanner.*

Pafko. Although he played behind four star players, he believed that a day on the bench in the majors still proved far better than a starting assignment in the minors. He produced sixty hits in 243 at bats during a season, which included nine doubles, three triples and six homers along with a .247 batting average, earning him the Milwaukee Braves Rookie of the Year Award. The 1955 team missed the pennant with a record of eighty-five wins and sixty-nine losses, a solid second to the Dodgers but not quite good enough.

Chuck's teammates and the coaching staff appreciated his can-do attitude and respected his hustle. When lucky enough to play in the outfield, he ran rather than walked back to the dugout at inning's end, frequently beating first baseman Joe Adcock to the bench.

Chuck's "I can't believe this is happening" naïvete sometimes even surprised himself. "They gave me six dollars a day meal money, and they took my suitcase when we went on our first roadtrip. I didn't want to let my suitcase go at first. I didn't believe them when they said it would show up at the hotel. I had my only jacket in there, but they told me not to worry, and when I arrived at the hotel, my suitcase was there—like magic."[8]

Chuck relished every moment with the Braves. "There I am standing with my teammates, the great Hank Aaron, who received the National League Most Valuable Player Award, and another player, the great Warren Spahn, who had won the Cy Young Award. It was like a dream come true to me."

As Chuck pulled down a major leaguer's salary, economics improved significantly for the Tanner family. The family designed a nice ranch house constructed by builder Patsy Carvella at 34 Maitland Lane in Neshannock Township in Lawrence County.

Ty Cobb with Chuck Tanner and Hank Aaron. *Bruce Tanner.*

Tanner's Maitland Lane home. *Photo by Michele Perelman.*

Off season, Tanner continued working for Hewlett-Packard Photographers of Atlanta, signing up high schools for class pictures, adding income to the family coffers, plus he enjoyed the job. "I liked meeting my customers."

Dr. Lew Grell, the principal of the Mahoning, Westside and West Pittsburg schools and a very proficient local outfielder who played competitively until age forty-four, handled the details for the class picture annual contracts. "The work part of my meeting with Chuck lasted maybe ten minutes," Grell said. "Then, we might spend an hour or so talking about baseball. What started as a business relationship turned into a lifetime friendship."[9]

When at home in New Castle during off seasons, Chuck frequently hit fly balls to the young neighborhood kids at the Walmo field across the street from his house. David "Fuzzy" Fazzone lived on Wilmington Road and Buena Vista and remembered this local hero lofting balls higher than he ever had seen. "I never had watched a major leaguer up close, and here was Chuck Tanner bigger than life."

Tanner received limited duty with Milwaukee in 1956, appearing in just sixty games, primarily pinch hitting. He put up just fifteen hits in sixty-nine at bats for a subpar .238 batting average with just two doubles and one home run.

Dr. Lew Grell. *Photo by author.*

On June 17, 1956, Braves owner Louis Perini replaced manager Charlie Grimm with Fred Haney following a 22-20 start. Haney finished the year with a sterling 92-62 record, just one game behind the Dodgers, who wrapped up their pennant victory on the last day of the season.

In 1957, Chuck played in twenty-two games with seventeen hits in sixty-nine at bats for a .246 average, with three doubles and two home runs. With a boatload of outfield talent, including newly added Wes Covington, the Braves considered Chuck expendable. On June 8, the team placed him on waivers. Several teams expressed interest, but the Chicago Cubs claimed him that same day. Chuck's release freed up a spot that brought Red Schoendienst from St. Louis to Milwaukee. With Red manning second and batting .310, the Braves finished the year by winning the pennant with a 95-59 record and the World Series in seven games over the New York Yankees.

Chuck later joked with his pal Fuzzy Fazzone, "We had lost a couple of games, and the Braves manager Fred Haney asked me what we should do. I suggested, 'Cut the dead wood.' That's when they released me."

Although the move to Chicago cost him a World Series ring, Chuck knew that rainy days often delivered rainbows. He upped his playing time

Chuck Tanner as a Chicago Cub.
Pittsburgh Pirates.

substantially with the new team. In a June 14 game against Pittsburgh, Chuck amazed himself with a four-for-five day in which he smacked a triple off Ron Kline and scored four runs. In a July 18 game at Forbes Field against the Pittsburgh Pirates, both Chuck and Ernie Banks hit inside-the-park home runs. Banks led off in the fourth inning with a round-tripper against starter Bob Purkey. Chuck hit his homer in the eighth off reliever Luis Arroyo in a 6–5 losing cause. He also drove home a run with a sacrifice fly and singled to go two for three with two RBIs for the day.

In the ninety-five games he played during 1957, Chuck produced four-hit games twice and three-hits on six other days. He stroked the ball at a healthy .286 clip with the Cubs during the season. His combined production with the two teams culminated in a .279 batting average for the year, with 19 two-baggers, 2 triples, 9 home runs and 47 RBIs in 387 at bats as a part-timer for Milwaukee and a semi-regular for Chicago, his best year ever in the big leagues.

While Chuck played in Chicago, New Castle friends and fans arranged a mini banquet in his honor. The colorful Pirates announcer Bob Prince emceed the event and introduced Chuck's parents; his wife, Babs; and sons Mark and Gary. "Bob Prince treated my family like you hoped people would treat your mother." The night remained a wonderful memory for the entire Tanner clan.

During his time in the majors, Chuck supported his hometown for every possible occasion. On Sunday, October 13, 1957, he helped the Jaycees organize a charity baseball game at Flaherty Field attended by 1,200 locals. The weather cooperated for a perfect sports day. Future Hall of Fame member and White Sox second baseman Nellie Fox, Pirates starting pitcher Ronnie Kline, Cincinnati pinch-hit specialist Jerry Lynch, Philadelphia Phillies catcher Joe Lonnett, Pirates shortstop and future batting champ Dick Groat, Pirates ace reliever Elroy Face and local minor leaguers Chet Boak, Gary Peters and John Swogger played for the major-league squad. Chuck handled first and pitched an inning in the exhibition won by the pros 5–2.[10] Dr. Lew Grell, a close friend of Chuck, roamed the outfield for the losing City-County All-Stars and got a hit in the game. Grell later went on to become a high school principal.

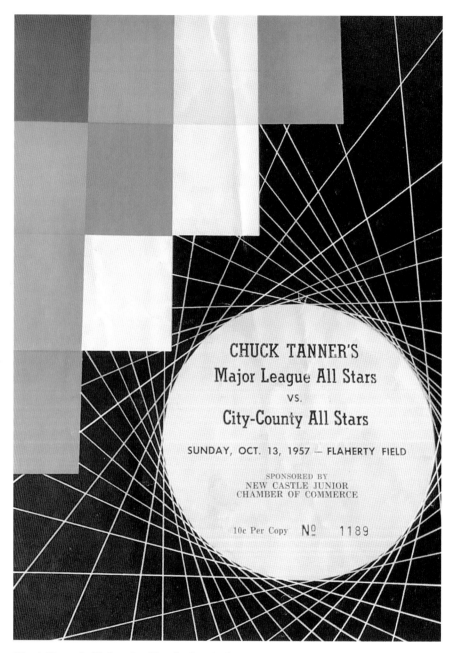

Chuck Tanner's All-Stars booklet. *Dr. Lew Grell.*

In 1958, Tanner's fifty-three pinch-hit appearances led the National League. He batted .262 with 23 hits in 102 at bats, which included six doubles and four home runs. On March 9, 1959, the Cubs traded him to the Boston Red Sox organization for journeyman right-handed pitcher Bob Smith.

Chuck played 152 games with the 1959 American Association AAA Minneapolis Millers under manager Gene March. He batted .319, the fourth-best average in the league, and his forty-one doubles led the division. He also connected for ten triples, twelve homers and seventy-five RBIs. His performance earned him a spot on the All-Star team.

The Cleveland Indians purchased Chuck's contract on September 9, 1959, from Boston, and he played in fourteen major-league games that month. He produced twelve hits in forty-eight at bats with two doubles, one home run and a .250 batting average.

Chuck remembered every detail of the games he played and his specific performance, sometimes successful and other times less so. With the Indians still in the running, his team faced the Chicago White Sox on Saturday, September 22. He watched future Hall of Fame player Minnie Miñoso face Early Wynn in the second inning. Wynn clipped the batter in the arm. Miñoso trotted to first like nothing happened.

"In the fifth, shortstop Woody Held had walked for us, and I pinch hit for third baseman George Strickland. I worked the count to a 3-2 count and fouled off several pitches. Early must have gotten tired of our cat-and-mouse game, because he tossed me a knuckle ball which darted and dropped every which way. I swung and missed. That shows the type of competitor Early was and why he later earned his place in the Hall of Fame. In a big game he had the confidence to throw that pitch on a 3-2 count."[11]

Chuck started in left field for the last game of the season on September 27 at Cleveland Stadium against the Kansas City Athletics. He managed two singles in five at bats, beating out a ground ball to short off Ned Garber in the first and stroking a sharp single to right off Marty Kutyna in the ninth. He played defense with no errors in a 6–5 losing cause.

In 1960, he played sparingly due to a ruptured Achilles' tendon that he received off season while slipping on his basement steps. "Good things have happened to me. Look, I ripped my Achilles' tendon, and I was still thirty-two games short of my pension."

Dr. Gerald Weiner's surgery left Chuck hobbling in a cast for six weeks and another six rehabbing. He tried to keep his operation a secret for fear that it might end his career before he qualified for his pension. He worked hard to bounce back and make the Indians team. His friend Lew Grell attended a Cleveland game where Chuck entered as a pinch hitter. Lew remembered him pounding a single through the infield and limping his way to first. Mercifully, his manager brought in a pinch runner.

Thirty-one-year-old Chuck Tanner managed just twenty-one games for the Indians that season, primarily as a pinch hitter. In twenty-five at bats, he had seven hits with one double and four RBIs for a solid .280 average.

The Indians sold Tanner's contract in 1960 to their AAA Toronto Maple Leafs farm club, allowing him to rehab his injury and making room for future Hall of Fame second baseman Joe Morgan, acquired in a trade from Philadelphia. Chuck played twenty-eight games in AAA ball and batted .293 with twenty-seven hits, including five doubles, two triples and four round-trippers. Somehow, he managed two stolen bases with his repaired Achilles' tendon.

In 1961, Chuck played seventy games for AAA Toronto and batted just .225 with forty-nine hits and fourteen extra bases. The Cleveland brass sold Chuck to the Los Angeles Angels AAA Dallas–Fort Worth Rangers on September 8. He played forty-eight games and batted .315 with twenty-eight doubles, two triples and five home runs, excellent stats.

Chuck ran into Fred Haney, general manager of the Angels and the former manager of the Milwaukee Braves, during his 1956–57 stay with the team. "He asked me how it was coming, and I told him I couldn't get a jump on the ball anymore and that I would never be the same. My leg still bothered me. Haney answered, 'You sound the same to me. The way you play you never could get a jump on the ball. You sound healthy as hell.' Haney promised to bring me up to the club."

Tanner managed to play seven games with the Los Angeles Angels during '61 and another seven in early '62, playing his final major-league game on May 8. He produced only one hit in eight at bats each year. He knew that his best years lay behind him. The 396 games he played qualified him for a major-league pension, thanks to Haney's assistance. He completed his career with a .261 batting average, 39 doubles, 5 triples, 21 homers and 105 RBIs, certainly not Hall of Fame statistics, but ones of which he could be proud.

Playing in the major leagues delivered a boatload of thrills over his career. He recalled many significant events. He thought about Brooklyn first baseman Gil Hodges blasting a grand-slam home run over his head and out of the park. He sat on the bench the day Hall of Fame member Stan Musial, a Donora native and a true gentleman, punched out his 3,000th hit. He played left field the day Ted Williams blasted his 500th home run over his head. As a rookie, he played left field with the great Hank Aaron beside him in right. He had pinch-hit for future Hall of Fame member Warren Spahn and called immortals like Ernie Banks and Eddie Mathews teammates and friends. His list of managers reads like a who's who: Charlie Grimm, Fred Haney, Bob Scheffing, Joe Gordon and Jimmy Dykes. He learned from each of them. The memories of his time in the big leagues would thrill him his entire life.

To make room for youngster players, the Angels had shuffled Chuck up and down between their minor-league Dallas–Fort Worth team and the bigs. General Manager Fred Haney, who liked Chuck and recognized his worth, called to offer him a part-time spot on the club for the next season as a fourth or fifth outfielder, promising, "I guarantee it." Chuck considered the opportunity to hang on for another season but realized that his playing time would be limited and short-lived. However, Haney also presented him with a second intriguing option: the opportunity to manage the Class A Quad Cities team in Davenport, Iowa.

Chuck opted for the second choice, accepting Haney's offer to manage. He looked forward to a new career path, one for which he felt both qualified and confident. Although his contract put him at the bottom rung of pro baseball, he believed that the opportunity to manage presented his best option for a future in baseball.

CHAPTER 5

MANAGING IN THE MINORS

I see great things in baseball. It's our game, the American game.
—Walt Whitman

A t the end of the 1962 season, manager John "Foghorn" Fitzgerald received a promotion to the AA Nashville Vols following a successful 74-51 record with the Class A Quad City Angels of Davenport, Iowa. This left the opening that Fred Haney presented to Chuck Tanner.

Los Angeles general manager Haney knew Chuck Tanner well, and he liked his "get up and go," baseball acumen and upbeat personality. Haney encouraged the aging outfielder to strongly consider the job. "Chuck, you have the tools and the temperament to relate to these kids and make them better. You would make a great manager, not just at Quad City, but up the line as well."

With his major-league career pretty much over, Chuck weighed various career paths, but he loved baseball. Spotting the upward mobility of the job, he opted for the starting salary of $6,000 to work at Class A baseball in a strange town at the bottom of the Los Angeles Angels organization, rather than accept the $18,000 Haney promised him as a minor-league player who would be brought up for a few games at the end of the season. He hoped that the downward step and reduction in pay would create a pathway that would allow him to remain in baseball and grow.

The new manager debuted in 1963 with Quad City of the Midwest League. The classic red-brick John O'Donnell Stadium, built in 1931 along the Mississippi River, served as the Los Angeles Angels affiliate's home field. Chuck vividly remembered the rumble of passing trains echoing throughout the stadium during games, as well as the loneliness of separation from his family and friends in New Castle while he lived by himself.

The Midwest League included teams in small and midsize cities in Wisconsin, Illinois and Iowa. The rookie manager opened his first season with a 66-57 mark as he climbed up the farm team ladder and earned his stripes. Six members of that 1963 team eventually earned a trip to the majors.

In 1964, the team performed comparably to the previous year, finishing third in the division with a 62-56 record. On a positive note, the Quad City Angels became the first in the league to draw more than 100,000 fans, reaching an attendance total of 108,129.

Tanner lived at least part of the season in a top-floor rented room on Fourth Avenue South in the home of the team's general manager, Fritz Colschen, a former Schlitz beer distributor. The ability to continue his career in baseball as a manager, even at the A level, provided him with a great deal of satisfaction along with a number of headaches. Although no longer throwing, catching or hitting, he relished the opportunity to work with younger players and help them reach their own dreams.

Over his first few months in the minors, Class A baseball's budgetary constraints, errors and miscues on the playing field, as well as the immaturity of the teenage players, angered and frustrated him. He developed a reputation for breaking furniture long before he became known as "Mr. Sunshine."

"I proved a hellion in my early years," Tanner confessed. Frustration and inexperience led to a lack of patience and bursts of temper. Supposedly, he once kicked over a tall locker after the team blew a close game. "I even slapped a player with a $50 fine for leaving his baseball spikes on the bench in front of his cubicle. I was a madman, not a manager," Tanner admitted.

"He and his coaches used to climb up fire escapes and peek into hotel windows when they made bed checks on the road," said Jim O'Brien, writing from his interviews with Tanner.[12] However, Chuck soon settled in and mellowed after a few months into the season. He remembered his own days as an impulsive eighteen-year-old rookie professional and developed the spirit of patience. He improved his skill of managing with each game, recognizing the futility of blaming his players for errors or mistakes, especially when they really tried. He developed the ability to mentor and support his troops rather than criticize them.

Chuck also came to recognize his own shortcomings in strategy and technique. Losing a game taught him never to relax his offense on the playing field. "We were up 9–0. Things could not be going better. I told our boys to cut out the base stealing and take it easy. While we quit running, our opponents didn't quit hitting. Well, we lost that game 10–9, and I never made that mistake again."

Roland Hemond, the Los Angeles Angels director of farm team development, spent many hours with Chuck while he managed the Quad City franchise. Together, they analyzed the potential of various players and discussed baseball in general. Chuck recognized that preparing his players to move up the ladder to AAA and eventually the major leagues remained even more important than winning games.

"That Llenas kid from the Dominican Republic has all the tools. He's only twenty-one and a decent fielder. I think I can help his progress," Chuck mentioned to Roland Hemond, who agreed with the prognosis. In fact, the two pros pretty much agreed on all of the team's talent potential. Hemond quickly gained respect for the young manager, who learned with every game. Plus, he seemed so damned likable. In short order, Roland and Chuck developed their baseball relationship into a close friendship.

As soon as the season ended, Chuck settled into the comfort of his ranch-style home at 34 Maitland Lane in Neshannock Township with his wife and four boys. It became a haven of tranquility. Chuck never considered moving from that house or New Castle. He intended to remain at that spot with Babs for the rest of his life.

With her husband away for much of the year, Babs raised the children and took care of the house like the Greek hero Odysseus's wife, Penelope, who patiently awaited her spouse's return from the Trojan War during his ten-year absence. Chuck enjoyed his work with the younger players, and he married the perfect wife who allowed him to do so. Babs relieved her husband from the day-to-day family matters in order for him to concentrate on his career. Chuck thanked the heavens for the sacrifices Babs had made for him every day of his life.

Chuck Tanner toiled for eight years in the Los Angeles Angels farm system and added to his repertoire with every inning. He nurtured his players and pushed them to become the best version of themselves. He treated each man as an individual, employing a knack for knowing which path would work best—sometimes total support and in other cases tough love. He developed self-control, communication skills and baseball strategy in his arsenal, and the Angels recognized his commitment to his players and growth as a field general. As a reward, the team promoted him in 1965 to the Class AA Texas League El Paso Sun Kings, with an appropriate raise. Dudley Field—an adobe-brick stadium named for a former mayor, built in 1924 and seating seven thousand—served as his second home.

The El Paso club finished with a dismal 53-87 record in '65 and a 62-78 record in '66. His bosses wanted winning stats, which, although important, proved secondary to advancing the team's top talent to the next skill level. Fifteen players from the El Paso '66 fifth-place team would spend time in the majors during their careers. The minor-league manager's primary job involved molding players into major leaguers, and Tanner coached some really good players during their formative years, such as twenty-year major-league outfielder Jay Johnstone, 114-game-winning pitcher Marty Pattin and top big-league relievers Ramon Hernandez and Bill Kelso. Almost to a man, the team members liked and respected their manager.

In 1966, Lawrence County honored Chuck Tanner with its Sportsman of the Year Award. At the time, he called it "the biggest thrill of my life… bigger than hitting a homer in my first time at bat in the majors…bigger than Rookie of the Year for the Braves…because this honor was given by my friends. I'll stick Lawrence County up against any in the nation for producing good athletes. You people don't realize what good athletic talent there is in the county, and that's because you know these athletes so well. As long as I live, I'll stay in Lawrence County. I think it's the greatest place in the world."

Chuck stood just under six-one and weighed in close to his playing weight at slightly less than two hundred pounds. His tree-trunk arms maintained their enormous strength. Although he learned to keep his temper in check, he used his physicality to make his instructions clearly understood. "In his minor league managing days, Tanner was known to grab players by their collars and lift them off the ground to get across his message."[13]

As soon as each season ended, Chuck raced back to his beloved New Castle family and friends. There, he frequented Valentine's Restaurant on Washington Street, chatting with pals like scout Fred Shaffer and Dr. Jim Snow. While chomping on a plate of stuffed cabbage or a sandwich, he pontificated about baseball or argued sports in general. The group gladly welcomed strangers and other topics of local interest, but Chuck ran the show.

In 1967, the Angels promoted Tanner to the Class AAA Seattle Angels in the Pacific Coast League. The team responded with an underwhelming 69-79 record and a fifth-place finish. However, Seattle produced a number of prominent major leaguers, including sixteen-year-catcher Ed Kirkpatrick, twenty-two-game winner Clyde Wright and reliever Tom Burgmeier, who ended his career with 102 saves and seventy-nine wins. Although the desired won-loss statistical performance appeared lacking, thirty-six players from the team would play at one time or another in the big leagues.

Jeff Pitzer, whose family ran Linger Light Dairy, delivered milk to the Tanner home on Maitland Lane during Chuck's minor-league years. Babs generally paid her bill in cash, and Jeff frequently chatted with her while collecting. When Jeff mentioned that he wanted to visit his grandparents in Cupertino, California, Babs suggested, "You should visit Chuck while you're out there. He is in nearby El Centro for spring training, and he would love to see you."

Jeff politely declined, thinking it might be too much of an imposition, but Babs persisted: "Really, Jeff, go. I know he would be thrilled to see a friend from New Castle."

When Jeff arrived in El Centro, Chuck proved the perfect host, providing him with a game ticket and putting him up in the team motel. While Jeff enjoyed California, the weather refused to cooperate. Rain ruined much of his trip. Since Jeff had never been to Hawaii and already had made it to the West Coast, he decided to fly to Oahu. When he arrived, he learned that the Seattle Angels had an away game against the Hawaii Islanders. He purchased a ticket directly behind Seattle's dugout. When Chuck looked up at the crowd, he spotted Jeff and kidded, "I thought I got rid of you in California."

Other New Castle friends also found their way to Hawaii. Dave Kennaday, a CPA with Carbis-Walker, and his wife, Carol, had attended an international Lion's Club convention in Tokyo. On their way home, they stopped in Hawaii and attended a ball game. Chuck apologized for not meeting them afterward due to another engagement, but he presented Carol with a ceremonial lei as a welcome. Dozens of New Castle citizens remembered similar kindnesses. Chuck never seemed too busy to offer a warm greeting, a signed baseball and a friendly handshake.

Chuck returned to the El Paso Sun Kings in 1968 and responded with a 77-60 record, leading the team to a first-place finish over the competition from Tennessee, New Mexico, Arkansas, Louisiana and Texas. A victory in the Texas League championship series earned him his first Minor League Manager of the Year award. Star first baseman Jim Spencer led the team with twenty-eight home runs. Spencer quickly moved up to the big leagues, where he enjoyed a successful fifteen-year career, winning two golden gloves and making the 1973 All-Star team.

On one occasion, Chuck served as a pinch hitter as well as the manager. He formally ended his last at bat as a player with an easy ground out. Over his minor-league career, he accumulated 1,669 hits in 5,328 at bats while playing in 1,454 games. He sported a sparkling .313 batting average with ninety home runs and 326 RBIs, proof of his prowess with a bat.

El Paso's first-place finish earned Chuck a 1969 promotion to the AAA Pacific Coast League Hawaii Islanders, where he delivered a 74-72 third-place finish, just one game out of second. Most importantly to the bosses, thirty out of the thirty-seven players he managed would eventually spend time in the big leagues, including star outfielder Floyd Robinson and two-time fifteen-game winner Tom Bradley.

The Hawaii team included flaky Bo Belinsky, a character with plenty of talent but limited dedication. When Chuck announced his rules to the team, which included promptness to all practices and meetings, ex–major leaguer Bo wrote out a postdated check and handed it to the manager. "I probably will be late for every meeting." The pitcher, who started his rookie season with a 4-0 record and a no-hitter before his big-league career fizzled, produced a 12-5 record and a sparkling 2.82 ERA for AAA Hawaii.

The major-league team executives pegged Chuck as a potential up-and-comer. The players drank in his positivity. His staff followed his lead and appreciated his loyalty, and he produced better than expected results with the available talent.

Los Angeles Angels general manager Dick Walsh placed his name on the shortlist for promotion and quizzed him on what changes he would make if he managed the team. Chuck answered, "I'd release Dick Stuart and Lou Johnson and bring up Jim Spencer and Ken Tatum, and we'd be fine."[14] The Angels considered Chuck as a potential interim replacement for fired manager Bill Rigney, but Chuck asked for a longer-term contract. The Angels opted to select Harold Ross "Lefty" Phillips instead, even though movie star owner Gene Autry would have preferred Chuck.

Los Angeles Angels scouting director and friend Roland Hemond telephoned Chuck to soften the blow of rejection. "Chuck, you should have gotten the job. My advice to you is just keep winning all you can win, and don't worry about anything else. Cream always rises to the top, and sooner or later you will hit the big leagues." Chuck gritted his teeth, took the setback in stride along with Roland's advice and persevered.

"You know, I had some satisfaction," Chuck told Fred Shaffer. "Although the Angels didn't hire me, they used my suggestions. They released Stuart and Johnson and brought up Spencer and Tatum. In fact, Tatum put up twenty-two saves and almost won Rookie of the Year."

With another season ended, Chuck returned to New Castle, where he took part in a stock club that met at the Travelers Restaurant on Washington

Street, a great spot for pizza, a beer and conversation. Since money proved tight with the Tanner family and most of the other members as well, the guys kept the dues manageable at about fifteen dollars per month. Paul Morrone, Chuck's former neighbor and part owner of Morrone Auto Wrecking, had invited his Carbis-Walker accountants Wally Cunningham and Dave Kennaday to join the stock club. Others included friends Bob Dean, a Shenango tax collector; Tony Ventarella; and Chuck's close friend, scout Fred Shaffer. Although no one made a killing in the stock market, the members had lots of fun. Chuck later joined a different group of investors with equally indifferent results.

Chuck's minor-league manager's salary made paying the bills challenging for a man with a wife and four children. In addition to his high school photography sales job and occasional work with his plumber father-in-law, Chuck served as the sports director for Youngstown's WFMJ TV. He handled the 6:00 p.m. and 11:00 p.m. broadcasts for $150 per week. From time to time, he allowed his cronies to appear as guests on the show. Chuck Ferris explained how his ex-neighbor had brought him on to discuss local sports.[15]

The Tanner family managed to make at least one trip to Hawaii while Chuck managed, son Bruce recalled. "But I was too young to remember much about it other than it took a long time to get there."

In 1970, Tanner led the AAA Hawaii Islanders, who started the season with a so-so 18-18 record, to a pennant-winning 98 wins in 146 games, the best record in all pro baseball. His victorious season earned him a second Minor League Manager of the Year award, an honor he shared with Tommy Lasorda, who led the Spokane Indians to a North Division pennant. Lasorda would gain lasting fame as the Los Angeles Dodgers manager for twenty years.

The Islanders finished the South Division a full thirteen games ahead of the second-place Phoenix Giants. Baseball historians Bill Weiss and Marshall Wright selected the 1970 Hawaii Islanders as the best-performing squad in the team's twenty-seven-year history. No other team had racked up more victories. In fact, minor-league experts selected the Tanner-managed Islanders as the thirty-eighth-best minor-league team of all time.

The Islanders and their successful manager proved immensely popular in Hawaii. The attendance at Honolulu Stadium ballooned to 467,217 paying customers versus 280,477 the previous year.

The Islanders possessed dominant pitching, and Tanner recognized that pitching created championships. Juan Pizarro, who would win 131 games in the majors over an eighteen-year career, sported a 9-1 record. Dave LaRoche chipped in with a 6-0 record and later would chalk up 58 wins and 126 saves during a fourteen-year major-league career. Tom Bradley produced an 11-1 record, and Dennis Bennett came through with 19-8 statistics. Both pitchers would play in the majors for more than seven years. The pitching staff finished second in the league in saves with thirty-eight, demonstrating a Tanner tendency toward a generous use of relievers, a hallmark of his strategy throughout much of his career. Future major leaguer Jim Coates led the way with seventeen saves. The team's ninety-four stolen bases, only one behind the South Division league leader, helped produce the highest run scoring total in the Pacific Coast League.

Baseball executives throughout the industry took notice of Chuck Tanner's outstanding year. Clubs with losing records scouted for new and dynamic leadership. Undoubtedly a team required skilled players to win, but success also required a results-driven manager to harness and motivate that talent into a winning lineup. During his decades as a player and manager, Chuck had proven his mettle, and his results at Hawaii made his name come up again and again as a potential major-league manager.

Chuck liked people, and people liked Chuck. That became one of his secrets to success—that and persistence. His affinity for finding the best in others drew people to him. During his years in baseball, his innate positivity delivered a coterie of fans and followers throughout the industry. At the head of the list of those who appreciated and respected him stood Roland Hemond, who considered Chuck among his favorites. Former minor leaguer Todd Alexander stated, "In baseball as in life it's often not what you know, but who you know," and Roland Hemond proved an important contact.

Chuck's capabilities had impressed Hemond. When he worked as the assistant director of scouting for Milwaukee in 1957, he witnessed firsthand Tanner's strong work ethic as a player and admired the way he got along with his teammates. Roland knew that Chuck would be the first to admit that other players possessed greater talent than he had, but few out-hustled him.

Later, when Hemond worked as the Angels scouting director, he marveled at Tanner's ability to grow major leaguers and build a team. Equally importantly, Roland took in Chuck's skill at getting along with his players and coaches. His resiliency at overcoming negatives and kicking despondency in the butt proved remarkable. "Chuck Tanner steered his ship like a consummate captain. He never veered off course regardless of whether the seas proved calm and easily navigable or twenty-foot waves buffeted his craft."

In baseball, nothing remains more constant than change. On September 1, 1970, the Chicago White Sox president, John Allyn, fired Ed Short, his veteran general manager for the previous nine years. The team had suffered through a dismal 49-87 record, with the playing season nearing its end. Attendance at Comiskey Park had plummeted to an average of only 6,115 fans per game, the worst in the majors. Allyn knew that he had to make an immediate change to survive.

The Sox owner hired Stu Holcomb, a former star Ohio State football player, Northwestern University coach and one-time manager of the Allyn brothers–owned Chicago Mustangs soccer team, as his new executive vice-president and general manager. One of Holcomb's first acts involved advising White Sox manager Don Gutteridge that he intended to replace him at the end of the season. Since his future with the Sox had come to an end, Gutteridge asked for and received an early release. With limited short-term options, Holcomb and Allyn appointed third base coach Bill Adair as the team's interim manager while the executives discussed who to select as a full-time replacement.

On September 4, Holcomb hired Roland Hemond, the Los Angeles Angels scouting director and a huge Tanner supporter, to head player personnel. Roland heartedly recommended Chuck for the vacant manager's position as the necessary cure for a sick team. Holcomb examined Tanner's credentials, liked what he saw and agreed to consider Hemond's suggestion.

With the minor-league season in its final days, the Hawaii Islanders team and its manager traveled to Arizona to play the Chicago White Sox's AAA farm club, the Tucson Toros. This allowed Holcomb the perfect opportunity to interview the forty-one-year-old candidate. If he harbored any doubts, Chuck's experience, warm smile, positivity and overall demeanor won over the general manager.

"Within ten minutes of speaking to Chuck, I recognized I had indeed made the proper selection," Holcomb said. "Chuck Tanner would make the ideal replacement for Gutteridge as manager."

As Chuck recalled the day's events, "Glenn Miller, the Sox farm club director, came over and said his club's new vice-president and general manager Stu Holcomb wanted to see me. We met, and Stu Holcomb offered me a two-year deal at $40,000 per year on September 4. Although I wanted three years, I naturally accepted." Another dream had been fulfilled. Chuck Tanner had just received his ticket to become the major-league manager of the American League's Chicago White Sox.

CHAPTER 6

MANAGING THE CHICAGO WHITE SOX

All things come to those who wait.
—Lady Mary Montgomerie Currie

The year 1970 had proven a disaster for the Chicago White Sox. Sporting the worst won-loss record in the league, the Sox attracted fewer than 500,000 fans. The team required a complete turnaround, and the tandem of Roland Hemond, Chuck Tanner and owner John Allyn, heir to the Francis I. Du Pont Brokerage firm, intended to clean house. After Tanner completed his season with Hawaii, he replaced interim manager Bill Adair, who had recorded a 4-6 record through September 13.

Chuck arrived in Chicago anxious to take over the team and move it forward in the standings, but first he intended to take stock of his players and hire staff. Chuck knew that he wanted his own coaches. "If this is going to be a Tanner team, I need my own guys." At just forty-one years of age, he intended to look at problems in different ways.

The new manager hired Johnny Sain as his pitching coach, an outstanding selection. Sain could be outspoken and difficult to handle, but he possessed undeniable talent. The Detroit Tigers had fired him the previous year, making him readily available. Chuck respected Sain, who had spent much of 1970 as a roving minor-league pitching instructor. This four-time, twenty-game-winning star pitcher for the Milwaukee Braves in the '40s and '50s had coached and produced a number of twenty-game winners over his career. As a player, his name had become synonymous with the saying, "Spahn and

Sain, Spahn and Sain, pitch them both and pray for rain." Several experts believed that his excellence as a coach exceeded his outstanding major-league career. One sportswriter stated, "If any pitching coach deserved a spot in the Hall of Fame, Sain's name should appear at the top of the list." Chuck anticipated that Johnny Sain's magic touch would increase the effectiveness of the 1971 pitching staff and dramatically lift the win total.

Tanner next picked Luke Appling, a two-time batting champ, seven-time All-Star and Hall of Famer, as his batting coach. He hired Alex Monchak to coach first base and Beaver Falls native Joe Lonnett to handle third. Years earlier, Chuck had promised his friend Lonnett that if he ever managed in the majors, he would find a place for him. After assembling a loyal and competent staff for the following season, he planned the necessary changes to solidify the team for the next season and crank up the win total.

Tanner's late September promotion to the Chicago White Sox for the final sixteen games of the season allowed him no time to get his feet wet. He approached the job like a kid with a pocket full of change in a penny candy store. Rain storms had delayed "Mr. Sunshine's" September 15 scheduled entry into major-league management until September 18.

Always the gentleman, Chuck visited with former manager Don Gutteridge before he left. He asked the departing manager if he could give him any tips. "Not really, I just left you three numbered envelopes in the top drawer of the desk in the manager's office. When the team is in a slump and you don't know what to do, open the first envelope. If that doesn't work, open the second. If nothing changes, fetch the third envelope."

During the next few days, losses mounted. Tanner went to the desk and pulled out envelope number one. Inside it read, "Blame it on your predecessor." At the afternoon press conference, Chuck did just that.

After more losses and sloppy play, he opened envelope number two. This one read, "Make a new lineup." Chuck did as instructed. During the final week of the season, one newspaper columnist called for another change in managers. Tanner opened envelope number three in hopes of coming up with an answer. The note inside read, "Prepare three envelopes." Tanner appreciated Gutteridge's sense of humor, but he intended to make certain that the next season showed improvement.[16]

The Tanner-managed team finished 1970 with a dismal 3-13 record, even worse than Gutteridge and Adair. Quite frankly, the last-place Sox just didn't have the horses. Slick-fielding Luis Aparicio starred at short and batted .313. Third baseman Bill Melton pounded out thirty-three round-trippers and catcher Ed Herrmann and outfielder Carlos May put up decent numbers, but the team lacked winning talent at several key positions. Tommy John and Wilbur Wood pitched okay, but the team ERA of 4.54 proved a disaster, the worst in the major leagues. The staff also finished dead last in total strikeouts and toward the bottom in almost every statistical category.

Although Chuck produced an even worse win-loss percentage than his two predecessors, the final sixteen games provided Chuck with the opportunity to scout his squad. He used those weeks to determine who belonged on the 1971 team and who didn't. At a team meeting, he announced, "Gentlemen, the pitching rotation is the same for the rest of the season. The only time you will see me is when I change pitchers. For the rest of the year do what you want. If you want to hit and run, fine. Steal, great. That's okay. It's up to you."

"I sat in the dugout with a notebook and watched, allowing me to determine who was a team player, whom I wanted to keep and whom I wanted to let go. I wanted to see who tried to sacrifice a man to third to gauge who was playing for himself and not the team."

He continued, "I intended to build on pitching and defense. We traded a few good players like Ken Berry and Luis Aparicio but got back guys each time who improved the team. Mike Andrews wasn't an All-Star second baseman, but he was better than what we had the year before," he told sportswriter Mark Liptak. The team also acquired or brought up Jay Johnstone, Luis Alvarado, Tom Bradley and Tom Egan.

"I was going to win or lose my way. I wasn't going to lose and get fired someone else's way," Chuck insisted. Director of personnel Hemond and Tanner sped toward change like a finely tuned race car gathering momentum on a straightaway. "We had worked together with the Angels, and we'd been in the Braves organization," Hemond reminisced. "In fact, we worked extremely well. At the first winter meeting of 1970, we moved sixteen players in the first eighteen hours of the convention. We improved by twenty-three games the first year. Then, we acquired Dick Allen and Stan Bahnsen in a couple of big deals, and we made a heck of a run at it in '72."[17]

Prior to spring training, Chuck received a good-luck haircut at Gomer Lewis's East Washington Street barbershop before heading south. "Gomer, how would you like to visit Chicago?"

"Sure would," Gomer answered.

"I'm going to arrange a couple of Sox seats for you and your wife during the regular season," he said, a promise the manager would keep.

In March 1971, sportswriter Al Abrams visited manager Chuck Tanner and executive vice-president Stu Holcomb in Sarasota during spring training. Chuck sprinted some two hundred yards to offer a warm welcome. Stu followed a few feet behind. Although the Sox may have finished last in the league the prior year, Abrams ranked them first in friendliness.

Abrams liked the upbeat spirit of the 1971 squad and wrote, "The White Sox finished dead last prior to the entry of Tanner and Holcomb. These two men became part of the sweeping changes in the organization.... Everywhere we looked there was evidence of the 'new look' the White Sox were sporting."

"We lost 106 games last year," Tanner told the reporter. "I'm sure we can do better than that. How much better depends on some young players coming along fast in the next two seasons. There is something I can promise—an aggressive style of play with lots of wild base running."[18]

Chuck intended to change the team from a singles-hitting, defense-oriented, opportunistic squad to a power-punching, base-running, high-scoring juggernaut. He planned on sluggers Bill Melton and Carlos May leading the way.

The White Sox executives considered Tanner a "dynamic force." Based on his success at Hawaii the prior year, they looked forward to an exciting season. They anticipated that his youth and upbeat disposition would rub off onto his players and staff. Chuck could also be tough when necessary. "I'm a disciplinarian, but fair and firm," he explained. "I'm for the ball players 100 percent when they give me 100 percent."

Chuck recognized that hustle and enthusiasm helped but failed to replace talent. The Sox team included some very fine players. Chuck pointed to long-ball hitters Carlos May and Bill Melton, whom he planned to convert from outfielders to full-time infielders. He also mentioned catcher Ed Herrmann and pitchers Tommy John, Joel Horlen and Jim Bradley. Chuck told the press that pitching coach Johnny Sain's skill and experience could improve the pitching staff by as much as 20 percent.

The Sox's entire team looked forward to changes in 1971. Equipment manager Larry Licklider from Ashtabula, Ohio; trainer Charley Said of the Wheeling-Steubenville area; and pitching coach Johnny Sain drank in the euphoria of the new regime. Bosses Stu Holcomb and Roland Hemond praised the skipper. "He was a pleasure to work with and for," Lonnett said. All of Chuck's coaches totally supported his actions and managerial philosophy.

Optimism soared during the preseason. Chuck Tanner put aside his king-size cigar and pontificated, "Being in baseball is like being in heaven. Just having the uniform on is like being a saint."[19]

The new manager intended to convert this ragtag losing team into respectability by employing "simplicity," an upgrade in talent and his own style of discipline. "I stress certain words like cut and relay." He emphasized that *cut* means cut and nothing else and ditto for *relay*. He pointed out that the fewer words the better. "For example don't say throw it to third or third base. Just say third. If a pitcher doesn't have sense enough to know third means third base, he doesn't have enough sense to pitch for me." Tanner explained to his players what should be done but also why.

During spring training, he experimented to position the best nine players on the field during the game. He tested power-hitting left fielder Carlos May at first. "We worked hard on fundamentals. We went through seven infield stations, twenty minutes at a time with five-minute rests in between. Each session ended with batting practice."

Pitching coach Sain considered Tanner's basket-of-surprises game plans as a breath of fresh air. He and Chuck counted on ace Tommy John, Joel Horlen and Tom Bradley to carry the pitching load, with Wilbur Wood handling relief. John had won twelve games the prior season. Horlen, a one-time 19-7 pitcher with a league-leading 2.06 earned run average in 1967, fell to 6-16 in 1970, but he "burned the ball" across the plate during his preseason outings. Bradley had put up an impressive 11-1 record with Hawaii, and big Bart Johnson performed well in practice. Rookie Terry Forster displayed a wicked fastball. With seasoning, he possessed the tools to be a great closer. Chuck believed that the Sox were well prepared and ready for action in the 1971 season.

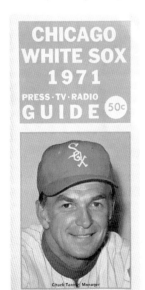

During the early weeks, the team performed poorly. Tanner planned to call up Mike Hershberger from the minors, where he was rehabbing from a pulled hamstring. Chicago scouts claimed that Hershberger gave off a bad attitude and didn't want to play. Chuck disagreed. "You know there's a reason Don Gutteridge isn't here as a manager anymore. It's because he listened to all of you. If Hershberger isn't brought back up, you'll be looking for a new manager....The point was I was going to win or lose my way, not the way someone else wanted me to."

The 1971 Chicago White Sox press guide. *Author's collection.*

Chuck considered himself a player's manager. He possessed the ability to communicate and let each man know exactly where he stood. His management style gave his guys every opportunity to shine. The writers told him that he would ruin the younger players like Jorge Orta, Bucky Dent and Goose Gossage by playing them too early in their careers. "Hogwash, I put the best players that I had available on the field. I inserted them in spots where they had an opportunity to succeed, both for themselves and the team."

"I had twenty-five different rules, one for each player on the squad," he explained. "Criticism belonged in the clubhouse, not for release to the media. Fines always remained a private matter, not for public knowledge." Chuck opted never to embarrass his players publicly.

Tanner's ability to calm the raging testosterone or soothe the hurt feelings of a team member at the proper moment proved exceptional. When right fielder Pat Kelly pouted over some perceived grievance or personal problem, Tanner watched the locker room suck in the negative vibes. Chuck acted to stifle the gloom before it spread. He walked over to Kelly, picked up the 185 pounder, backed him against a locker and said with a twinkle in his eye, "Hey, Pat, lighten up and smile." Pat got the message. "Okay, Skipper," he grinned, and the clubhouse relaxed.

When Bucky Dent struggled and feared a demotion, Tanner reassured his player, "You are a major-league shortstop. You are not going back to the minors." Dent loosened up and started playing better. Wilbur Wood noticed that Chuck always found time to work with those players experiencing the most severe problems.

Injuries play a key role in a winning baseball season. Starting pitcher Joel Horlen tore his knee sliding into second in early April, a huge loss for the Sox. Tanner had counted on him as a mainstay. New Castle confidant and scout Fred Shaffer reminded Chuck that Wilbur Wood had been a legitimate starter in the minors before becoming a reliever. "Remember, Wilbur won fourteen games a few years ago at AAA Columbus." When Chuck broached the idea with his pitching coach, Sain gave his "let's give it a try" nod of approval.

Wilbur Wood initially balked at the idea of converting from a successful role as a reliever to a starting role. "Chuck, you know I had twenty-two saves last year."

"Yea, I know. You were a terrific reliever, Wilbur, but you know a starter earns a lot more money? Do you like money?"

"Sure," came back the reply.

"Well, I intend to pitch you every third or fourth day. In fact, I plan to pitch the hell out of you, and you can become a star."

Wood agreed to try the change and responded with twenty-two wins to lead the club that year. He would produce four twenty-game winning seasons in a row and be named as an All-Star three times.

Tanner crowed, "You know what's funny? Harry Caray and all the writers in the Bard Room at Comiskey talked about how it wouldn't work. A few months later, I'm having a beer, and these same guys are talking about how great a move it was. You know what made me feel especially good? Owner Allyn later came over to me toward the end of the season, patted me on the back and said, 'Chuck, you saved the franchise.' That's how I knew I was doing my job."

Chicago White Sox locals raved about Chuck. His attentiveness and courtesy created friends throughout the city. He recognized the importance of interacting with fans. Chuck never turned down anyone seeking an autograph. Game attendees Jules and Beam Wolff spent several minutes with him after a game. The couple boasted how he didn't brush them off and seemed to care about what they had to say. They would not be an exception; friendliness and consideration proved Chuck's *modus operandi* for promoting positive public relations.

New Castle native Gerry Mitchell remembered Chuck coming to a sales manager's lunch for Universal Rundle held in Chicago. "He preached his philosophy of what it takes to make a winning team, and he didn't expect a fee for his advice."

After toiling in the trenches as a minor-league player for nine years and as a manager for another eight, Chuck remembered his roots. He understood the futility of criticizing a player who struck out or committed an error on the field. He avoided second-guessing a pitcher's selection of curves, fastballs and change-ups. The offending player generally regretted his mistake already—why make him feel worse? A good manager supported his players and helped them to reach their own personal and team goals, just as others had helped him. That was the Tanner way. He intended to become the best manager he could be.

During the 1971 season, the Tanner family spent six weeks in Chicago, staying at the forty-story Executive House on Wacker Drive, a corporate housing facility. "When Muhammad Ali walked through the lobby bigger than life, my mom was awestruck and so was I," Chuck's youngest son, Bruce Tanner, reminisced. "Many evenings we ate at a rib house, but during game nights, we usually went to the Bard's Room at Comiskey Park—the dining room for VIPs, investors, front office executives and the media—for a snack and a drink. After forty-five minutes or so, we would return to the hotel." The excitement and electricity of big-league baseball pulsed through the veins of Chuck's eleven-year-old son during that Chicago season.

Lawrence County residents ardently supported the White Sox and Chuck Tanner—that is, when not rooting for the National League's Pittsburgh Pirates. Lew Grell described a visit to Comiskey Park. "Chuck arranged Sox tickets for me, my daughter and her roommate. As we approached the front of the ball field, we discovered their seats lay directly behind the dugout, possibly among the best locations in the house. Chuck peeked up from the dugout and greeted us with a friendly welcome and the question, 'How do you like those seats?'"

"Chuck made us feel like a million dollars," Dr. Grell beamed. Dozens of attendees provided similar stories about his hospitality toward hometown guests before, during and after games.

The year 1971 delivered improved results for the Sox, who ended with a 79-83 record, good enough for a third-place finish behind Oakland and Kansas City. Bill Melton led the league with thirty-three home runs and the team with eighty-six RBIs. Carlos May batted .294 and topped the team in hits, but the Sox work on the mound accounted for the greatest uptick. Newly converted ace Wilbur Wood's 22-13 record and incredible 1.91 ERA over 334 innings paced a pitcher's year. Tom Bradley, Tommy John and Bart Johnson each chipped in with twelve or more wins, accounting for the statistical improvement of the 20 percent that Tanner predicted. Team ERA dropped to an outstanding 3.12, and the staff strikeout record rose significantly. The performance upgrade excited the fans. Attendance at Comiskey Park jumped from just 495,355 the previous year to a more acceptable figure of 833,891.

New Castle fans rewarded its native son with a banquet at the Elks Club on Mill Street on December 9. The *New Castle News* called him "the most popular guy in the area." More than two hundred people showed up to honor Chuck. Guests of honor included his close friend, major-league scout Fred Shaffer, also a local, and third base coach Joe Lonnett from neighboring Beaver Falls. Lonnett lauded his boss as "the greatest manager in baseball....I'm not saying that because he is sitting here. Chuck Tanner can motivate a ball player better than any man I've ever seen. It is a real treat to be associated with him."

On the podium, Chuck modestly said, "I think I have the easiest job in the world managing a major-league team. My coaches do all the work. I just stand around, watch nine innings of baseball, take my shower and go home." Everyone knew Chuck lived and breathed the sport twenty-four hours a day, but he shared his successes with his staff and players and accepted blame for any failures.

To the question from the crowd, "Will you win it all next year?" Chuck refused to make a firm prediction, couching his words: "I don't know how many games we'll win in 1972 or how high we'll finish. I only know that whenever you pay to see the White Sox play, you'll see a team that will be giving 100 percent and hustling all over the field."

Chuck joked, "I was only thrown out of three games all season, and in every instance I was right and the ump was wrong, but somehow I always ended up paying the fine."

Chuck reiterated his forgive-and-forget managerial philosophy: "If I get upset at a player one day, I erase everything at nightfall. When the sun comes up the next morning, it's a new day, and we start fresh. I treat my players like men as long as they behave like men....There's only one boss. That's me. On the other hand, if a player has a suggestion to make, I'll listen to it. If I use it, I give him credit."

Chuck found another reason for optimism in 1972. His twenty-one-year-old son Mark, after playing ball and finishing his studies at Penn State, began his own professional baseball career with the Chicago Cubs rookie-level affiliate of the Gulf Coast League in Bradenton, Florida. Walt Dixon, a former minor leaguer who once batted .415 with thirty-seven home runs and 165 RBIs, managed the Gulf Coast Cubs team, and future Hall of Fame reliever Bruce Sutter became a teammate. Mark appeared both as a pitcher and a first baseman. His best year would come in 1974 with the Class A Gastonia Rangers of North Carolina, where he posted an 8-1 pitching record in fifteen outings under manager Rich Donnelly. The club led the league with an 84-48 record. Six members of that squad would make their way to the majors, led by Len Barker, who would win nineteen games for the Cleveland Indians in 1981, throw a no-hitter in 1982 and lead the American League in strikeouts both years.

Friend Jack Zduriencik, a minor-league second baseman and one-time general manager of the Seattle Mariners, remembered Mark well from their high school days. "He played for Neshannock, and I played for New Castle. In the summer, we both took part in American Legion ball. Mark played for another team. We always were opponents, but he was a great player. He was a talented right-handed pitcher and a strong left-handed batter who looked like Robert Redford." Unfortunately, neither Jack nor Mark progressed beyond the minors.[20]

Young Bruce Tanner, Chuck's youngest son and a future major-league pitcher, relished every moment of his time in Sarasota's Payne Park during 1972's spring training. "I was a little leaguer, and pitching coach Johnny Sain watched me throw and gave me a tip or two on my grip. Dick Allen hit some grounders to me, and I shagged balls in the outfield. I also got to be a bat boy, and that was great! The players were really nice to me, a sign of their respect for Chuck. After workouts or games, I cleaned shoes for the equipment manager and performed other tasks. I received homework from my teachers and spent a few wonderful weeks in Florida with the team. What more could a youngster want?"

A strong spring training psyched up the White Sox team. They appeared ready for action. Unfortunately, a player walkout lasting from April 1 to April 13, the first such strike in baseball history, delayed the opening day of 1972 by two weeks. The season only began after the owners agreed to a $500,000 increase in pension benefits and added salary arbitration to player contracts.

The White Sox opened in Kansas City with disastrous consequences, dropping all three games in the series, but in their opener at Comiskey, the Sox stunned the Texas Rangers with a fifteen-hit, fourteen-run performance led by Carlos May's six RBIs and Wilbur Wood's three-hit pitching.

As the season progressed, the team excelled. Tanner's leadership and some strong performances by the pitchers propelled the White Sox to a second-place finish in its division, five and a half games behind Oakland. The fans responded accordingly, and paid attendance at Comiskey Park swelled to 1,177,318.

Chuck rode his ace 24-17 knuckleballer Wilbur Wood through 376⅔ innings of pitching, a modern season-high record. Wood and 21-16 Stan Bahnsen started an amazing ninety games during the season, the highest number since Hall of Famers Christy Mathewson and "Iron Man" Joe McGinnity appeared in ninety-nine for the 1904 New York Giants. Workhorse 15-14 Tom Bradley added another forty starts. Chuck's folksy small-town style, positivity and confidence had inspired his players to perform at their best.

The addition of first baseman Dick Allen proved a major factor in Tanner's 1972 success in Chicago, but Allen never would have come to Chicago without a push from Chuck. Chuck had played basketball and baseball against Dick's older brother Coy Craine, and the Allens lived just twenty minutes away from the Tanner family's Shenango Township home. All five of Era Allen's boys had been outstanding high school athletes, and three ended up playing major-league baseball.

Dick Allen's elder brother, Harold (or Hank, as many called him), remembered Chuck from the days in which he had set up Wampum High's class pictures with Seavy Photography. When Chuck bumped into Hank, who played for the Milwaukee Brewers at the time, prior to the start of a game at County Stadium in 1971, Tanner remarked after some chitchat, "You know, Hank, I intend to bring your brother to the White Sox if I can work out a deal with the Dodgers." Hank considered the move a pipe dream or at best a Tanner joke, but he smiled and said, "Lots of luck. Always great to see you, Chuck."

In a December 2, 1971 blockbuster deal, the Sox traded ace pitcher Tommy John and infielder Stephen Huntz to the Los Angeles Dodgers for star first baseman Dick Allen, considered in baseball circles as a strong-willed player. He had hit .295 during the previous year with twenty-four home runs and ninety RBIs, far from his best year, but still quite good.

Allen appeared unhappy with the trade and his entire career in the majors. He refused to report and strongly considered retirement, even though the Sox management dangled a hefty $120,000 salary as an enticement. Fed up with the vicissitudes of baseball life, Allen explained, "I lived from age one to eighteen without money. So, why not go and make $100 a week out in the country where I can live in peace."

Chuck visited Dick and his mother, Era, in Wampum to try to convince them that Dick and the White Sox would make a nice fit. "I knew Mrs. Allen. Back home everybody knew about Mrs. Allen and her boys. She was a wonderful lady, a tough woman raising all those boys. I said to them, 'Look, Dick, Chicago will be your last stop. You're going to make it with us. You're the guy who can make us a winner.'"[21] Dick listened quietly, but Chuck failed to convince him. He returned to his farm in Perkasie, thirty-five miles north of Philadelphia, with the intent of retiring.

Mrs. Allen called her son at his farm and asked him to come home to discuss the matter in further detail. A week or so later, Dick came home, and his mother said she had thought a great deal about their talk with Chuck.

"Why would I want go to a team that was in last place a year ago?" Dick sulked.

"Well," his mother answered, "I trust Chuck, and I know he will look after you. It might be a blessing in disguise." Dick eventually listened to his mother and joined the team. He never regretted his choice.

Many considered Dick Allen a "problem"—too high-strung and hard to control. Some Chicago sportswriters and announcers jeered at Tanner's decision to bring his fellow Lawrence County resident on board, but Chuck possessed a knack for dealing with so-called difficult players. As promised, he treated his new first baseman with respect, and Dick Allen flourished as a team leader. He became the team's senior statesman and Chuck's go-to guy.

Chuck watched out for Dick just like he told Mrs. Allen he would. "When I wanted to demonstrate the proper way to take a lead from first base, I used Allen." Dick responded to Chuck's special treatment by nourishing and supporting his younger teammates.

When Chuck consigned Jorge Orta to the Southern League's Knoxville Sox to work on his hitting, the young Mexican broke down and sobbed in broken English, "But I have no money. What will I do?"

Allen pulled a wad of cash from his pocket and handed it to his teammate. He then added, "Jorge, you'll be back up here before you know it." That is the Dick Allen his manager saw and admired.

A sportswriter nudged Chuck about playing Dick Allen. "Do you really think you should be starting a guy who skipped batting practice?" Chuck blasted back, "If you were the manager, would you rather play a nice guy who batted .240 or a man with a chip on his shoulder who smacked forty or more home runs and hit for a .300 average? Why don't you tell me what you would do?" The manager explained his philosophy in three words: "communication not regimentation."[22]

Chuck recognized that each player on the team deserved special attention. "If I tried to box Dick Allen in, I wouldn't get results. He'd be unhappy and so would I. I valued a player's worth on the ball field not at public events or practice sessions."

Like Chuck in New Castle's Shenango Township, the Allen brothers had starred in high school basketball, four of them earning all-state honors. Dick developed into one of Chuck's all-time favorite players—"an altar boy, not a bad boy."[23] In return, Allen credited Tanner for much of his success: "It's like playing on a college team." Chuck had shown him the respect he felt he deserved, and he responded in kind. The two became more than manager and player. They became lifelong friends.

Allen led the 1972 Sox offense with a .309 batting average, a league-leading 99 walks, 37 home runs, 113 RBIs and 19 stolen bases. His outstanding year culminated in his winning the American League's Most Valuable Player award (MVP).

On July 31, Allen thrilled the crowd by becoming the only person ever to hit two inside-the-park home runs in a single game during modern times— and against future Hall of Fame pitcher Bert Blyleven of the Minnesota

Chuck Tanner and Dick Allen.
Bruce Tanner.

Twins. According to Tanner, "Dick was the leader of the team, the captain, the manager on the field. He watched over the young kids, took them under his wing, and he played each game as if it were his last day on earth."[24] Chuck always considered Allen as one of the finest players he ever managed, deserving of a spot in the Hall of Fame at Cooperstown. "Dick is well worth his $120,000 salary and more." In fact, he received a well-deserved increase for the next season.

With the exception of first baseman Dick Allen's big bat, left fielder Carlos May's .308 average and right fielder Pat Kelly's thirty-two stolen bases, the offense appeared subpar. A .238 batting average forced the Sox's powerful "Big Three" pitching staff to carry much of the load during the 1972 season. Ace Wilbur Wood's twenty-four victories earned him the American League Pitcher of the Year Award from the *Sporting News*.

Tanner also assembled a capable relief staff. He had called up twenty-year-old Rich "Goose" Gossage, an 18-2 fireball-throwing starter for Appleton in the Class A Midwest League, the previous year. The manager opted to convert him to a reliever despite his 7-1 record as a starter. Tanner and Sain helped Gossage add a wicked curve to his arsenal, enabling him to become one of the major league's strongest all-time closers. Although only collecting 2 saves in 1972, Gossage would earn the Fireman of the Year Award in 1975 after leading the league with 26 saves. Eventually, his 124 wins and 310 lifetime saves earned him a spot in the Hall of Fame.

In addition to his technical skills, baseball ambassador Tanner's outgoing nature produced a wonderful public image. His big heart and enthusiasm spread to everyone he met. He possessed the unique ability to motivate any who dealt with him. He claimed that he never had a bad day in baseball. "I thought I had it made even when I didn't have it made."[25]

Chuck expected effort, and the team responded. After taking over that horrendous 56-106 team of 1970, the worst record in baseball, the 1972 squad attained a winning 86-67 record just two years later. Baseball experts recognized how he had turned around a loser into a pennant contender in a short period of time. Several well-deserved awards followed to celebrate his success.

Chuck Tanner easily outpointed Eddie Kasko of the Boston Red Sox in a December 27 213–149 vote to win the Associated Press American League Manager of the Year award for 1972. Hall of Fame manager Sparky Anderson of the Cincinnati Reds earned the corresponding National League award after leading the Western Division with a 95-59 record.

The *Sporting News* selected Tanner as the Major League Manager of the Year. Along with the prestigious award, he received a state-of-the-art Bulova Accutron II watch and a trophy. Manager Dick Williams of Oakland told the media, "There's no question that Tanner is the Manager of the Year. With the defense he had, I don't know how he had his team up there, but somehow he hid those weaknesses."[26]

The *Sporting News* also named Chuck's friend Roland Hemond, the personnel director of the White Sox, as the Baseball Executive of the Year several weeks earlier. The duo had formed a sensational alliance. Chuck performed well above expectations, even with the loss of his number-four pitcher Bart Johnson prior to the opening of the season and of Bill Melton, the 1971 American League home run champion. Melton suffered two herniated discs while breaking the fall of his son from a garage roof. The injury caused him to miss one hundred games and forced Tanner to substitute Ed Spiezio and Hank Allen in his place.

Chuck's Lawrence County friends intended to honor its native son for the past season's accomplishments. This was a man who never forgot his hometown, and New Castle resolved to remember his success.

The breakfast crew at Valentine's Restaurant met to plan a formal banquet for their friend. Attorney Francis X. Caiazza and Walter Smith agreed to chair the committee for a Saturday evening, February 17, 1973 dinner at the Holiday Inn on Route 422. Planning sessions generally took place at the house of Roselee Caiazza, who penned a commemorative ode to Chuck and the committee:

> *The boyhood dreams of heroes were only what they knew.*
> *Perhaps they can at last identify with you.*
> *For you're their inspiration, and your ideals have been instilled.*

Mike Leitera covered the event for the *New Castle News* and estimated an attendance of about seven hundred, one of the largest banquets in the area. Monsignor Joseph F. Fabbri, pastor of St. Vitus Church, opened

Roselee and Judge Francis
Caiazza. *Judge Francis Caiazza.*

with an invocation. Star first baseman Dick "Sleepy" Allen flew in from Oakland to announce, "He's more than just a great manager. He's a great guy." Allen's brothers Harold, Ron, Coy and half-brother Caesar Craine, all basketball stars at Wampum High School under Coach Butler Hennon, along with their mother, Era Allen, joined the festivities. Tanner responded to an Allen compliment with one of his own: "There's no one in the game who can do what he can do. I predict we can win it all next year if I don't screw it up."

Co-chair Walter Smith gifted Chuck with a portrait of his parents for placement in his office at Comiskey Park. The American Legion Perry S. Gaston Post 343 awarded a certificate of recognition. Representatives Donald Fox and Tom Fee of the Pennsylvania House and Tom Andrews of the Pennsylvania Senate presented congratulatory resolutions. Mayor Francis Rogan gave Chuck a proclamation from the city.

The Shenango China Company produced special platters for the event. Company officer Dave Parillo handed them individually to Chuck Tanner, Dick Allen and Roland Hemond. Team owner John Allyn's wife, Marjorie, received a complete set of Castleton china dishes.

Local sports promoter and gravel-throated barber Pete "Figo" Carvella presented recognition plaques to Coach Joe Lonnett, a Beaver Falls native; scout Fred Shaffer; Dick Allen; and Roland Hemond. White Sox coaches Joe Lonnett, Jim Mahoney and Alex Monchak; California Angels scout Nick Kasmec; and Cleveland Indians farm club director Bob Quinn, the brother-in-law of Roland Hemond, each stepped to the microphone and offered a brief tribute.

John Carmichael, a Chicago sportswriter for forty-one years, served as the keynote speaker and told the crowd, "I've been asked who was the greatest manager I've ever seen. I'll have to admit Jimmy Dykes was the best, and I think Chuck Tanner is another Dykes."[27]

Chuck thanked everyone for the evening and for making February 17 a night he always would remember. Reverend Richard Salley, pastor of St. Nicholas Orthodox Church, closed the evening's festivities with a benediction.

Tanner joked after the dinner, "People made fun of my optimistic outlook. They said that if I were the captain of the *Titanic*, I would tell my passengers we were stopping for ice."[28]

In an article for the *New Castle News*, Chuck told the reporter that if Bill Melton had not suffered a herniated disc, Chicago would have taken the pennant.

On February 27, the Sox demonstrated their appreciation for Dick Allen by making him the highest-paid player in baseball with a three-year $675,000 contract, equal to about $4,671,000 today.

Chuck held a special fondness for the members of the Allen family. Hank Allen needed fewer than forty-five days on a major-league roster to earn his pension. Chuck told his Western Pennsylvania friend he thought he could bring him up for a few games at the end of 1972 to help him along. Hank answered that he appreciated the help, but Chuck didn't have to do it. With the season almost over for Chicago, Chuck called Hank up in late September and told him to catch a plane to meet the team in Dallas. Hank started in left field and went 0 for 4. "My timing was off from a lack of play and the long trip, but it felt great to be back in the big leagues."

During spring training in 1973, veteran thirty-three-year-old Hank Allen's reaction time might have slowed a tad. Unbeknownst to Hank, his brother approached Chuck and told him that he appreciated everything he had done for his brother, but he expected no special favors. Chuck looked up from his desk at his star first baseman and scolded him, "Don't tell me who I should put on this team. I am the manager, and that is my decision. You should just worry about whether you make this team." Of course, Chuck added a quick smile to soften the message.

Hank still required a few more games in the majors to earn his pension. Hank had an excellent baseball mentality, and he realized that Chuck probably had better options than to keep him on the team. He popped into Chuck's office and, like the gentleman he was, said he understood if Chuck cut him from the roster. Chuck thought back to the twilight of his own career and the kindness that allowed him to play enough games to earn his own pension. He looked up from his desk into Hank's eyes, a man whom he really liked, and barked, "You get your butt out of here and work your tail off, and I will decide who I will keep." Hank worked hard and had a great spring. Chuck used him at every position—second, third, outfield and even as catcher.

"Other than batting practice, I never had caught professionally. Chuck played me at catcher for a fourteen-inning game. I had no passed balls, but

Hank (40) and Dick (22) Allen of Wampum High School in 1958, State Class B Basketball Champions. *Lawrence County Historical Society.*

my legs really ached the next day. Another time, he played me on a split squad game against the Pirates. After completing my innings, I returned to find the other game tied. In those days, all games were played out to the end. Although I was shot, he put me in left. Chuck must have known what he was doing since I got a hit in the second game after completing the first," Hank remembered.

"I worked hard and had a strong spring, but I didn't know if I made the team. I actually considered going to Japan to finish my career as an alternative. Then Joe Lonnett told me I had made the team. When I told Chuck he didn't have to keep me as a favor to my brother Dick, he looked me squarely in the eye and told me, 'This was no favor. You earned it.' Chuck placed me on the squad as a utility infielder."

Hopes ran high for a Sox pennant in 1973. The team's makeup had changed somewhat over the previous year. Management had traded outfielder Walt Williams to Cleveland for shortstop Eddie Leon, replacement for light-hitting Luis Alvarado. Pat Kelly started full time in right field. Ken Henderson opened in center, and Jorge Orta manned second. With Dick Allen anchoring first, Carlos May in left, Bill Melton on third, Ed Hermann catching and a strong pitching staff, the Sox looked like a solid contender.

The year started well. During a close-fought battle against the Indians at Cleveland Stadium in the first game of a June 10 double-header, Chicago held a 5–3 lead in the ninth. The White Sox had played through catchers Ed Herrmann and Chuck Brinkman. With limited alternatives, Chuck called in Hank Allen, a player who had only caught a few games in the minors, to handle the final inning. "Hank, you can do this. You'll do fine," Chuck reassured him.

Fireballer Terry Forster threw bullets, and Hank caught each one. The opposition managed just a single hit off Forster, and the reliever earned his eleventh save of the season. Hank played flawless ball. At the completion of the game, Chuck congratulated winner Steve Stone and reliever Terry Forster for a job well done, but he picked up and hugged Hank Allen and shouted, "I knew you could do it! I knew you could! You saved the game!"

"You would have thought I had hit a bases-loaded home run rather than just catching an inning." In the second game, a losing cause, Hank played a few innings at third. Only after he received enough time to receive his pension did Chuck release him to AAA Hawaii to finish his career, a gesture Hank never forgot.

Problems buffeted the 1973 team. Pitcher Stan Bahnsen had refused to sign his contract. He had been promised a significant raise based on how well he performed following a terrific 1972 season. His twenty-one wins provided a huge lift to the Sox, and he anticipated a substantial increase in his 1973 salary from its current rate of $38,000. Instead, Chicago general manager Stu Holcomb played hardball. He handed Bahnsen a contract with a $5,000 increase, far less than the pitcher anticipated. Bahnsen complained to his manager about the unfair treatment by the GM, but Holcomb refused to budge. The pitcher went home and told his wife he planned to quit.

As Roland Hemond explained, "Holcomb was supposed to handle the owner's soccer team, but when that folded, Allyn had to find something for him to do, and he named him the GM of the Sox. He didn't handle things well at all, and Stan Bahnsen said he wasn't going to pitch unless he got a new contract."

Both Hemond and Tanner sided with Bahnsen, a key pitcher on the squad. They had seen more than enough of Holcomb's take-it-or-leave-it strategy. "He's dismantling the team. We can't allow this to continue," the manager carped. Hemond, now promoted as special assistant to the president, recognized the damage Holcomb had created.

The pair approached President Allyn, who also sided with the complainants. Holcomb retained a stiff-necked attitude and refused to budge. He "retired" under pressure on July 27, and Allyn promoted Roland Hemond to the GM spot.

Although Bahnsen received a new contract with the salary he requested, the disruption created hard feelings and damaged the player-management interrelationship. The team's mojo fizzled.

Team star Dick Allen started the season where he had left off the prior year, appearing well worth every penny of his team-high salary. That is, until June 28, when Allen reached for a high throw from third baseman Bill Melton, and six-foot-three, 225-pound Oakland first baseman Mike Epstein struck him in full stride and broke the fibula beneath his knee. After Allen brooded for nearly a month, Tanner allowed him to rest and recuperate at his farm in Perkasie in Bucks County, Pennsylvania.

The Sox record at the time of Allen's injury stood at a respectable 37-32, one game out of first. Without its star first baseman, the team slid to a 77-85 losing record and a fifth-place finish, seventeen games behind the Oakland Athletics, who would win their second World Series in a row.

In an injury-shortened year, Dick Allen still managed to bat .316 with sixteen home runs in seventy-two games. Bill Melton and Carlos May each hit twenty home runs. Steady Wilbur Wood supplied a 24-20 record over 359⅓ innings. Stan Bahnsen put up 18-21 win-loss statistics. Mexican reliever Cy Acosta produced a career year with a 11-6 record, eighteen saves and a 2.23 ERA, but overall the Sox pitching staff failed to perform as anticipated.

The following year, 1974, produced a so-so 80-80 finish, good for fourth place. Pitcher Jim Kaat, whom the team picked up on waivers the previous year, led the staff with a 21-13 record and an earned run average of 2.92. Wood won twenty games for the fourth year in a row but against nineteen losses, and starter Bart Johnson won ten games against only four losses with a sterling 2.74 ERA.

Dick Allen started the season slowly, as his damaged leg hampered him. Nonetheless, he led the team with a .301 batting average and a league-leading thirty-two homers. Ken Henderson and Jorge Orta put up good statistics as well, but the Sox lacked the talent at a few key positions to overtake the pennant-winning Athletics.

Injuries and intra-squad turmoil further complicated the season. Dick Allen and recently acquired third baseman Ron Santo feuded incessantly. Each star believed that he deserved the position of team leader. Allen did not like how Santo treated the younger players, and Santo considered Allen lazy. The constant bickering destroyed the team's cohesion. Tanner feared that the animosity might percolate into a full-scale eruption. He summoned both veterans in his office to warn them that their feud was killing the Sox. "There's only room for one man to run this team, and that's me," Tanner barked.[29]

Sportscaster Jerome Holtzman criticized the Sox first baseman for failing to earn the $225,000 the team had been paying him and called him "a cancer in the clubhouse." Chuck stuck by Allen. "Just because you read it somewhere doesn't make it true. I think Allen has taken a bum rap in the press, and he doesn't deserve it. I think he's the best ball player I have ever seen, and when his playing days are over, I think he'll be a great manager if he decides to do it." Tanner added that he thought Dick was a "great teammate," who helped the younger players with their hitting.

Dick Allen had played through injuries and pain. His leg ached continually. A bad back forced him to leave the team with two weeks left in the season. Despite his election to a third All-Star team in a row and a strong season, Allen announced his intention to retire on September 14. With his skills slowing, his health in doubt and the planned retirement, the team traded him to the Atlanta Braves on December 3 for $5,000 and a player to be named at a later date.

With Allen gone, 1975 proved a weak year. Jim Kaat won twenty games against fourteen losses, and Jorge Orta batted a healthy .304. Little else worked well that season. Even reliable knuckleball pitcher Wilbur Wood slumped to 16-20 with a 4.11 ERA. Two-time twenty-game winner Claude Osteen had been picked up as a free agent from the Cardinals as a third starter but proved a bust with a 7-16 record and a 4.36 ERA. The Sox lost eighty-five games against seventy-five wins and ended up in fifth place. Tanner's frustrations during that losing season generated a career-high six game ejections.

During his time in Chicago, White Sox announcer Harry Caray and Tanner had sparred over his management style and a pitching change he made during a game against Boston in June. With the bases loaded and no one out in the sixth, Tanner brought in Jim Kaat. Caray remarked that the next six Red Sox batters due up were righties and that percentages militated against such a change. Boston hammered Kaat, initiating a dispute between the manager and the sportscaster.

With the team's record on the decline, Caray mouthed the frustration of the fans, which further depressed the team, its manager and owner. "Some of the guys are so worried about what Harry Caray is going to say on the air, we can't relax and play our game," groused third baseman Bill Melton. The furor exploded into a Caray-Melton shouting match in a Milwaukee hotel lobby that made sports headlines.

The animosity between Caray and Tanner festered to the point that owner Allyn, who sided with his manager, barked, "Either Harry's got to

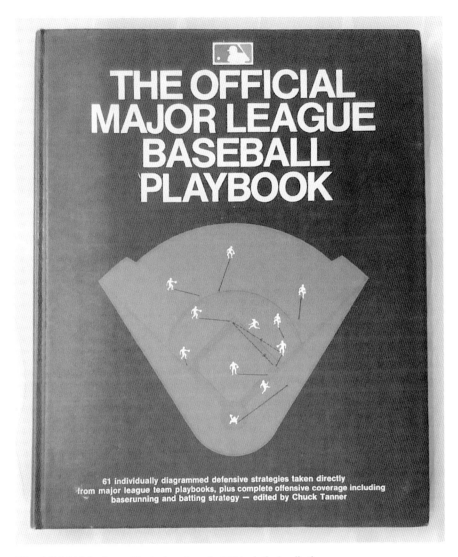

The *Official Major League Playbook*, written in 1974. *Author's collection.*

go or the team's got to go." Allyn announced that he would fire Caray at the end of the 1975 season. The fans liked the outspoken Harry Caray far more than the owner. The public viewed Caray's criticism as that of an ardent fan who loved the team but could blast the manager in the heat of the moment for one decision and praise him in the next. Chicago refused to allow Harry to go. One columnist wrote, "He could make a ping-pong match interesting."[30]

Owner John Allyn had been good to Chuck. He recognized that the club had personnel shortcomings but liked his manager. As a sign of his confidence, Allyn extended Tanner's $60,000 contract for three more years to guarantee stability.

However, following a catastrophic dip in attendance to 750,802 from 1,149,596 the previous year, financial contingencies forced Allyn to sell the Sox for $14 million. On December 16, 1975, "Sport Shirt" Bill Veeck, a handsome and controversial maverick whose wooden leg frequently concealed a pack of cigarettes, bought the Chicago team for a second time.

In 1959, Veeck led a consortium that purchased the franchise from the Comiskey family. Due to health problems, he sold the team to John and Arthur Allyn in 1961 for $2.5 million. Now Veeck owned the Chicago White Sox once again.

Popularity in professional sports remains a transitory factor. Yesterday's hero can quickly become tomorrow's goat. The new owner claimed, "I try not to break the rules, but merely test their elasticity." He promptly replaced 1972 Manager of the Year Chuck Tanner with former major-league catcher and one-time Atlanta Braves general manager Paul Richards, known throughout the trade as the "Wizard of Waxahatchie."

Chuck, who still had three years owing on his $60,000 annual contract, turned down lucrative executive and scouting options with Chicago in order to collect the balance of his contract and find employment for his services as a manager elsewhere.

Chuck expressed few regrets about his release. He had enjoyed his time in Chicago and knew that he did not want to remain with Veeck. "I was fortunate. The fans took us under their wings. Mayor Daley was a big White Sox fan. He supported us a lot.…People say Chicago is a Cubs town.… That's garbage. It's a White Sox town, too."

CHAPTER 7

MANAGING OAKLAND

If you find a path with no obstacles, it probably doesn't lead anywhere.
—Frank A. Clark

Chuck's dismissal as the Chicago manager brought a host of confusion and complications, but he refused to back away from challenges. As skipper of the White Sox, Chuck had received a lucrative $25,000 annual advertising contract with the Olympic Savings and Loan Bank. Once Veeck removed him as manager, the bank unilaterally rescinded the contract. Chuck immediately called his attorney, Francis Caiazza, to represent him against the financial institution. With little notice prior to arbitration, Caiazza hired a Chicago lawyer to draw up the necessary documents. Walter Smith, a cousin of Caiazza's, served as the investigator and picked up the paid-for memorandum prior to the hearing.

Since the contract failed to provide the bank with a clear-cut out clause, the mediator found in Chuck's favor. In gratitude, Chuck escorted Walter and Francis to his favorite tailor for a made-to-order suit as a gift, followed by a celebratory breakfast at the tony Palmer House Hotel. The men immediately recognized a celebrity sitting at a nearby table: three-time Golden Globe–winning actor and bridge columnist Omar Sharif. Within minutes, Sharif and the talkative baseball manager struck up a lively conversation. Sharif happened to be a big baseball fan, and the pair spent several happy minutes swapping stories.

Since the baseball industry recognized Chuck Tanner as a quality, proven major-league manager, he believed he would find a new position within a few months. The opportunity came quickly. General Manager Charlie Finley of the Oakland Athletics and his manager, Alvin Dark, had spent the 1975 season at loggerheads. Although Dark had won the American League West division with a 98-64 record and a World Series ring the prior year, Finley constantly criticized Dark about his "religion first/baseball second" approach. The owner questioned his manager's commitment—"You're too busy with church matters." Also Finley knew that Dark had banned the speaking of Spanish in the clubhouse and on the field, dividing and segregating his players. Hispanic stars like Orlando Cepeda, who had played for Dark in the mid-'60s, felt that his manager disrespected him. Possibly Finley recognized that Dark might be alienating his Cuban and South American players. When disagreements festered to a boiling point, Finley fired Dark.

Since Chuck still had money owing on his contract, Charlie Finley offered free agent Tanner a three-year chump-change contract with the Oakland Athletics at $10,000. Tanner naturally balked and negotiated the ante up to $25,000 with the assumption that he would continue to receive the balance of his $60,000 annual salary owed by the White Sox.

Attorney Caiazza watched Charley Finley draw up the contract with Chuck. The Oakland owner, who disliked Bill Veeck, bragged to the press, "I won't say how much I'm going to pay him, but if I give him $10,000 per year, Bill Veeck will have to pay him the other $50,000.[31] This "arrangement" led to a huge brouhaha.

Disagreements regarding pay culminated in a dispute between Tanner, Finley and Veeck as to who owed what to the new Oakland manager. Veeck argued that once Tanner accepted a job with Finley, the White Sox contract became null and void. Finley assumed that part of Tanner's $60,000 salary would be covered by the White Sox and that he had purchased a bargain-basement manager.

Matters festered until Veeck ceased paying Chuck once he started work with the Oakland Athletics, stating, "Chuck Tanner's new contract with Oakland has invalidated the prior one with Chicago." Caught in the middle of the impasse, Tanner appealed to the president of the American League, Lee MacPhail, to arbitrate the issue.

Attorney Francis Caiazza, Roland Hemond, Chuck and Bill Veeck met with President MacPhail but failed to reach a consensus. MacPhail viewed both Charlie Finley and Bill Veeck as intransigent mavericks. After much give and take, MacPhail ordered Veeck to pay Tanner his full salary for one year. The parties would have to come to some mutual agreement regarding years two and three. Chuck left the meeting with his pay for 1976 resolved but with no idea how 1977 and 1978 would work out for him.

Even though hampered by the mercurial Charlie Finley's disruptive antics, Chuck managed a respectable 87-74 Oakland second-place finish. He retained nine-year veteran reliever Wes Stock as his pitching coach and seven-year veteran first baseman Bobby Hofman as his batting coach, but he brought along Sox cronies Joe Lonnett to man third and Alex Monchak to coach first. He convinced twenty-eight-year veteran scout and friend Fred Shaffer to join Oakland as well.

Jim "Catfish" Hunter, a twenty-five-game winner in 1975, had signed with the New York Yankees following a contract dispute with Finley, a huge loss to the team. Tanner relied on balanced pitching, strong defense and speed on the bases to win his games. Pitching ace Vida Blue, a twenty-two-game winner in 1975, led the team in 1976 with eighteen wins and a stellar 2.35 ERA. Starter Mike Torrez, obtained in a trade with Baltimore, chipped in with sixteen wins, and reliever Rollie Fingers won thirteen games and saved twenty, adding to his future Hall of Fame credentials. All in all, the staff put up a respectable 3.26 ERA.

Chuck gave his players a directive: "Run! Whenever you can, run. Run in the first. Run in the ninth. Run when you are ahead, and run when you are behind. Just run."[32] He would become the only major-league manager with teams producing 180 or more stolen bases in four consecutive years.

During the season, the team racked up a major league–leading 341 stolen bases in 464 attempts, the most recorded since 1911, when the New York Giants stole 347 bases. Speedster Billy North led the team and the entire American League with 75. Bert Campaneris swiped 54 bases. Claudell Washington added 37 and Phil Garner 35. All in all, eight Oakland players stole 20 or more bases, and four of the eight swiped 35 or more. Even part-time utility speedsters Matt Alexander and Larry Lintz managed 34 steals between them.

The starting lineup failed to put up a single .300 hitter. North led the team with a .276 batting average, and Joe Rudi batted .270. As a team, Oakland hit for an unimpressive .246 average. Sal Bando supplied twenty-seven round-trippers, and Joe Rudi produced ninety-four RBIs. Tanner tinkered with his strong fielding, speedy lineup and excellent pitching staff to eke out wins. Detractors believed that Chuck managed by whimsy. Supporters appreciated his innovation and aggressiveness.

Tanner, like his predecessor Alvin Dark, had difficulty coping with the mercurial Charlie Finley, who intended to cut salary costs, even if that meant dismantling a competitive team in a "fire sale." On June 15, with free agency on the horizon for several of his star players, the Oakland owner sold star pitcher Vida Blue to the Yankees for $1.5 million and outfielder Joe Rudi and relief pitcher Rollie Fingers to the Boston Red Sox for $1 million each.

Commissioner Bowie Kuhn voided the transactions for the "good of baseball." Finley and his attorney, Neil Papiano, sued the commissioner, but the courts backed Kuhn, ruling that he possessed the power to void the transaction. Nonetheless, Finley's actions generated enough negative energy to sink the morale among the players and staff. The owner's interference and cost-cutting sabotaged Tanner's ability to deliver a pennant to Oakland.

Finley cooked up other irritants to his manager as well. He often called the dugout with his "suggestions." Chuck did not appreciate such intrusions into his realm of expertise. Once Phil Garner overheard the owner tell Tanner to remove a player from the game. Chuck answered his boss with a challenge, "If you want him out that badly, you can fire me, and then you can take him out yourself."

Even with Finley's incessant tampering, Tanner managed a respectable second-place American League West finish, just two and a half games behind the league-leading Kansas City Royals. Unfortunately, team attendance dropped from 1,075,518 to 780,593 as the Athletics failed to make the playoffs for the first time in five years. Although the owner could be irksome, Chuck enjoyed California, his team and the Oakland–Alameda County Stadium.

At the end of the season, Chuck relaxed with his friends at Valentine's Restaurant. He could be found at his favorite table, kibitzing with his buddies, spinning yarns and enjoying life. While Ray and Ted Valentine manned the kitchen, sisters Flo Morella and Emma Mazzocca waited on customers. Mary Starsinic, although not a member of the Valentine family, always remained on hand to pour coffee and chime in with a comment or two about what Oakland and Chuck could do differently to improve the team's chances. Chuck welcomed one and all to his table, even making strangers feel like important members of the group.[33]

Discussions over coffee about horse racing and local politics occasionally occupied the participants, but basic fare centered on baseball, with Chuck umpiring any arguments to ensure that nothing got out of hand.

As a youngster, Victor Stefano, whose mother owned the beauty parlor near Valentine's, considered Chuck as the closest person to a celebrity he had or ever would know. Wherever Chuck sat, Fred Shaffer generally could be found nearby. Clyde Stefano, Bonesy DeLorenzo, Francis Caiazza, Henry the barber and, of course, Ray and Ted frequently joined the table to "chew the fat." The crew had lots of fun mocking one another and the world in general.

Side bets on baseball games and other sports added spice and humor to the morning get-togethers. Victor recalled his dad, Clyde Stefano, and "Tempy" Temperato arguing about the potential outcome of a baseball game. "Sometimes the wagers could move to the crazy side. In one case, Tempy boasted, 'Clyde, if I lose, I'll drive you in a wheelbarrow down Washington Street.' When he lost, Tempy pushed him through the downtown as promised."

Tom DeLorenzo Jr. reminisced, "My dad—they called him Bonesy—Ray and John Valentine, Henry 'the Barber' Giamatteo, and Chuck drove to Avalon Lakes in the mid-'70s for a game of golf. As each man ponied up his greens fee, the pro at the desk recognized Chuck. 'Hey, Chuck, you get to play on the house.' My dad, who also happened to be Chuck's accountant, groused, 'Hey, he's the only guy with the money. Why does he get to play for free? Is that fair?' Chuck burst into a wide grin and joked, 'Well, we celebrities merit special treatment.' Chuck roared with laughter, and the group joined in with him. Chuck possessed that special ability to ingratiate himself with everyone regardless of the circumstances."

Luck plays an important part in every baseball executive's life. With the popular Danny Murtaugh due to retire at season's end due to ill health, Pittsburgh Pirates general manager Joe L. Brown sought a replacement. Chuck Tanner's name stood at the top of his list of potential candidates. Brown put out feelers to Charles Finley about obtaining Tanner for his team. Finley appeared cooperative but demanding. He stipulated a draconian price for his "outstanding" manager. "Chuck is exactly whom you need. He will bring you a pennant, but I need a front-line player in return—plus cash….If I am going to run a finishing school for managers, I want to be paid for it."

Like Murtaugh, Brown also intended to retire at the end of the season, and the Pirates tagged Harding "Pete" Peterson—a one-time major-league catcher, minor-league manager and Pirates farm team director—to take over for Brown as general manager. Peterson likewise wanted Tanner as his manager. Chuck fit the Pittsburgh blue-collar mold. In addition to being a native Western Pennsylvanian, he held a solid reputation as a phenomenal motivator and an aggressive manager.

Peterson received the authorization from the Pirates ownership to offer either a player or $100,000 as payment. When Finley demanded both $200,000 in cash and All-Star catcher Manny Sanguillén, Tanner lost confidence that the deal would come to fruition. He assumed that the cost-conscious Pirates would never go for so expensive an arrangement.

As expected, Pittsburgh balked at the offer. The frugal Pirates refused to accept the trade as offered. The loss of a top-notch player plus a $200,000 kicker seemed far too exorbitant a price to pay for a manager, regardless of his credentials.

CHAPTER 8

THE PIRATES' 1977 AND 1978 SEASONS

When you think positively, good things happen.
—Matt Kemp

L uckily for Chuck, his intuition proved wrong. The Pirates reached a compromise with Finley. On November 5, 1976, Pittsburgh acquired the rights to Chuck Tanner from Oakland for $100,000 rather than the initial demand of $200,000, plus catcher Manny Sanguillén, only the second such trade in the history of baseball.[34]

Bragging about his shrewd bargaining skill, Charley O. Finley smirked, "I would trade a manager any day of the week for Manny Sanguillén and $100,000. I can get $250,000 for Sanguillén, and that means I would be making $350,000 for having a manager someone else wants."[35]

Danny Murtaugh, no. 40, had led the 1976 Pirates to a second-place finish with a strong 92-70 record, but still nine games behind the pennant-winning 101-60 Philadelphia Phillies. Ill health forced the popular fifty-nine-year-old to retire at the end of the season in October after a fifteen-year career and 1,115 victories. He would pass away in December from a stroke, after which the team permanently retired the number forty.

Pitcher Kent Tekulve remembered Murtaugh fondly as a great manager who had delivered two Pirates World Series championships to the Steel City: "Although he spoke to us frequently off the field, during game time he switched to an all business mode. He was an institution, but I can think of only one time he ever spoke to me during the game other than a specific instruction. It was toward the end of my second season when he took the time to compliment me on an appearance with the words, 'Nice job.' He made me feel I belonged. In contrast, Chuck and I would chat all the time."

General Manager Harding Peterson had set his sights on Chuck Tanner as the perfect replacement for Danny Murtaugh. Chuck possessed working-class grit, diamond know-how and the even personality the Pirates wanted. In addition, folks considered him a local, with New Castle situated only fifty miles north of the stadium.

Tanner delivered a whole new sense of energy to the team. He possessed what New Castle native and Milwaukee minor-league head of scouting Jack Zduriencik called a great "PMA"—a positive mental attitude. His infectious enthusiasm and zest for success proved to be two of his strongest assets.

Attorneys Carmen Lamencusa and Francis Caiazza drove Chuck to Pittsburgh's Three Rivers Stadium for a formal signing ceremony and his introduction to the media. The brass quickly separated Chuck from his legal advisors to maintain control of the carefully designed public relations program. Chuck already had negotiated his own deal, happy to be away from the clutches of Charlie Finley and Bill Veeck and thrilled to be with the Pirates, just an hour's drive from his family and hometown.

That cold November night, the stadium sign glowed with a warm welcome to the Pirates new manager. The click of cameras and the rapid-fire questions from the reporters circling around him magnified the excitement of the evening. Chuck grinned like the proverbial Cheshire Cat. This was the moment he had wanted all his life. Francis Caiazza heard Chuck call across the field to General Manager Harding Peterson, "You won't regret this. I'm going to bring a pennant home for you." In a separate comment, he told the press, "I can't wait for spring training. This is such a thrill. It's a dream come true."[36]

Chuck's timing for a move from the Oakland Athletics to the Pirates proved impeccable. Finley decimated the California team's talent following the '76 season. He traded or sold most of the club's stars and backups, including Sal Bando, Mike Torrez, Denny Walling, Gene Tenace, Rollie Fingers, Joe Rudi, Bert Campaneris, Don Baylor, Claudell Washington, Billy Williams, Phil Garner, Tommy Helms, Chris Batton, Jim Todd, Gaylen Pitts and Willie McCovey. In their place, he brought in an out-of-shape Doc Ellis and an injured Dick Allen as replacements, both players well past their prime. Allen batted just .240 with five home runs, and Ellis put up a miserable 1-5 record and a 9.69 ERA. Rookie Mitchell Page and Manny Sanguillén numbered among the few to put up strong offensive numbers. The pitchers

Left: Jack Zduriencik. *Wikimedia Commons.*

Right: Attorney Carmen Lamencusa. *Photo by author.*

combined for a 4.04 ERA, and 10-6 Doc Medich proved the only starter with a winning record.

Finley's slicing and dicing caused a powerful Oakland team to plummet to a disastrous 63-98 last-place record in 1977. Attendance sagged from 780,593 in 1976 to just 495,578 the following year—the worst of any club during the '70s. On June 10, Finley fired Chuck's replacement as manager, Jack McKeon, following a 26-27 record. McKeon's replacement, Bobby Winkles, performed far worse and quit the next season due to Finley's incessant second-guessing and harping.

In contrast to the strained relationship he experienced with Finley, Chuck formed a close bond with the owners of the Pirates. Majority shareholder John W. Galbreath, an Ohio construction contractor and successful horse breeder, would meet with his manager, general manager, minority partners and a few key personnel for preseason budgetary and planning sessions. Once spring training began, he turned the day-to-day decision making over to the experts, his GM and field manager. When asked what Mr.

Three Rivers Stadium. *Pittsburgh Pirates.*

Galbreath was like, Chuck answered, "He was a true gentleman and a pleasure to be around."

Mr. Galbreath also whetted Chuck's growing interest in horses, an avocation he would relish for much of his life. Minority Pirates shareholder Tom Johnson, a New Castle native, arranged a board seat for the new manager at Citizens Bank, which lasted until the bank's formal merger with Mellon on January 7, 1985. Although Chuck rarely attended meetings, he received an inscribed Bulova watch as a parting thank-you gift for his service along with the bank's other board members, who included my father, Lawrence Perelman; Bruce Waldman; and a neighbor, Chester Lapinski Sr., among others.

The Pirates made several moves in the off season to strengthen the team's relief squad. Harding Peterson traded starting outfielder Richie Zisk and pitcher Silvio Martínez on December 10, 1976, for Chicago White Sox relievers Terry Forster and Goose Gossage, an eventual member of the Hall of Fame in Cooperstown. The team would miss the strong bat of Zisk, an All-Star in 1977, but Gossage developed into one of the finest relievers in baseball, producing a remarkable 1.62 ERA, twenty-six saves and eleven wins along with a team-leading 151 strikeouts for the Pirates. Terry Forster ended up as a useful spot starter who accumulated a 6-4 record and one save. Both Chuck and his GM recognized the necessity of assembling a strong relief staff for a pennant contender—considering the latter innings of the game every bit as important as hitting and defense and key to developing a winning team.

As an additional plus, the 1974–78 Pirates minor-league system teemed with strong prospects working their way onto the big league squad. Twenty-seven players from the 1975 Charleston farm club advanced into the big leagues. Outfielder Omar Moreno displayed tremendous speed on the base paths, decent control with the bat and good defense. By 1977, he had become the Pirates' regular center fielder.

Pitcher Kent Tekulve required more time to develop, but his wicked sidearm delivery showed potential. While playing for West Virginia's AAA Charleston Charlies, Teke initially drew a strong dose of discouragement from management. He stood six-foot-four but weighed less than 160 pounds, far from the optimum physique for a pitcher. His unusual delivery and advanced age of twenty-seven militated against his success.

Like Chuck, Teke worked hard and eventually convinced his detractors that he indeed possessed a major-league arm. He would spend sixteen years in a highly successful career as a reliever, appearing more than one thousand times. In 1975, he pitched in thirty-four games, and his importance increased significantly over the next several years.

Among the starting pitchers, John Candelaria raced along the quickest track. He proved a phenom with the Charleston Charlies in 1975. Recent college graduate and eventual baseball executive Joe Safety said, "John never did anything halfway. He was an amazing pitcher and an equally amazing man." Safety had visited his West Virginia University fraternity brothers in Charleston and took in a game at the Walt Powell Stadium from the friendly confines of the KFC box. He watched Candelaria and thought that he possessed awesome skills. Later that year, after a sterling 7-1 record and an ERA of just 1.77, the twenty-two-year-old, six-foot-seven Candelaria found himself promoted to the majors for a rookie season, producing eight wins and a spiffy 2.76 ERA. Safety would intern in the Pirates public relations department that same year.

Another fine player, Ed Ott, performed admirably as a top-notch minor-league outfielder. Once he realized that the Pirates outfield consisted of Dave Parker, Al Oliver and Bill Robinson with minor leaguers Miguel Diloné,

Tony Armas and Omar Moreno in the wings and others ready to back them up, he switched to the catcher's position, a smart move on his part. He quickly developed into a very proficient defensive player with offensive skills.

Teke admired Ed's instincts: "He possessed the ability to make minor adjustments in a pitcher's technique without the need for verbal communication." During 1977, he caught 104 games for the Pirates.

The 1978 Columbus Clippers in the International League possessed some backup talent as well. Mike Easler pounded out a .330 average with twenty-six doubles and eighteen homers. He inched his way up to the big leagues primarily as a pinch hitter in 1979. Third baseman Dale Berra, Yogi Berra's son, batted a solid .280 in the minors. He developed into a major-league utility player and third baseman in 1977. The Pirates' 1973 number-one draft pick, catcher Steve Nicosia, batted .322 and displayed decent power as he alternated between the minor and major leagues during the season. Pitcher Ed Whitson demonstrated enough flashes of ability to bob up and down between the minors and the main squad as a reliever until traded in 1979.

Managing in the '70s required far more than game and practice supervision from a manager. The position involved scheduling, room assignments and a variety of small details today covered by the traveling secretary. Tanner's handpicked crew included a pitching, bullpen, batting and two base coaches, as well as a trainer. Chuck retained Spanish-speaking José Pagán from Murtaugh's staff as his batting coach and interpreter. Third base coach Joe Lonnett and first base coach Alex Monchak came with him from Oakland. Larry Sherry, a skillful reliever from the late '50s and early '60s, handled the pitchers. Tony Bartirome, who played one year in 1952 as a first baseman for the Pirates, stayed on as the trainer. Chuck and his handpicked crew hustled to keep a team of twenty-five well-paid and rambunctious guys happy and motivated but, most importantly, productive.

Shepherding the Pirates meant a lifetime goal had come true for Chuck. Plus, his new role allowed him to spend more time with Babs and the kids in New Castle as a commuter manager. He ate at Valentine's Restaurant with increased frequency. He'd often order the stuffed cabbage, but he spent so much time talking to his local fans and friends that he frequently didn't get to finish his meal. Folks lined up in droves to talk baseball with Chuck, and he never disappointed. This hometown hero spoke to everyone.

Dewey Lutz, who worked a few buildings away from Valentine's at Spencer Paints, ate breakfast with Chuck and his gang two or three mornings per week. "We always talked sports, usually the topic centered on the Pirates

Top: Joe Lonnett. *Pittsburgh Pirates.*

Bottom: Chuck Tanner jersey. *Chuck Tanner's Restaurant.*

and baseball. I drove Chuck to the ball park for several night games, and I enjoyed our time together. Win or lose, Chuck was always a pleasure."

Excitement poured through the Bucco players at spring training in Bradenton, Florida's Pirate City. Chuck's zest for the game cut through the doubters and created converts. The team possessed the talent to win a pennant, and with luck, 1977 could be the year. Chuck's hopes ran high and realistically so.

Lawrence County had lined up to show its appreciation to Chuck Tanner for enhancing the reputation of the area. Various organizations and clubs honored his achievements. As an example, the Neshannock supervisors presented the "Lumber and Lightning Crew's" manager with a citation as the city's goodwill ambassador.

Chuck made every effort to accommodate his fans. Friend Fuzzy Fazzone recalled the day a few guys from Youngstown, Ohio, met up with him before a Florida practice game. "Hey Chuck, I remember you from a golf game at Yankee Run. You were playing slowly, and you let us go through your foursome."

"Sure, I remember that. Did you guys have a good game?" Once the conversation ended, Chuck whispered to Fuzzy. "You know, I never played Yankee Run in my life," but he had made two fans feel important, and that mattered to him.

Pittsburghers bragged about the autographed baseballs Chuck had given them as souvenirs. Dozens of people have contacted me about the treasured mementos they located in a relative's sock drawer. He had handed out so many that these balls seem commonplace.

During spring training, the Tanners rented a place on Anna Maria Island that once belonged to U.S. Senator (and later governor of Florida) Lawton Chiles. The family joined Chuck for several weeks of sun and fun.

Young Bruce Tanner loved his time in Florida with his dad. "Trainer Tony Bartirome would pick me up at five many mornings for the twenty-minute

Signed Chuck Tanner baseball. *Collection of Dr. Gary Snow.*

drive to Bradenton. A couple of days a week a backup catcher caught my pitches. Once in a while, I took batting practice with Joe Lonnett. I even warmed up John Candelaria."

Bruce attended games almost every day and during practices. He might even receive a tip or two from the coaches or the pros to improve his own play. The teenager felt lucky to get to skip school and watch his heroes, although his mom made him tackle his assigned homework in the evenings.

Chuck proved a wonderful host to visitors. Ginny Slater, once a school nurse at Shenango Elementary School, and her husband, Fred, had retired to Bradenton. When they stood in line to buy tickets for a preseason game, Chuck happened to see them and called out, "Hey Ginny and Fred, you don't need tickets. Come with me!" Then he escorted them into the stadium. He also arranged for the couple to receive an autographed Willie Stargell baseball.

As soon as spring training ended, Pirate City reverted to the home of the rookie league for the Bradenton Pirates, and McKechnie Field—some five miles away and what Kent Tekulve called one of the worst playing surfaces in Florida—became available for local use or sat dormant. However, for

Phil Garner and the Crew.
Pittsburgh Pirates.

the six weeks of spring training, Bradenton seemed like baseball magic to sixteen-year-old Bruce.[37]

On March 15, 1977, Charlie Finley traded starting second baseman "Scrap-Iron" Phil Garner, Tommy Helms and Chris Batton to the Pirates for six players, some pretty good—Doc Medich, Dave Giusti, Mitchell Page, Rick Langford, Tony Armas and Doug Bair. Tanner had managed Garner at Oakland the previous year and liked Garner's rough-and-tumble, hard-nosed Pittsburgh style of play. The trade worked, and Phil became an infield fixture with the Pirates during the next five years.

Although Pittsburgh paid a steep price for Garner, Tanner never regretted the trade. He called him the glue that held the team together and referred to him as the best number-eight batter in baseball and his "second cleanup hitter." Chuck and Phil cemented a mutual trust and friendship that grew even stronger over the years. Once Garner retired and became manager of the Milwaukee Brewers, he and Chuck remained in touch and frequently exchanged notes on strategy.

In June, the Pirates picked up veteran All-Star infielder Jim Fregosi in exchange for utility player Ed Kirkpatrick as backup insurance for the infield. Chuck believed the squad contained a solid bunch of players, capable of challenging any team in the National League.

Each day, Chuck thanked his lucky stars for the opportunity to return to Western Pennsylvania. He now managed his beloved Pirates, lived in his comfy Maitland Lane home, spent more time with Babs and his family and visited with close friends in his second home at Valentine's Restaurant. The years had been good to him, well worth the arduous climb up the ladder.

At Chuck's go-to restaurant, Ray Valentine manned the stove from early in the morning until two or three o'clock in the afternoon six days per week, every day but Sunday. Brother Ted arrived at around noon or one o'clock and took over until closing. Chuck might stop in for coffee and breakfast before practice or for a late dinner, but always for lots of conversation, most of it concerning baseball. Bruce remembered, "I spent lots of time at the restaurant, kibitzing with waitress Mary Starcinik or watching the goings-on in the kitchen."

Wednesday nights in New Castle often meant poker at Tom Andrew's house. Joe Abraham, a Neshannock teacher and football coach, liked playing with Chuck, not only because he was a great guy but also, more often than not, because "he bluffed and lost."

Chuck could not walk the streets of his hometown without someone greeting him. Whether he was sitting in the sauna at the YMCA, kibitzing with his cronies at Valentine's, getting tickets for a friend, speaking at the Rotary Club, golfing with his radiologist friend "Doc" Frank Raynak, watching a Little League game or just sitting at home with Babs, he loved life in New Castle.

Whenever he could, Chuck threw a favor to his fellow New Castle citizens. Jim McKim, a former Mohawk music teacher, remembered how Chuck arranged for his barbershop quartet, the Last National Bank, to sing the national anthem at Three Rivers Stadium on several occasions. "We were especially welcomed when the Montreal baseball team came to town because we knew the Canadian national anthem. A highlight involved us singing before a Cincinnati playoff game in 1979."

Son Bruce remembered fondly the holiday family meals at the Tanner household on Maitland Lane. "We had lots of good-natured ribbing. Mom's sister Thelma McGary and her three kids added to the family crowd. After dinner, we sometimes played basketball, and the kids accused Chuck of cheating when he grabbed their shirt tails, but it was all done in good clean fun, although Chuck was a highly competitive guy."

Bruce remembered his older brother Mark and a friend challenging Chuck and Fred Shaffer to a golf match. "Well, Chuck fed his opposition lots of booze and told them tee off would be promptly at 8 a.m. Chuck was a decent golfer who generally shot in the high 70s or low 80s at the area's local golf courses, including Stonecrest, Greenville Country Club, Tam O' Shanter, Castle Hills and Mohawk Trails. His game plan worked. He and Fred outplayed their younger competitors, who had been slowed by a late night of way too much fun."

As a manager, Chuck often came up with the unexpected, both in the treatment of his players and his strategy on the field. He performed like the Sinatra hit song "My Way." Some criticized his leniency with his players, but he offered his own explanation: "Well, Paul Waner used to wander into the lobby at 1 a.m., and Babe Ruth always managed to find a little spot to have some fun. I think if someone had slapped a curfew on them, there might be two empty spaces in the Hall of Fame today. The thing is you have to handle people like they are men."[38]

Some managers, like Dick Williams, maintained a single set of rules for everyone—not so with Chuck. He allowed certain players to question his decisions, and discipline became an individual and situational matter. He bent the rules depending on the infraction and the person involved. He also followed another important axiom, "I always remember the players are human beings first."[39]

When Frank Taveras found himself mired in a batting slump, Willie Stargell and Phil Garner approached Chuck and asked if they should speak to him. Even worse, the shortstop's defense had declined. Chuck believed that confronting Frank might further aggravate his stress. Chuck advised Willie and Phil, "I don't think we should say anything. Leave him alone, and he will snap out of it in a few days," and he did. Chuck believed in giving a player his space, but he also knew to intercede when the situation called for active criticism or a helping hand.

Most fans considered the 1977 season successful. The Tanner managed team ended with a strong 96-win, second-place finish, the team's highest total since its victorious 1971 World Series year. Unfortunately, the Philadelphia Phillies beat the Pirates by five games with 101 victories.

Starter John Candelaria chalked up a 20-5 record with a league-leading 2.34 earned run average, and Jim Rooker added fourteen wins. Closer Rich "Goose" Gossage supplied eleven wins and twenty-six saves. Dave Parker, Candelaria and Gossage all had been named to the July 19 All-Star squad that played at Yankee Stadium, where the National League pulled out a 7–5 victory.

John Candelaria. *Pittsburgh Pirates.*

Kent Tekulve supplied a strong 10-1 record while appearing in seventy-two games. As Teke modestly explained, "The starters kept the game close. When I came in to a tied or close game in the middle innings, our big guns pounded out a few well timed runs. Chuck would bring in Gossage to close the show. Gossage would get the save and me the win."

The Pirates' "Lumber and Lightning Crew" displayed both power and speed. Although their pitching was good, their hitting proved even stronger. Star right fielder Dave Parker, the epitome of the team's lumber, won a batting crown with a .338 average while also leading the league with 215 hits and 44 doubles. In addition, he earned a Golden Glove for his defensive skills. Second baseman Rennie Stennett batted .336, just a few points behind Parker. Left fielder Al Oliver stroked the ball at a .308 clip, good enough for the tenth-best average in the league. First baseman Bill Robinson put up the best year in his career with a batting average of .304, 26 home runs and 104 RBIs.

Base-running, the lightning, provided another Pirates competitive advantage. Shortstop Frank Taveras led the majors with 70 steals. Center fielder Omar Moreno posted 53. Rennie Stennett added another 28. Third baseman Phil Garner stole 32 bases and scored 99 runs, second on the team to Parker's 107 runs. All in all, the Pirates stole 260 bases, the most by any Pirates team in the last seventy years.

Chuck added the proper touch to that Pirates team. He knew how to deal with his bunch of wild and crazy guys. The players liked and trusted him, and his enthusiasm rubbed off on the players.

The 1977 squad competed solidly though fell short of winning the National League East. An early season-ending elbow injury to Willie Stargell in a bench-clearing brawl against Philadelphia might have led to the shortfall. However, Stargell's replacement, Bill Robinson, put up remarkable stats.

Without a doubt, Tanner displayed effective managerial skills during 1977. His team and the owners respected his ability to win games. He knew strategy and tested the opposition. Because of his strengths on the field, his engaging smile, fine sense of humor and down-home personality, the fans, owners and team members recognized him as the perfect replacement for Danny Murtaugh.

Chuck's popularity in New Castle knew no bounds. The library presented a free movie about him made while he managed the Chicago White Sox. Nonprofits lined up to request his services as a guest speaker, and Chuck rarely disappointed them. On January 17, 1978, Chuck opened the YMCA membership kickoff meeting. Rotary Club Number 89's members enjoyed his folksy sports banter at a Monday lunch meeting.

Tanner's optimism spread through Pirate City with 1978's spring training in Bradenton like hot fudge oozing over French vanilla ice cream. The squad possessed talent and spirit, a strong combination. Chuck's motivational skills and energy fired up the players. He pushed his team to steal bases with abandon and swing freely and ordered his pitchers to throw aggressively.

Chuck also enjoyed parlaying his celebrity status. Florida restaurants proved crowded during the spring training season as snowbirds flocked to the South for the weather. Many Western Pennsylvanians came to Bradenton to watch preseason games. After a full day of practice, Chuck might appear at the most popular restaurants around 6:55 in the evening and announce to the host or hostess, "Reservations for Tanner at seven." The person at the counter invariably responded, "I'm sorry sir, but we have no reservation listed." Chuck would then lay down his ace card: "I am the manager with the Pittsburgh Pirates, and they advised me a reservation had been made in my name. Please check again." The ruse always worked, and the restaurant would find seats for the Tanner family. Poor Babs just rolled her eyes and shook her head from side to side with that "what am I going to do with him" look.

Once the Florida sun had chased away the chill of the North, Pirate City's four practice fields became the stage for the players to strut their stuff. Comfortable hotel housing and a cafeteria overflowing with tasty food presented the guys with the opportunity to relax after a full day of practice. The refreshing aroma from the nearby Tropicana orange juice factory scented the air with a healthy Florida aura.

Most of the previous year's starting team and pitching staff felt secure in their jobs. The Yankees had tempted closer ace Goose Gossage with a six-year, $2,748,000 free-agency contract, but Chuck felt that Kent Tekulve and Grant Jackson possessed the stuff to fill the void. The Pirates had signed free-agent pitcher Jim Bibby on March 15, and the big guy looked terrific. The starters just needed to tone up their muscles and regain their timing for opening day. Rookies and veteran journeymen alike fought for the handful of open spots on the team. Those without a chance worked hard in order to impress the manager and his coaches enough to be called up later in the season. Chuck liked what he saw on the field. It was going to be a great Pirates year.

Coach José Pagán had watched twenty-year-old Don Robinson tear up the AA leagues in Puerto Rico. "Chuck you should take a look at this kid. He's got a great arm."

Chuck approved an invitation for the twenty-year-old six-foot-four Kentucky-born, West Virginia–bred native to come to spring training for a tryout. When Robinson demonstrated his speed and control in the late innings, Chuck gave him additional work, and the righty performed well. Pitching coach Larry Sherry took the candidate aside and told him to keep doing what he was doing. "You know, the skipper is watching, and Don, you might even have a chance to make the team."

Shortly before spring training ended, Chuck took Don aside and told him, "If we can make a trade, we might be able to keep you." Sure enough, on

April 4, the Pirates traded pitcher Elías Sosa and infielder Miguel De Leon to Oakland, bringing back catcher Manny Sanguillén along with a player to be named later, who happened to be Mike Edwards. Manny served as a backup catcher and provided pinch-hitting strength. Oakland probably received the better end of the deal, as Sanguillén was entering the tail end of his career. Both DeLeon and Sosa put up some very good numbers for other teams, but Manny supplied several key pinch hits along the way.

The next morning after the trade, Chuck called Don into his office at McKechnie Park. "Have a seat." Don sat. "Son, we weren't sure whether we wanted to keep nine or ten pitchers. Unfortunately, you are number ten. We could send you to AAA." Chuck paused. Don's heart sank with disappointment. Chuck smiled, "But we are not. We are going to keep ten, and you are going north with the team." The pitcher the vets named "Country Boy" had become a Pirate.

When General Manager Harding Peterson questioned the selection of Robinson as a squad member, Chuck refused to back down from his decision. In fact, he threatened to quit if Harding overruled him. The Pirates manager had chosen wisely, as Robinson would post an outstanding 14-6 record and a strong 3.47 ERA while completing nine games in thirty-five outings during the 1978 season. He also earned a $21,000 major-league salary—not bad for a young man barely out of his teens.

Recently promoted twenty-three-year-old public relations director Joe Safety missed the first week of spring training due to a string of unfortunate personal issues. His father, Vincent Safety, had died of a heart attack at age fifty-three the previous Labor Day. Then his mother passed away at the start of spring training. Funeral details and family matters kept Joe in St. Marys, West Virginia, for several days.

Upon his return to Bradenton, Joe visibly struggled as he inched his way down the hall to his office, crushed by the loss of his mother and uneasy about the responsibilities of his new job. As he eased past the manager's office, he heard Chuck end a phone call. "Let me get back to you a little later, I have something important to take care of."

He called out, "Hey, Joe, can you come in my office for a minute?"

"Sure, Chuck."

The manager offered Joe his condolences, but more than that, he asked what else he could do—and he meant it. "We spoke for nearly a half an hour. Chuck took me under his wing and became the parent I needed at that particular moment. I never forgot his kindness. There was a reason Chuck Tanner was so highly respected," Joe said. "Other players and friends provided their own stories of the leadership and kindness Chuck projected, but I experienced his concern personally."

Teke, a freakishly thin beanpole nicknamed the "Human Drainpipe" by the press, took a terrible hazing as a twenty-seven-year-old rookie back in 1974. When announcer Bob Prince, "the Gunner," first saw him, he croaked, "That man's so thin he could tread water in a test tube."

Teke only played in eight games and put up a stratospheric ERA of 6.00, an ominous start. He asked old pro Stargell why the veterans beat so hard on the new guys. Stargell answered, "You want to know why? I'll tell you. If the rookies can take it, they probably will perform in the clutch."

Teke quickly learned a cardinal rule: rookies should be seen but not heard. By 1976, he performed amazingly in the clutch with a dominant 2.45 ERA, a winning record and nine saves. Teke lasted twenty-two years in professional baseball, well into his forties. Through much of his colorful career, he took part in a series of "fun-filled give-and-take repartees" with Chuck during their nearly nine-year player-manager relationship.

Joe Safety marveled at Teke's peculiarities, and like all great relievers, he exhibited his share. "He rarely entered a game before the seventh inning. He would stay in the locker room many days to watch the game on television in some state of undress and add to his uniform as each inning progressed so he would be fully clothed when needed."

If Chuck felt his pitchers had given their all, he complimented them regardless of the outcome of the game. One day after Teke had been hit hard, Chuck told him, "You were throwing the ball good." Teke replied, "If I'm throwing the ball good, and I get hit hard like this, what happens when I throw bad?" Chuck smiled, shook his head and walked back into his office.

Teke recognized, "Chuck was different in a better way. He liked people, and people liked him. His knack for building confidence among his players converted the 'I' individual into a 'we' person. This skill set proved one of his most enduring gifts."

With the opening of spring training in Bradenton prior to his second season in Pittsburgh as the Pirates manager, Chuck expected his 1978 team to excel. The squad presented a star-studded lineup. "We have the horses, and I believe the Pirates could very well win the pennant." He always looked for the best in his players and tried to put them in the right spot to shine. If a Pirate gave his all, Chuck could be the easiest manager in the league for whom to play.

During that spring, Pittsburgh fans flocked to Florida, and Chuck served as the perfect host. He greeted visitors as if they were guests in his home.

The Snow brothers with Chuck Tanner. *Collection of Dr. Gary Snow.*

Close friend and dentist Dr. John Snow remembered with excitement how Chuck allowed him to coach third base while wearing one of John Milner's uniforms. After games and practice, Doc Snow mixed with the players making him feel like an honorary Pirate.

Spring training also included a brief trip to Puerto Rico for inter-team play. The great star right fielder Roberto Clemente had died in a plane crash on December 31, 1972, while delivering emergency relief supplies to Managua, Nicaragua. All baseball mourned his loss, and Pittsburgh fans and executives intended to honor his memory.

Election rules for entry into the Hall of Fame required a five-year waiting period following retirement, but Roberto's untimely death created the need for an exception to the rule. Clemente's statistics and character had been exemplary—three thousand hits over an eighteen-year career, four batting championships and a .317 lifetime average. A special dispensation allowed the baseball writers to elect Roberto posthumously in 1973.

Shortly thereafter, the major leagues agreed to sponsor two preseason games each year in San Juan, Puerto Rico, for a minimum of a ten years. Ticket proceeds from the games supported a Clemente pet project called Sports City, which promoted the island's youth baseball program. The Pirates volunteered to send one of the teams for the first five years.

Tanner and his preseason team had completed their first game against the Boston Red Sox in San Juan on Tuesday, March 28. A Puerto Rican bus driver motored the team toward the Condado Beach Holiday Inn after the game but got lost along the way. The players booed and jeered the driver, and the Hispanic contingent on the vehicle told him "which way to go" in Spanish. An argument ensued, and the driver pulled off the road and walked off the bus. Shortstop Frank Taveras calmly took the wheel and maneuvered the vehicle to its proper destination, to the accompaniment of cheers and clapping among the riders.

Once at the hotel, Chuck asked Joe Safety if he would like to join him and Boston manager Don Zimmer for an early breakfast. "Sure," Joe said. "Don had stuffed a wad of tobacco in the side of his mouth which slurred his speech, and Chuck offered an entertaining story. The day proved bright and sunny, and we were having a great time. As we were about to enter the restaurant, we saw a huge crowd jamming the street even though it was only 7:30 in the morning. Most of the people gawked at something in the sky. The three of us shielded our eyes from the sun and looked up to see what was happening."

Safety continued, "More than one hundred feet in the air a man stood on a tightrope carrying a balancing pole and walking between the two towers of San Juan's Condado Hotel. The man had no safety net beneath him. Suddenly, the daredevil teetered to and fro as he made his way across the rope. Swirling gusts of wind caused him to lose his balance. We watched him topple from the tightrope, falling ten stories to his death against the concrete pavement, landing less than twenty feet from where we stood."

The victim of the fall happened to be none other than the world-famous, seventy-three-year-old German American acrobat Karl Wallenda, founder of the world-famous Flying Wallendas. "The event seemed like something from the *Twilight Zone*. Years later, on separate occasions, both Chuck and Don questioned me, 'Did that really happen?' It had, and the three of us never forgot that strange morning," Safety explained.

Back home in New Castle after spring training, and when not at Three Rivers for an evening game, Chuck frequently watched the Little Leaguers play baseball across the street from his house. At one game, he greeted a proud parent, "Hey, aren't you the mother of that little all-star?" The mother beamed at the compliment. His special knack made strangers feel like lifelong friends. Chuck, never "Mr. Tanner," always proved approachable, willing to take a minute to build up a person's ego and add to their self-importance. Even his own children called him Chuck rather than Dad. This Pirates public relations agent provided incalculable benefits to the team, the owners, his community and the Pittsburgh fans in addition to his superior managerial skills.

Scores of people witnessed and appreciated his many kindnesses. Judge Caiazza watched him load his car with bats and balls to take to a terminally ill child in Edenberg. Bruce Pickel, who lived a few blocks up the road from Chuck on Maitland Lane, exchanged pleasantries with him at the Pennzoil gas station and mentioned that his wife's favorite player was Phil Garner. The very next day, Chuck showed up at the Pickel house with a signed "Phil Garner" baseball.

Tanner served as the perfect emissary for the Pirates—always courteous and considerate to fans. Kids loved his come-hither personality, and he never refused an autograph. Young Kirk Oleskyski stood above the dugout before the start of a game. When Chuck peeked up and recognized Kirk, he popped into the dugout, grabbed a ball and flipped it to the New Castle boy's outstretched hands—just another case of making a young fan feel special.

"No one gave me the book on how to manage. I just worked from my gut and my head," Chuck confessed. He put a lot of faith in a strong staff of relievers. If the openers could keep the game close, he believed that his finishers could shut down the opposition. His runners would steal bases, and his strong bats would bang out hits in the late innings after the other team removed their starters.

Teke joked that the Pirates enjoyed watching the other dugout, where the players sat smugly, assured that they held the upper hand. He explained, "Look at them—up 4–2. They think they're winning. They're going to remove their starter. They don't know we've already got three runs we haven't scored yet. Our relievers will shut them down, and they are about to lose." The confidence of the Pirates team soared with every game as the season progressed.

Chuck prioritized relievers as a key input to his team's strength. He'd gladly exchange an average starter for a strong reliever. Both he and the baseball experts considered the Pirates mop-up crew as one of the best ever assembled.

Chuck knew baseball and strategy. He recognized that a pitcher's velocity counted as a powerful element toward his success, but he recognized that movement on the ball meant even more than speed alone. In Chicago, Wilbur Wood's zany knuckleball delivered far more success than his curve or fastball. Nolan Ryan might have been one of the few pitchers playing in 1978 who consistently threw the ball one hundred miles per hour and dominated with speed.

With Teke, if his ball reached much above ninety miles per hour, his sidearm sinker didn't sink and his slider hung. Speed actually became his enemy. On one occasion, Chuck asked his reliever how he felt, Teke told his manager, "Don't worry, you won't wear me out. I'll let you know if I need a rest." The two agreed that Teke would rarely pitch more than three days in a row, and Chuck almost never would allow him to sit out more than two days. Chuck used him in ninety games or more during 1978 and '79 and seventy-two or more between 1980 and 1984, with the exception of 1981.

Chuck managed his pitching staff differently from many managers. He kept five starters and five relievers. He had great confidence in his staff but rarely allowed his starters to go more than five or six innings. When Chuck arrived to the big leagues as the Chicago White Sox's manager, the team had a weak bullpen. Chuck converted Goose Gossage and Terry Forster from starters to relievers and added some hitting, and the team blossomed. Chuck set a goal of building a strong relief staff with the Pirates as well.

Chuck appreciated the psychology and physiology behind relief pitching. "A reliever generally warms up with thirty throws. If the reliever can hang in for two or three innings instead of one, he saves another pitcher from those thirty warmups, translating to a more rested staff during the second half of the year, especially important if using four or five relievers and an alternating closer."

Tanner did everything in his power to make his players feel comfortable. They quickly learned to trust him. When Teke first encountered Chuck's optimism, he questioned if it might be fake. How could anyone remain so positive under adverse conditions? After several months of his manager's continued positivity, the pitcher recognized that the "act" was for real.

Teke stated that '70s baseball was much different than that of today. "Managers could not demonstrate a flaw or hitch in the windup or delivery with mechanical aids such as video replay. We relied on self-evaluation. My roommate Ed Ott possessed the uncanny knack of communicating from his catcher's position without words. In most cases a minor tinkering adjusted any problems I had—a tiny tweak of a screwdriver rather than a complete overhaul. Chuck recognized and appreciated this skill and rarely interfered with his catchers."

When coach Jim Frey of the Kansas City Royals asked Teke if he would look at fellow submarine reliever Dan Quisenberry's delivery, Chuck okayed the program since both men pitched in different leagues and side armers were such a rarity. Teke watched and marveled at the younger pitcher's control. "Don't change a thing," he advised. As a thank-you, Quisenberry sent Tekulve some argyle socks and a tie for Father's Day.

Shortstop Jim Fregosi recently had been purchased as an insurance backup utility player. At spring training the following year in Bradenton, he played an early game and headed to the bench for a rest.

"Hey, Jim, I need you to play in another game," Chuck called over to him.

"Okay, Chuck, you got it."

"Then they needed me in a third game. I was thirty-six and beat. Tanner nearly killed me," Fregosi later joked, but he liked playing for him.

Third baseman Phil Garner related how Chuck overlooked a serious breach of the rules in his favor. "At one point during the '78 season, I was struggling at the plate. We were playing out west, and Ed Ott suggested we go to TGIF's for a few drinks to help me forget my slump. I think I overdid it. I bought tequila shots for everyone and somehow ended up in my hotel room, probably with Ed's help. We had a game the next day requiring a short plane trip, but I was hung over and slept through the wakeup call. I missed our Pacific Southwest team flight. Luckily, I caught a later flight and made it to the ballpark around 1:45 p.m. prior to game time. I tried to sneak in, but damned if Chuck didn't catch me. I told him I was sorry, and he could fine and bench me. 'Oh, no, I'm not going to fine or bench you, but you sure as hell better play well today,' he said. I threw up before the game but also came up with a couple of hits. The slump had ended."

Jim Bibby recalled his first start of the season on his fifty-first day with the club. During a shaky May 28, 1978 first inning against the Montreal Expos at Three Rivers, Tanner screamed from the dugout at the imposing six-foot-five, 225-pound pitcher, "Close your eyes and throw. Don't worry about anything." The advice must have worked because Bibby ended up pitching a four-hit complete game, winning by a 5–2 score.

In baseball, rookies are supposed to keep their mouths shut and never show up vets. During one game, Don Robinson held a 5–1 lead, but the bases were loaded. Shortstop Frank Taveras dropped a routine pop-up, and two runs scored. The young pitcher scowled and mumbled something under his breath. Totally unnerved and out of his pitching rhythm, he gave up another hit, and two more runs scored to tie the game. Tanner yanked Robby, but the Pirates eventually won the game 15–5.

Tanner thought that Robinson's facial expression and mumbling embarrassed Taveras. After the game, he grabbed the pitcher and pushed him into a corner. "Don't you ever show up a vet again. You are just a rookie and lucky to be playing here. I can bury you in the minors and make sure you never see the light of day. Do you understand?" Robinson recognized that rookies had to earn their stripes, and errors must be forgiven and forgotten. He also learned that a rookie should never show up a vet.

Chuck consigned Robinson to the bullpen, where he relieved Bibby for eight and one-third innings to gain a hard-fought win. After the game, Chuck put his hand on Robinson's shoulder. "I guess you are out of the doghouse now." Robinson returned to his role as a starter.

The 1978 season produced eighty-eight wins against seventy-three losses and another second-place finish, a strong season but less than hoped for by Chuck and the fans. Bert Blyleven (who had come to the Pirates in a four-way trade from the Texas Rangers), Don Robinson and John Candelaria provided a steady starting threesome, although none won more than fourteen games.

Blyleven led the team in ERA, strikeouts and innings pitched, while tying Don Robinson for the most wins with fourteen. Kent Tekulve nailed down thirty-one saves. While most of the team's batting declined from the previous year, Parker won a second batting crown with a .334 average. In addition, he pounded out 30 home runs and 117 RBIs, earning him the National League's Most Valuable Player award.[40]

Chuck cared for his players and looked after them. He told the press, "When Dave Parker went through his 0-for-24 slump, he didn't kick helmets or throw bats.…He removed his helmet, placed it on the bench, replaced his bat on the rack, sat down and rooted like hell for the next batter." Parker appreciated Chuck's support, and in his autobiography he stated that he never thought he would like a manager as much as Danny Murtaugh, but Chuck reached that level.

"Pops" Stargell, who played only sixty-eight games the previous year due to a pinched nerve, returned to form with twenty-eight homers and ninety-seven RBIs to win the National League Comeback Player of the Year. His overall fighting spirit also earned him the Hutch Award, named in honor of

Willie Stargell. *Pittsburgh Pirates.*

the inspirational manager Fred Hutchinson. Willie became Pittsburgh's sole member of the All-Star team.

The '78 squad proved especially speedy. Omar Moreno led the charge with a league-leading 71 steals. Frank Taveras ran for 46. Phil Garner put up 27, and Dave Parker added another 20. All and all, the team produced 213 stolen bases. On August 12, the Pirates found themselves eleven and a half games behind Philadelphia after a horrible 4-17 stretch. Always optimistic, Tanner told his troops, "This may not be the end; it may be the beginning."[41] By September 19, the Pirates had climbed to second place.

My son Sean, eleven at the time, became a huge Pirates fan during that summer. On Sunday, I took him to a game. After a slew of popcorn, hot dogs and lots of fun, the game ended in a win. Sean asked if we could get some Pirate autographs.

"Sure, why not?" We waited outside the door to the dressing room as the players bolted out the door. A nervous young boy thrust a paper in front of Dave Parker, and he signed. He greeted the rest of the disappointed waiting crowd. "Sorry, I'm in a hurry. No more today."

Most of the rest of the team scurried past the young fans without a hint of acknowledgement. Lastly, Chuck Tanner walked out the door and waved. The young fans encircled him.

"Okay kids, let's take it easy. Don't worry. I am going to sign for every one of you." I leaned over to Sean and whispered, "Let's let the line thin out." As promised, Chuck signed for every kid, possibly fifteen or twenty who waited. When our turn arrived, I approached Chuck. "Hi, we are from New Castle."

"I know who you are." I had spoken to him on several occasions at the YMCA, and he served on the board of Citizens Bank with my father.

"It was really nice for you to hang around and sign for all the fans."

"No, that's just my job." How could one help but respect a man with that kind of attitude? Chuck took the time to listen to and talk with everyone. He made me and my son feel important.

Jeff Pitzer, his former milkman, while buying gas at the Sunoco Station on Maitland Lane and Wilmington Avenue, ran into Chuck filling his tank. Jeff mentioned that his aunt Mae VonGraff thought he pulled his starters too quickly. Chuck laughed. He had thick skin. He signed a ball he had in the car to Mae, who treasured that autographed ball for all her days. In New Castle, Tanner autographed balls for hundreds of fans.

Bruce Tanner remembered how much his father had taught him about baseball and life. "He spoke a different language. He came up with simple solutions to difficult problems, and I began to think 'Why couldn't I have thought of that.' The older I got, the more I came to appreciate Chuck as a person and as a father."

During his junior and senior years at Neshannock High School, Bruce Tanner pitched extremely well. Several colleges expressed interest in the six-foot-three, 220-pound, hard-throwing right hander. Bruce seriously considered a scholarship to Penn State, where his older brother Mark had

Dave Parker.
Pittsburgh Pirates.

played. Chuck recognized his son's potential and offered his own advice: "You can go to Penn State, where you will get to play six months out of the year and freeze three months, or you can go to Florida State, which also is interested in you, where you can play in the sun all year long." Bruce followed Chuck's advice and chose FSU.

On the final game of the 1978 season at Three Rivers, the crowd applauded their Pirates for another successful season. While the championship Phillies watched, Tanner replaced Parker during a meaningless game. Chuck stood on the field and clapped as his star right fielder jogged toward home plate. The entire team congratulated him for his second batting championship in a row. Tanner considered Dave Parker as the best player in all baseball— intelligent, hardworking and a great fielder, base runner and hitter.

Philadelphia eliminated the Bucs on the next-to-last day of the season. The experts felt that Chuck had performed admirably, and the *Baseball Bulletin* named him as its Manager of the Year.

Tanner summed up the season: "We would have taken the whole enchilada if we had Enrique Romo." The increased attendance figure at Three Rivers of 1,237,349, versus 1,025,495 the previous year, testified to the growing popularity of the "colorful, free-spirited and confident" Pirates and their always optimistic manager.[42] The increase in the sales of hot dogs, popcorn, soft drinks and beer put a smile on the faces of the owners and vendors alike and added some extra cash in their pockets.

At the end of the 1978 season, the Pirates made two coaching changes. Larry Sherry, a former reliever and Chicago White Sox minor-league manager, had handled the pitching staff for the previous two years. He moved on to the Los Angeles Angels. Chuck replaced him with former three-time All-Star pitcher Harvey Haddix. Bob Skinner, a nine-year-veteran Pirates left fielder and three-time .300 hitter in the late '50s and early '60s, took over for José Pagán as the batting coach. Joe Lonnett and Al Monchak remained glued to their spots on third and first.

CHAPTER 9

THE 1979 SEASON

My motto was, "Always keep swinging."
—Hank Aaron

T he 1979 season shaped up as special for the Pirates. Chuck knew that the team possessed all the tools to compete in the division and possibly even take the pennant. "We just missed last year. We can do it in '79."

On February 10, prior to spring training, St. Vitus Church presented Chuck with a banquet and a citation. When Chuck rose to speak, he told his audience, "I'm going to say this, everybody picks Philadelphia, but we can win it." He added with a broad grin, "If those Philly players were so good, they'd be playing for us in Pittsburgh."

The Bucco's squad sported outstanding hitters such as Dave Parker and Willie Stargell along with fleet-footed base stealers like the 1978 National League leader Omar Moreno. Kent Tekulve and Grant Jackson provided the team with a duo of top-notch closers.

Since starting pitching appeared a tad thin, Tanner recognized the need for a quality long reliever to control the important fifth, sixth and seventh innings. On December 5, 1978, the Pirates traded with the Seattle Mariners for Mexican-born Enrique Romo to act as the set-up man for his closers. The Romo acquisition created an important upgrade. He would produce the best season in his six-year major-league career.[43]

The team arrived at spring training in Bradenton during mid-February hyped to play. "I'm not surprised that almost all our guys arrived here in

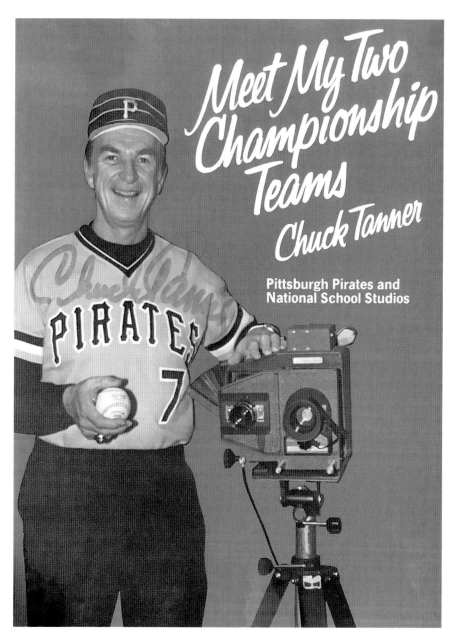

Chuck Tanner and National School Studios. *Pittsburgh Pirates.*

great condition. Most of them didn't have to work off season. When I played, the day after the season ended, like most of my teammates, I was either looking for work or already had a job....Today, a player makes enough money so he can take it easy during winter....All a guy has to do is visit the gym every day."[44]

Chuck felt comfortable in his no. 7 Pirate uniform. He liked his owners, his coaches, the players and the Pittsburgh fans. He purchased a condo on University Parkway so his family could feel at home during the preseason in Florida. Always positive about his chances, he held a special premonition about his team's shot at a division title in 1979.

Although Dave Parker came in a few pounds overweight after a few months on the banquet circuit, Chuck knew that he would be in top form within a few weeks. The "Cobra" may have possessed destructive appetites, but his massive talent overcame any shortcomings. He put together five Hall of Fame years between 1975 and 1979, never batting less than .308. Chuck considered him one of the finest players he ever managed.

Chuck complimented his players through good times and bad. While Bill Robinson and Phil Garner tossed the ball back and forth, Chuck spoke to a sportscaster and pointed to the field. "Look at Robby over there. Bill's going to be thirty-five in June, but you'd never know it by looking at him. Robinson has outlasted plenty of players who are considered better than him....It's his dedication. He's a winner."[45]

"If everyone does their part, we'll have a good year." Tanner recognized that team wins far exceeded the importance of individual stats. The "we" trumped the "I" every time. Even Bert Blyleven bought into the system that year and had fun playing ball for the Pirates. Kent Tekulve summarized the camaraderie of the squad: "The twenty-five guys on the team, be they Mexican, Panamanian, Dutch, American, Dominican, Black or White, these men were like Chuck's younger brothers or sometimes his children. He stood by them, and they backed him to the hilt."

Chuck's goals for the year included winning a pennant. To succeed, he put forth three basic tenets:

1. Always do the right thing. Your team will know it and trust you. Besides, you'll feel better about yourself.
2. Care for others and look out for the team's best interests. This will make your players perform to the best of their ability.
3. Work to improve yourself and those around you. This will pay dividends for you and your players.

During spring training, David "Fuzzy" Fazzone joined Chuck for an away game at Payne Park in Sarasota against the Chicago White Sox. "He introduced me to bigger-than-life Bill Veeck, and I told Mr. Veeck how much I enjoyed his book *Veeck as in Wreck*. The Sox owner thanked me and pontificated, 'Well, my boy, come sit with me in my box, and we can talk.' We spoke about baseball the whole game, and I had a wonderful time, thanks to Chuck."

In March 1979, the umpires went on strike during spring training. Pay for a major-league umpire topped out at $40,000 for up to 170 games per year of work. The umps lacked health insurance and job protection and received a minimal pension. In contrast, a National Basketball Association referee received $60,000 for fewer than 100 games. The grounds crew and other workers sympathized with the umpires and honored their picket lines, forcing teams to use local talent. The walkout lasted through mid-May.

A substitute umpire from New Castle with a wooden leg named Nicky Lucas manned first base in an away preseason game at Payne Park in Sarasota against the Chicago White Sox. Even in spring training, Chuck demonstrated his competitive spirit. Omar Moreno had dribbled a weak grounder and appeared to be out by a mile. Chuck must have thought the first baseman had missed his foot on the bag because he raced on the field and got in Lucas's face to argue about the call.

"Chuck, he was out. Why are you doing this to me?" After a sixty-second rant, Chuck returned to the dugout. Then the next batter, Willie Stargell, smacked a liner to right field that careened off poor Lucas's wooden leg. When the ump ignored the pain from the shot, Chuck announced to the dugout, "You see how tough New Castle guys are."

Tanner ruled over a rough-and-rowdy bunch of fun-loving flakes with a calm but nurturing hand. However, he pushed the action on the playing field to the edge. His free-swinging and wild base-stealing approach drove other teams off-kilter. Manager Sparky Anderson of the Detroit Tigers called the Pirates "aggressive in everything they do: hitting, fielding, pitching and running. They do everything with abandon, because that's the way Chuck Tanner wants it. He's an aggressive manager who doesn't go by the book. That's why Pittsburgh's such an exciting team."[46]

Public relations director Joe Safety explained that the Pirates of the '70s produced highly successful results for a small-market team. "Chuck operated without the huge checkbook of the big-city teams like the Yankees and the Dodgers, but he made the most of what he had. Management, the players and the fans enjoyed his style of play. They liked and trusted him." Safety summed up the manager of the Pirates in the single sentence used by many others: "If a guy couldn't play for Tanner, then who could he play for?"

Joe Safety later left Pittsburgh and moved on to George Steinbrenner's New York Yankees, a big-market team. "Steinbrenner only cared about winning, and he proved tremendously good at it. The management of the Pirates wanted to win, but they also maintained a close relationship with their players as well."

As in the past, John W. Galbreath and the other minority stockholders met with key executives such as Harding Peterson and Chuck Tanner the week prior to the opening of the season to hammer out budgets and overall business strategy. The majority owner then returned to his horse farm in Galloway, Ohio, to allow the professionals to run the team. Unlike owners George Steinbrenner and Charlie Finley, the Pirate brass rarely interfered with day-to-day activities, clearing the way for Chuck to do his job, and he loved it.

On the field, Chuck made liberal use of his entire squad, including pinch runners and hitters, and he used his bullpen with regularity. In the 1979 opener against Montreal, Blyleven pitched a strong seven innings and left unwillingly. Tanner brought in Romo, who pitched a scoreless eighth. Tekulve came in the ninth and pitched a scoreless inning, but in the tenth, a hit batter and two errors brought home the winning run, and Teke took a hard loss. Blyleven, aggravated at being pulled while he still had his stuff, griped at Teke, "You know I've never had much luck with relievers." Teke snapped back, "You know, Bert, I'm going to save a hell of a lot more games for you than I lose." Blyleven realized he was out of line after some of the players spoke to him, and he apologized to Teke the next day.

During the third game of the season, Bruce Kison struck out ten in six and a third innings against Montreal and was leading by a 2–1 score. Tanner brought in Enrique Romo, who gave up three hits in the inning. Tekulve relieved and got the final out in the seventh, but three runs had scored. When the Pirates hitters evened the score at four, Tanner brought in Ed Whitson for the eighth and ninth. He pitched okay but gave up the winning run. The fans booed Tanner unmercifully. How could the manager pull Kison when he was throwing bullets? What they didn't know was that his elbow had tightened, and he threw in pain.

On April 19, eleven games into the season, the Pirates sent starting shortstop Frank Taveras to the New York Mets in exchange for "Crazy Horse" Tim Foli, a highly spirited slick-fielder. On paper, the deal looked terrible. Taveras had led the league with seventy stolen bases in 1977, and he scored eighty-one runs in '78. On April 18, Foli sat on the Mets bench with a sore knee while sub Doug Flynn started.

Foli possessed a volcanic temper. "He could start a fight in a monastery," reported an ex-teammate. The press called General Manager Harding Peterson an idiot for trading a proven starter who had led the league in steals, but the deal worked. Chuck helped Tim rein in his temper. Foli's rough-and-tumble persona fit in perfectly with Pittsburgh. His strong play at short solidified the team's defense. He claimed that Tanner's support gave him the confidence to perform with the best offensive statistics of his career—a .291 batting average and seventy runs scored, the third highest on the team. His nineteen sacrifices and low strikeout ratio made him a valuable scoring tool, and his defense proved a vast improvement over that of Taveras.[47] Tanner called him "the best second-place hitter I have ever seen in the big leagues, and he makes the ordinary plays extraordinarily well." Foli's hardscrabble play provided exactly what Pittsburgh needed at short, and his teammates appreciated his mental and physical toughness. During the entire season, Foli, an excellent contact hitter, struck out only 14 times in 525 at bats.

The walk-out of the umpires that had started during spring training continued through all of April and part of May. As the strike persisted and no contract appeared in sight, pitchers and batters struggled through questionable ball-and-strike calls by the minor-league "scab" umpires. The subs missed plays, and the early weeks of the season proved unsettling for the players. Sometimes the mistakes worked to the Pirates' advantage and sometimes not.

The early part of the season included its share of fireworks on the field, especially due to the ersatz umpires. On May 9, the Pirates played the Atlanta Braves at Fulton Stadium. Pitcher Whitson had difficulty locating the home plate. After giving up a hit and a few walks, a wild pitch struck opposing pitcher Phil Niekro on the shoulder. "Take your base," the umpire bellowed. Whether or not the pitch hit Niekro's bat first became a bone of contention. Tanner exploded, convinced that the ball had ricocheted off the bat before hitting Niekro in the shoulder. Tanner refused to leave the field, and the ump threw Tanner and coach Lonnett out of the game. Luckily for the Pirates, ten runs in the final three innings led to a 17–9 victory and made the brouhaha of little significance.

On May 12, down by a 2–1 score against Cincinnati in the seventh, Chuck called on Willie Stargell to pinch-hit for pitcher Jim Bibby. Pinch runner Matt Alexander stood on second and Phil Garner on first. Pitcher Frank Pastore caught two quick strikes against Stargell. On the next pitch, Pastore threw a ball. Willie started to swing and tried to hold up. Replacement first base umpire Harry Smail, a 350-pound hulk of a man, signaled no swing. The Reds disagreed. A rhubarb ensued, and Pastore labeled it the worst umpiring he had ever seen, but to no avail. The call stood. Stargell and Moreno followed with hits, and the Pirates won the game 3–2. Future Cincinnati Hall of Fame second baseman Joe Morgan claimed that Stargell later joked about the incident: "How can he call me out when last night I sent him two pizzas, a half-gallon of beer and a hamburger on the side? Tomorrow, I'm going to send him a double order."[48]

The strike eventually ended on May 17 after forty-five days, with the umpires gaining a $7,000 annual increase in pay. The season returned to normal, and the players could count on a higher degree of accuracy in the calls on the field.

During a June 15 game against the Los Angeles Dodgers, Bert Blyleven, "the Dutchman," had only given up four hits in seven and two-thirds innings. After a single to Bill Russell, a strike-out and a walk to Steve Garvey, Tanner pulled his starter and brought in Teke to deliver a third out. However, in the ninth, Teke gave up a two-run homer to Joe Ferguson. Although Blyleven won the game, he sulked about losing his potential shutout when he still had his "best stuff."

Blyleven believed that he performed better in a three-man rotation than a four-man. He ranted, "If I'm going to pitch every five or six days, get me out of Pittsburgh." Tanner refused to publicly embarrass his pitcher, telling the sportswriters, "If I was the pitcher, I'd want the shutout and complete game. But I'm the manager, and I have to get the win for the team. I like Blyleven. I like his competitiveness." Privately, Chuck bristled at his ace pitcher's lack of team spirit and his negative interview with the media.[49]

The final piece in the Pirates puzzle cemented a bunch of individuals into a pennant winning team. The San Francisco Giants dumped two-time batting champion "Mad-Dog" Bill Madlock on June 28 to the Pirates, along with infielder Lenny Randle and pitcher Dave Roberts, in exchange for pitchers Fred Breining, Al Holland and Ed Whitson.

The Pirates desperately needed starting third baseman Bill Madlock. Second baseman Rennie Stennett had slowed significantly, and Chuck moved the previous year's third base starter, Phil Garner, to second to strengthen the infield.

Madlock would pound the ball for a .328 pace through the 1979 season, and he covered the third base line like a ravenous cat snatching a mouse for its breakfast. Newly acquired pitcher Dave Roberts chipped in with a solid

5-2 record, one save and an above-average 3.26 ERA as a spot starter and reliever. The Pirates sold Randle to the Yankees on August 3. Catcher Ed Ott believed the addition of Bill Madlock made all the difference during the pennant run.

In San Francisco, Bill Madlock had a reputation for an explosive temper. His outbursts against umpires, teammates, coaches and his manager pushed the Giants to trade this valuable commodity in a fire sale for the good of the squad. He once tore up a scorecard and threw it in the face of manager Joe Altobelli.

After Altobelli benched him, Madlock demanded a trade. Three weeks later, he received his wish, but before the season ended, San Francisco fired Altobelli.[50]

The arrival of the hard-hitting third baseman thrilled Chuck. His formula for handling so-called difficult players employed the development of mutual respect. He had earned Dick Allen's allegiance in Chicago by treating him as an adult and a leader. As a result, Allen performed like a superstar, and the two men bonded into a lifelong friendship. He did the same with Tim Foli, and he intended to win over Bill Madlock as well.

Once his new infielder arrived in Pittsburgh, Chuck welcomed him warmly with a firm handshake and a broad smile. "Bill, glad to have you here. You are now my third baseman, but if you tear up a program and throw it in my face or disrespect me, I'll put your head in my hands and squeeze it." Tanner waited for an argument, but Madlock calmly answered, "Skip, I'll do whatever you want me to do. I'm just glad to leave that zoo in San Francisco."

When Tanner placed him sixth in the batting order, Madlock bellyached, "But I am a batting champion." However, he did as told, and the manager got along famously with "Mad-Dog," allowing him to use his bat and glove to do the talking. Madlock proved a wonderful asset to the team. He received the latitude to swing or steal at will. "It was a pleasure playing there," Madlock told the press. Bill liked the team, and the team liked and appreciated the energy he brought to the field. The Bill Madlock acquisition—virtually a steal—proved to be one of Harding Peterson's finest trades. The Pirates had assembled one of their strongest teams ever with a strong bench and few weaknesses at any position.

The 1979 year provided outstanding results. Willie Stargell's 32 home runs earned him a co-MVP trophy along with first baseman Keith Hernandez of the St. Louis Cardinals, the league leader in doubles, runs scored and batting average. Dave Parker chipped in with a solid .310 average, 25 home

Chuck Tanner and
Bill Madlock. *Pittsburgh
Pirates.*

runs and 109 runs scored. Pitchers John Candelaria, Bert Blyleven, Bruce
Kison, Kent Tekulve, Jim Bibby and Enrique Romo each added ten or more
victories to the kitty. Kent Tekulve racked up 31 saves, second in the league,
and Grant Jackson posted an additional 14 saves, both career bests. Oddly,
no single pitcher on the team reached the fifteen-win level, although six
achieved ten or more victories and no batter drove in more than 94 RBIs.

Like past Tanner teams, wild base running played an important role in
the offense. Moreno led the league with seventy-seven steals in 1979. Bill
Madlock had twenty one, Dave Parker twenty, Bill Robinson thirteen and
pinch runner Matt Alexander thirteen. The combination of the team's
speed and power gave proof to the sportswriters' nickname for the Pirates
offense as the "Lumber and Lightning Crew."

Chuck motivated his team to play top-notch baseball. He stuck to only
two hard-and-fast rules: be on time and play hard. The players would have
followed their "terminally optimistic" manager anywhere he asked.

Thirty-nine-year-old senior statesman Willie "Pops" Stargell acted as
Chuck's "co-manager," smoothing out the team's high testosterone levels
and stroking the egos of the star athletes. Willie proved the perfect man for
the task. His "Stargell Stars," which players affixed to their caps, became
treasured mementos for a job well done—signifying a key hit, a timely
sacrifice fly, a defensive gem or a scoreless inning.

Calls occasionally went the wrong way against the Bucs, driving Chuck to
distraction. John McCollister in his book *Tales from the 1979 Pittsburgh Pirates*
describes a July 25 game where Lee Lacy ran toward second on a 3-1 count

to Omar Moreno. The pitch missed the plate for a ball. Cincinnati catcher pegged the ball to second, and umpire Dick Stello thumbed Lacy out, even though the walk entitled him to second base.

After being declared out, Lacy headed toward home, and second baseman Dave Concepción tagged him again. A rhubarb ensued, but the umpire insisted that Lacy was out. The Pirates lost 6–5. Tanner filed an official protest with National League president Charles Feeney, who refused to overturn the umpire's bad call.

The season also held its share of humor. Pitcher John Candelaria, during a phone call from his home in Davidson, North Carolina, near Lake Norman, described an incident in Candlestick Park in San Francisco. He had pitched the prior night, and the press subjected him to a long interview the next day before a game. The discussion lasted longer than anticipated, and "Candy" missed the snack served in the clubhouse. He returned to the dugout hungry, with the game about to start. Unfortunately for the pitcher, Chuck had issued a no-eating-in-the-dugout rule.

Candelaria peeked his head out of the dugout and spotted a boy eating a hotdog. It looked delicious, and he was starved. He took a baseball in his hand and called the youth to him. "Kid, here's a five-dollar bill. If you get me one of those dogs, I'll give you this ball with some autographs."

"Really!?"

"You bet."

The boy took the five and raced through the stands to get Candelaria his snack. As he returned, Chuck happened to be making his way back to the dugout. He glanced up into the stands to see a youngster looking for Candelaria, who had ducked into the dugout as soon as he saw his manager coming. The boy shouted, "Hey Mr. Candelaria—Candy Man—number forty-five. Where are you? I have your hot dog." No answer. As the boy spotted Tanner about to enter the dugout, he called out, "Hey number seven, tell number forty-five I have his hot dog and want my ball."

Chuck looked toward his pitcher. "Candelaria, this kid has your $250 hot dog."

Candelaria appeared, sheepishly took the hot dog, gave the kid the ball and disappeared inside the dugout.

Chuck stared at his pitcher and asked, "What do you think you're doing?"

"Well, I am going to eat my $250 hot dog," and he did, but the fine stuck.

The month of May finished with a healthy 16-10 record. June proved weaker, with the Bucs eking out 14-13 stats, but Madlock just had joined the team as the starting third baseman. By July, the team had caught fire, and the Pirates finished the month with a respectable 57-45-1 record. However, in August, the team members appeared poised to strut their stuff.

Willie Stargell, no. 8, the team captain and its leader, first discovered Sister Sledge's hit song "We Are Family" during batting practice in St. Louis in June. Dave Parker suggested adopting "Ain't No Stopping Us Now," a disco hit by Gene McFadden and John Whitehead, for the club song. Team captain Willie Stargell stuck with Sister Sledge's "We Are Family," and Parker voiced no objection. Pops called public relations director Joe Safety to purchase the right to use the record and adopt it as the team's theme song.

Win or lose, the song reverberated through the clubhouse after games. Fans joined in an oft-times off-key performance of "We Are Family" during the seventh-inning stretch after the rendition of "Take Me Out to the Ball Game." Walkers in the downtown area could hear the lyrics of Kim, Debbie, Joni and Kathy Sledge, accompanied by the chorus of thousands in the stands:

> *We are family.*
> *I got all my sisters with me.*
> *We are family.*
> *Get up everybody and sing.*
>
> *Everyone can see we're together*
> *As we walk on by.*
> *And we fly just like birds of a feather.*
> *I won't tell no lie.*
>
> *All of the people around us they say,*
> *Can they be that close?*
> *Just let me state for the record,*
> *We're giving love in a family dose.*
>
> [Chorus]
>
> *Living life is fun and we've just begun*
> *To get our share of this world's delights.*
> *High hopes we have for the future,*
> *And our goal's in sight.*

No, we don't get depressed.
Here's what we call our golden rule,
Have faith in you and the things you do.
You won't go wrong.
This is our family jewel.

We are family.
I got all my sisters with me.
We are family.
Get up everybody and sing.
Get up, get up, get up and sing it to me.
Have faith in you and the things you do.
Get up, get up, y'all.
I got all my sisters with me.
We are family.
I got all my sisters with me.

Sister Sledge, Cotillion Records, Bernard Edwards, 1979

The Bucco players idolized Pops Stargell as their father figure and loved Chuck Tanner as their patriarch and leader. Pitcher Don Robinson explained Stargell's importance: "During my time with the Pirates, I had very few meetings with Chuck. Willie Stargell quietly but forcefully took care of almost everything."

Teke said, "Parker and Garner were the two loudest guys on the team, but every member added his special spice to the Pirates stew. It was every man for himself, but only Chuck could mold a winning combination from twenty-five unique personalities from different countries, backgrounds and temperaments. We had a United Nations team. We actually had three Panamanians. No other squad had three Panamanians."

Willie Stargell added, "We all may be different, but when we put on our uniforms, we're all Pirates." Like Teke said, Chuck molded this hodgepodge of professional individualists into a formidable team. He recognized that the 1979 champions had what Phil Garner called "a depth of personality." Sportscaster Stan Savran pointed out that the Pirates were the most charismatic team he had ever seen, with "more characters per square inch than you could ever imagine."

Tanner allowed his players a great deal of latitude. He encouraged the "family" theme. In fact, he said, "I loved it." This was a veteran-laden group, and he believed they merited freedom. He recognized that the team makeup contained more than enough internal leadership and maturity to keep the ship afloat.

Sometimes, Chuck employed a soft touch. Other times he used a firm hand. The high-strung and emotional Enrique Romo proved an excellent pitcher and a challenge. When he relieved Jim Bibby following a brilliant outing, the crowd released a torrent of hisses and boos. Romo assumed that he was the object of the fans' displeasure. He looked out into the crowd and stewed, unsure of whether or not to pitch. Tanner came to the mound to calm his pitcher. "Enrique, calm down, they are not booing you. They are booing me for taking Bibby out of the game. Just pitch like I know you can."

Although Chuck could play loose with his rule book, he also showed a tough side when needed. He red-lined certain borders of conduct, and players who crossed that invisible line found themselves facing a tough customer.

In one game after a rough outing, the skipper yanked Romo, a talented Mexican reliever with a fierce screwball. Romo slammed the ball in Tanner's hand and stormed off the field, disgusted at his performance and angry for being pulled.

When the game ended, Romo kicked over a trash can in the locker room and unleashed a machete, which he pointed at Steve Nicosia. "He acted crazy," Phil Garner recalled. Romo made no actual threats, but Tanner iron-fisted Romo's throat and shoved him against a wall. "If you ever bring a knife into this locker room again, I'll shove it up your butt. Now cool down and apologize." Chuck allowed the incident to pass. He rarely held grudges, especially against a man like Romo, who always gave 100 percent.

"Chuck's smile could fool you," Dave Parker warned. "If he was upset with you, I would suggest you never go in a room alone with him by yourself because he might be the only one who will come out." Chuck knew how each of his players would react to discipline. Ed Ott might respond well to a tongue lashing, but Omar Moreno would mope for days. Chuck knew he had to hug some guys and kick others in the rear.

Mike Easler, nicknamed "The Hitman" for his ability with the bat, also found himself in a heated run-in with his manager. Easler called Chuck "one of the strongest human beings I knew. If you are wrong or say something back to him, he could pick you up by the shirt. He did that once to me. He got me against the wall and picked me up and said, 'Who's your boss?' I said, 'You are, sir,' but I always loved Chuck. He was the most positive man I ever met."[51]

Garner appreciated Tanner's aggressive style. He pushed hitters to hit and runners to run. Coach Joe Lonnett said, "You'd think I'd know what he's going to do, but I don't. He has no pattern."[52] One thing everyone agreed on about Chuck was that he possessed unparalleled communication skills along with his naturally upbeat nature. He pushed the entire Pirates team to deliver a winning attitude and to provide a great experience for the fans.

Jim Rooker respected Chuck's ability as a manager "to handle players. He took a mesh of guys, be they Black, White, Latin or Puerto Rican, who couldn't talk to each other very well, couldn't understand each other—but he knew one thing—how to make them play baseball."

Chuck considered individual statistics unreliable predictors of a team's success. The key was building a winning outfit. "We may not have the best players in baseball, but we have the best team," he told the press.

Tanner appreciated each and every player's special talents, He marveled at Willie Stargell's physical strength and his ability to hit the long ball. On July 29, the first baseman smacked a ball in the ninth off Steve Rogers to deep right field, estimated at traveling 535 feet. "He hit the ball so far they painted the seat gold. I went up there the next day and sat in that seat, and everyone on the field looked like puppets. That's how far it traveled."[53] Willie, besides being nicknamed "Pops" and the "Captain," earned the moniker "Chicken on the Hill Will" for his prodigious home run shots. In fact, Stargell had blasted seven of the eighteen balls ever hit over the eighty-six-feet-high, right field wall at the old Forbes Field, the predecessor to Three Rivers Stadium. Chuck recognized that Willie's thirty-nine-year-old legs ached, and he would ask him how he felt, resting him as necessary.

At the All-Star break, the team sat in fourth place, 4 games behind the Montreal Expos. By August 4, after a 17-7 run, the Pirates sat 17 games above .500 and led the league by half a game. They won 86 out of the last 133 games. As Stargell told the guys, "The cream always rises to the top." During that madcap season, Chuck made some off-the-chart moves that defied the odds but often paid dividends.

On Sunday afternoon, August 5, during a home game at Three Rivers Stadium, the Phillies had beaten up Bert Blyleven and staked ace Steve Carlton to an 8–3 lead. Somehow, the Pirates rallied on Lee Lacy and Steve Nicosia home runs and a few key hits off reliever Kevin Saucier. In the ninth, the score sat knotted at eight runs each. Parker grounded to second, and Robinson flied out to right. With two outs, Lee Lacy singled to center, his second hit of the day. Bill Madlock and Phil Garner each walked to load the bases.

The Phillies manager Dan Ozark brought in All-Star lefty Tug McGraw to face right-handed catcher Steve Nicosia, who had gone four for four with two doubles and a home run during the game. Tanner operated on a hunch. He substituted for Nicosia. His gut told him to bring in left-handed hitter John "the Hammer" Milner. Traditional managerial tactics dictate to avoid having a lefty batter face a southpaw pitcher whenever possible. The crowd of forty thousand hooted and hollered in disbelief. "Dumb move, Tanner," came a cry from the stands. When Chuck looked into the crowd, he thought he saw his wife, Babs, leading a chorus of boos. "Too late now," he muttered to himself.

On the first pitch, McGraw threw a fastball ball down the middle, which Tug jokingly called "his Pearl in the Prell," since his fastball proved average at best. Milner's bat struck the ball. *Crack*! The sound echoed throughout the stadium. The crowd's mood quickly changed from anger to glee as the pinch hitter knocked the ball out of the park for a grand-slam homer to deep right field. The boos became cheers as most of the 46,006 fans in the stands screamed their approval. The Pirates left the field a 12–8 victor.

Nicosia, who batted .248 in his career, refused to second-guess his manager. "What are the chances of a guy like me going five for five?" Tanner later told the press that McGraw's screwball proved almost "unhittable" for a righty. "With a lefty, I took his screwball, his bread-and-butter pitch, away from him."

The roar of the crowd actually shook the stadium, and team members lifted Milner onto their shoulders and into the locker room in celebration. The Pirates had beaten the Phillies' top pitcher, Steve Carlton, and their number one reliever, Tug McGraw. The victory convinced the Pirates that nothing could stop them from winning the division. They had crushed the spirit of the Phillies. Parker knew that the team would take the second game of the double-header, and they did by a 5–2 score with Romo getting the win and Teke the save. Chuck's Bucs had carried the day. The Milner grand slam made Chuck look like a genius. Of course, the crowd reaction would have been quite different had Milner struck out rather than homered.

On August 7 at Wrigley Field in Chicago, the Cubs were chewing up the Pirates. Tanner called on veteran Joe Coleman, a two-time twenty-game winner for Detroit, to relieve battered starter Jim Rooker on a boiling ninety-degree afternoon. This would be Coleman's final season in an illustrious fifteen-year, 142-win career. Rook had given up six runs and looked terrible. This was not his day. The bullpen had been beaten up, and Tanner hoped to rest his relievers, especially for an out-of-reach game. Coleman labored over five and a half innings while throwing a load of pitches and giving up eight earned runs on thirteen hits. His teammates worried about his health with every pitch.

Tekulve volunteered to relieve for the last inning, but Coleman refused. Blyleven, a starter, also offered to step in, but he again said no. When Coleman stepped off the mound after a 15–2 shellacking, Tanner greeted him like a conquering hero. "You just won the division for us." He had given the relief staff a badly needed rest. Although Coleman failed to make the postseason roster, the team rewarded him with a World Series ring that read, "We Are Family." Coleman recognized that's who his teammates were—family.

Prior to another game at Wrigley, Blyleven threw perhaps fifteen balls to the spectators in the stands. After Don Robinson watched, he thought that tossing out a few balls looked like fun. Chuck came marching over. "Hey Robinson, baseballs don't grow on trees."

"Blyleven was doing it, and I just was copying him."

"Well, you're not Blyleven. If you do it again, it's going to cost you $100 per ball."

Although Chuck could be a disciplinarian, Don Robinson, like every other player under his control, liked and respected him. "I'm not sure I would have made it to the pros without him, and his positivity pushed me to be the best I could be."

John McCollister called the Saturday, August 11 away game against Philadelphia pivotal, especially since the Pirates would eke out their end of the season divisional victory by only two games. The Phillies had shelled Jim Rooker and Joe Coleman and led 8–0 after three innings. The day appeared hopeless. That is, until captain Willie Stargell told the guys, "Quit your pouting. We are on national television. We can either kiss our butts goodbye, or we can show everybody what the Pirates are made of." Someone on the bench seconded Willie and shouted, "Let's do it." Tanner clapped his hands and announced, "Go get 'em."[54]

A Moreno home run in the fifth cut the lead by one. After Foli singled and Parker walked, a Stargell single scored Foli. Milner followed with a single, bringing Parker home. Then timely hits by Madlock and Ott scored Stargell, and Milner tightened the score to a more manageable 8–5.

A Parker home run in the seventh followed by Madlock, Ott, Garner and Easler hits delivered a 9–8 Pirates lead. Tug McGraw's eighth-inning hanging curve resulted in Ed Ott's first bases-loaded home run with Stargell, Milner and Stennett aboard, bumping the score to 13–8 in favor of the Pirates. Although Pittsburgh gave up fifteen hits and eleven runs, they pounded out twenty-three hits and scored fourteen runs for an unbelievable comeback win, solidifying the importance of a combative never-say-die spirit. Moreno, Foli, Stargell, Milner, Madlock and Ott all accumulated three or more hits that day.

After the Bucs took that Saturday's game in a slugfest, with Romo earning the win and Tekulve the save, rain postponed Sunday's game. As a treat, Chuck accompanied New Castle brothers Jim and Dick Snow, Fuzzy Fazzone, trainer Tony Bartirome, coach Joe Lonnett and Willie Stargell for dinner at Cous Little Italy, a well-known South Philadelphia Mafia hangout and fine dining eatery.[55] Leonard Tose, the owner of the Philadelphia Eagles football team, a man known for his compulsive gambling and massive alcoholic intake, had presented the restaurant with a giant green-granite eagle to highlight the front of the restaurant. The Pirates contingent enjoyed a memorable and riotous evening prior to the "Lumber and Lightning Crew," assisted by Jim Bibby's able pitching, crushing the Phillies the following Monday by a 9–1 score, greatly enhancing the weekend's fun.

Chuck implemented more than his share of "cockeyed decisions" as a manager. Teke stated, "Chuck wrote his own book on strategy." Some sportswriters and second guessers considered him too quick to pull starting pitchers for a reliever. However, writer Bill James credited the 1979 Pirates as having one of the top-ten relief staffs of all time.

When Tekulve appeared in an amazing 94 games, he asked Chuck if he knew the names of any of the other pitchers. However, Romo entered 84 games and Jackson 72, 250 appearances in all for his three top relievers. Teke joked, "If Chuck had to use a pay phone, he wouldn't have called us relievers so often." When Teke asked if he would get paid overtime for all the games he worked, Chuck gave it right back to him. "Teke, we played 172 games this year if you count the post season. You only worked 101. So the way I look at it, you owe us for the 71 games where you just sat on your butt."

Chuck needed, used and respected his relievers. He repeated his statement to the press about the prior year, "As I said before, if I had Romo in 1978, the team probably would have won the pennant." Chuck opposed the use of the designated hitter, which removed "a key strategic aspect of the game." His bias against the designated hitter developed based on his experience in the majors as a career pinch hitter. Relievers and pinch hitters served as key tools in carving out 1979's success.

On the other hand, Chuck on occasion surprised his starters by keeping them in the game rather than pulling them. John Candelaria was pitching in

Chicago and having a rough day: "The swirling winds had been blowing the ball out of the park. None of us wanted to pitch on a day like that. Anyhow Chuck walked out to the mound and put his hand on my shoulder. I handed the ball to him after giving up a handful of runs, but he surprised me. I knew the relief staff had been overused, and the game already appeared out of hand. Chuck looked up at me and handed me back the ball, saying, 'No sir, you're it.' I became the sacrificial lamb that day. Baseball has a way of humbling even the best, but with Chuck, if you screwed up one day but had given your all, the following morning brought another day and a clean slate."

One of Chuck's wildest moves involved Kent Tekulve in the first game of a double-header at Candlestick Park in San Francisco on September 1, late in the season. The Pirates led 5–3. Chuck had called in Teke, who pitched a scoreless eighth. In the ninth, Teke forced the first two batters, Bill North and Jack Strain, to ground out. Then, Jack Clark reached first on a bunt single, and third baseman, power pull-hitter Darrell Evans, a player who Teke thought resembled the puppet Howdy Doody, came to bat. Tekulve had trouble with Evans in the past, so Chuck came to the mound, took the ball from his pitcher and brought in reliever Grant Jackson. "I thought I was done for the game, but Chuck removed John Milner and put me in left field. I hadn't played the outfield since Little League."

"Grant, pitch him on the outside of the plate," Tanner suggested.

"Hey, Skip, if I pitch outside, that ball may go to left, and you know who you just sent out there?" Jackson reminded his manager.

"Just do it!" Tanner ordered.

"Okay, if that's what you want," Grant dutifully answered.

Omar Moreno yelled instructions from center about the wind and where to stand, but Omar's heavy accent made it tough for Teke to make heads or tails out of whatever he was saying. The center fielder picked up a few blades of grass and tossed them in the air to show a lack of wind.

"Hell, he yelled at me in Spanish, but I couldn't understand him. Lo and behold, Grant pitched outside, and the ball flew to me in left. I didn't move more than a few steps, and I caught it. The game ended, and we won."

Tekulve joked that he considered dropping the ball so he could come back in as the pitcher and get the save. "Actually, we Pirate pitchers shagged balls during batting practice, and I felt very comfortable in left. The team cheered me as I trotted toward home, congratulating me instead of Grant for saving the game."

Teke continued, "I enjoyed agitating Chuck, so later I walked past his office and told him, 'You do things that defy logic. It played out okay this time, but I'm not sure you should ever try it again.'" Chuck grinned from ear to ear, turned and disappeared back into his office.

Teke continued, "I used to tell him, 'You make the dumbest decisions in the world, and then we make you look pretty good.'"

The following week, Teke kidded Chuck again about the move he made in San Francisco. "Hey, if you plan to put me in left again, give me a heads up first."

"I would have, but I thought it might make you nervous," the manager responded. Chuck enjoyed the banter with his veterans and they with him. He made playing baseball even more fun than it already was.

Roger Angell, the *New York Magazine* sportswriter who lived to the ripe old age of 101 years, "credited Chuck Tanner for the carnivalesque clubhouse atmosphere with lots of people shouting at one another in apparent rage and then collapsing in laughter…a cacophony of various cultures eating, drinking, joking and playing games together with a mix of music from rock to salsa constantly blasting in the background."

Sportscaster Bob Prince, the gravel-voiced "Gunner," pegged the Pirate players with crazy nicknames like "Caveman," "Cobra," "Hitman," "Mad-Dog," "Scrap-Iron," "Pops," "Candy Man," "Crazy Horse," "the Hammer" and "Rooster." The fans loved that madcap team like no other.

If the team lost a close one, Stargell and Tanner rallied the troops with some rose-colored pronouncement. "Let's get over it. We lost today. No worries, no need to panic. We'll get them tomorrow."

Phil Garner brought up the famous Yogi Berra–Phil Linz "harmonica" story as a direct contrast to the Pirates' upbeat philosophy of dealing with losses.

On August 20, 1964, the New York Yankees rode the bus to O'Hare Airport after losing all four games to the White Sox. Ace Whitey Ford had just dropped a 5–0 decision, and an aura of glumness permeated the vehicle.

Reserve infielder Phil Linz started practicing his harmonica. When he played a noisy version of "Mary Had a Little Lamb," manager Yogi Berra, already in a foul mood, screamed, "Knock it off. Things are bad enough without that stupid harmonica."

Linz did not hear his manager and asked Mickey Mantle what Yogi had said. Mantle added fuel to the fire by answering, "He said play it louder!"

When Linz continued playing, Berra stomped to the rear of the bus, seized the harmonica from his player's fingers and threw it across the bus. It accidentally struck nearby first baseman Joe Pepitone, causing a slight cut on his hand.

Berra fined Linz $250 for insubordination, a not insignificant sum for a utility infielder earning $14,000. The sportswriters in the bus had a field day with the incident. With a ton of negative publicity, Yankees owner Dan Topping soured against Berra, questioning if his manager had lost control of the team.[56]

In their next away game, Fenway Park fans in Boston heckled Berra and the Yankees with a kazoo and harmonica serenade of "Mary Had a Little Lamb." Linz paid the fine but had the last laugh. The hullabaloo created a huge increase in harmonica sales, and the Hohner Company signed Linz to a $10,000 endorsement contract that far exceeded his fine. Linz apologized to Berra, and neither the manager nor the player held a grudge. When Linz signed a new contract, he received a "$250 harmonica bonus" as part of his package.

With Chuck, win or lose, boom boxes blasted out music, and the Pirates took each game in stride. The players knew the next contest probably would produce better results.

If nothing else, the Bucs assembled a fun team, full of gleeful agitation—twenty-five guys, most of them with a wild streak but all united in a will to win. Tanner tolerated all sorts of shenanigans off the field as long as they didn't affect the performance on the field. "If the guys play harder during games than in the bars, I will cut them some slack."

Teke called Candelaria, one of the quieter Pirates, a "silent instigator" and lots of fun. Candy, always modest for such an outstanding athlete and a future 177-game winner, performed some offbeat stunts. In Philadelphia, since he was not scheduled to pitch at the Vet, he asked pitcher Jim Bibby if his brother Henry, a star guard for the Philadelphia 76ers, could score a free ticket for him at that night's game in the Spectrum. Candelaria, a top notch amateur basketball player as well as a baseball star, figured that Chuck would never miss him in the dugout.

Just in case, Candy donned a running suit over his uniform and wore a trench coat when he made his way across the street to watch the game. When Teke went in to relieve, he spotted Candy remove his trench coat and sweat pants and hot foot it back to the dugout as if he had been there the entire game.

On another occasion, during a home stand, Candy, not scheduled to pitch, headed up Mount Washington to the Tin Angel along with the Pirate Parrot, Kevin Koch, for a few beers and to obtain a better view of the fireworks. After several hours, he and Kevin noticed that the stadium lights were still lit. "Bartender, would you turn on the tv? I want to see how the Pirates did."

The television showed the game tied in the twelfth inning. Recognizing that Chuck might be light on pitchers, Candelaria headed posthaste to the clubhouse. When he reached the dugout, he received notice to loosen up in case needed. Luckily, the game ended and he didn't have to pitch, and no one caught him playing hooky. Public relations executive Joe Safety believed that Chuck knew where Candelaria was, but since he didn't plan to use him, he let it slide.[57]

Candy could be up for anything crazy. Once, on a five-dollar bet, he jumped from the second floor of the Pirate City building during spring training, bad back and all, but on the field he became all business.

Salaries in 1979 appeared ridiculously low by today's standards. Dave Parker received the outlandish sum of $775,000 in 1979, toward the highest in the league. Bert Blyleven and Willie Stargell each earned $500,000, Bruce Kison $223,000, Kent Tekulve $110,000 and Phil Garner $121,000—good salaries for the time. Steve Nicosia, Enrique Romo and Dale Berra only earned $21,000 per man. As a comparison, in 2022, the minimum major-league minimum salary stood at $700,000, the average at $4.4 million and a handful of stars like Max Scherzer earned more than $40 million per year.

Three Rivers ticket prices appeared to be a bargain averaging just $4. A hot dog cost $0.75, a small popcorn or a soft drink $0.45 and a can of beer $0.85, quite a difference from today, where a PNC Park hot dog runs $7.50, a beer $6, a grandstand seat $20 and an average premium seat around $59.

The Pirates' 25-11 record during the last thirty-six games of the season slotted them in first place in the 158th game of the 162-game season. While thirty-nine-year-old Willie Stargell only played in 126 games during the year, he served as the heart and soul of the team. Players treasured their "Stargell Stars," given by the first baseman for above-and-beyond effort. Each winner wore them proudly on his cap like a military medal won in combat for valor. Willie's can-do attitude tattooed the team with the drive to excel. Although his batting average tailed off in the latter part of the season, he slugged eight home runs during the last month, connecting twice in a September 25 10–4 victory against Montreal to provide the Pirates with a tight lead over their rivals. If Chuck served as the field general, Willie acted as his aide-de-camp.

The Pirates cinched the pennant on September 30 with a 5–3 win over the Cubs. Kison worked a solid six innings, Teke picked up his thirty-first save, a club record, and Willie Stargell smacked his thirty-second home run. Stargell's two RBIs lifted him past the legendary Honus Wagner in the club record books.[58] The 42,176 fans on hand cheered their team's division victory, and champagne flowed freely in the clubhouse following the game.

The Pirates' 98-64 record edged Montreal by two games to win the National League East. Chuck recognized that his team possessed talent, but they also commanded a winning attitude—and yes, they required good luck and health thrown in the pot as well. The 1979 attendance of 1,435,454 showed a distinct improvement over the previous year's figure of 964,106 and stood as the highest since 1971, when the team won the World Series.

The Western Pennsylvania fans went wild after the division victory. Signs reading "Beat 'Em Bucs," "Chuck's Bucs Are Number One" and "The Pirates—No One Does It Better" covered the entire region.

The pitching staff combined for a respectable ERA of 3.41, although none of the Pirate starters cracked the top ten in this statistic. No pitcher on the team won more than fourteen games, but the team's fifty-two saves led the National League. Kent Tekulve topped both leagues with ninety-four appearances and came in second in the league in saves behind future Hall of Game member Bruce Sutter. Jim Bibby's 12-4 record led the league with a .750 won-loss percentage, while Bert Blyleven's 12-5 finished a close third, winning .706 of his games.

The Pirates accrued a solid .264 batting average, and their 774 runs scored topped all their division rivals. Dave Parker's seventy-seven extra base hits led the National League. Bill Madlock batted .328. Tim Foli's amazing strikeout ratio of just one in every thirty-eight at bats easily outclassed the entire major league. Omar Moreno produced a league-leading seventy-seven stolen bases, and his 110 runs produced a second-place league finish behind co-MVP Keith Hernandez. The "Lumber and Lightning Crew" had excelled.

With the National League East's division in their hands, the Pirates faced manager John McNamara's 90-71 NL West's "Big Red Machine" for the pennant. The bookies considered Cincinnati a heavy favorite. The Reds featured future Hall of Fame players Joe Morgan, Johnny Bench and Tom Seaver, as well as All-Stars George Foster, Dave Concepción, Ken Griffey Sr. and Ray Knight. Beating the Reds presented a formidable task for Chuck's Bucs.

Tanner penned in John Candelaria to start at Cincinnati's Riverfront Stadium for the first playoff game on a chilly October 2 evening. He announced to the press that his "money" pitcher appeared rested and ready to face Tom Seaver. A boisterous crowd of 55,006 jammed the seats, ready for action.

Chuck dedicated the game to his parents, especially his ailing mother. Candy didn't disappoint that night. He battled severe back pain in a gutsy

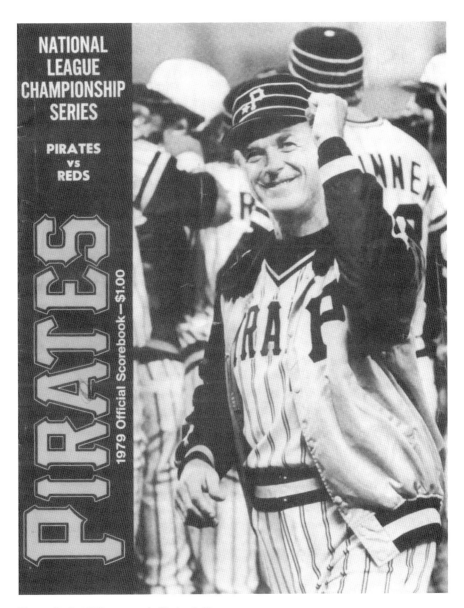

Pirates-Reds 1979 scorecard. *Pittsburgh Pirates.*

performance through eight innings against ace Seaver, the Reds' leading pitcher with sixteen regular-season wins. In the third, Phil Garner led off with a home run. After Candelaria struck out, Omar Moreno tripled. Tim Foli drove Moreno home with a fly to deep right, and the inning ended with a 2–0 Pittsburgh lead.

In the bottom of the fourth, Cincinnati returned the favor. Dave Concepción singled, and George Foster brought him home with a home run. The game remained tied at 2–2 through the eighth, when Candy left the game in pain after his back stiffened.[59] Manager Tom McNamara removed Seaver and brought in Tom Hume, who quieted the Pirates' bats in the ninth.

Relievers Romo, Tekulve and Jackson held Cincinnati's bats at bay through the tenth, while Tom Hume did the same for Cincinnati. In the eleventh, Tim Foli caught a single off Hume. Tanner brought in the speedy Matt Alexander to pinch run. Dave Parker followed with another single, landing Alexander on second. The number three batter Stargell clubbed a three-run homer off reliever Tom Hume, scoring Alexander and Parker to give the Bucs a 5–2 lead.

When the inning ended, Tanner made some defensive changes. Rennie Stennett took over at second. Phil Garner moved from second to short, and Bill Robinson replaced John Milner in left. With two outs and Grant Jackson in relief, a Dave Concepción single and a walk to George Foster led Tanner to bring in Don Robinson, primarily a starter with a wicked curve ball. Robinson promptly walked Johnny Bench to load the bases, forcing a confrontation against the always dangerous Ray Knight with the potential winning run at bat.

Robinson performed like a seasoned pro rather than a twenty-two-year-old sophomore. He struck out Knight, a .318 hitter during the regular season. When the batter swung and missed, catcher Ed Ott dropped the ball from his mitt but reacted quickly. Ott pounced on the ball. He should have touched home for the force-out to end the game. Instead, he threw the ball to Stargell at first, nipping Knight by an eyelash. The Pirates had escaped with a roughly fought away-game victory.

Tanner opted for Jim Bibby, a twelve-game winner with a sparkling 2.84 ERA, for game two to face rookie Frank Pastore. A sell-out crowd of fifty-five thousand filled Riverfront Stadium, anxious for a comeback victory.

The key play occurred in the fifth with the score tied 1–1. Garner led off with a sinking liner to right. Dave Collins bolted for the ball and appeared to make a diving catch, but second base umpire Frank Polli ruled Garner safe. Apparently, Collins had trapped the ball, or at least the umpire thought so. Manager McNamara stormed onto the field, creating a huge ruckus, but to no avail. After Bibby laid down a perfect sacrifice bunt, Garner landed on second. Moreno flied out, but Tim Foli drove a double down the left-field line to score Garner and give the Pirates a 2–1 lead.

Replays indicated that Collins probably had caught the ball. When former Yankee shortstop Tony Kubek questioned Frank Pulli about the call, the umpire cursed and said, "Don't you tell me about damn replays." Case closed, and a lucky break for Pittsburgh.

Bibby held the Reds to one run through seven, leaving the game with a single-run lead. Chuck could see his starting pitcher's neck hurt. He called in Grant Jackson, who retired Joe Morgan on a ground out. Tanner next brought in Romo, who promptly surrendered singles to Dave Concepción and heavy-hitting George Foster. The Pirates inserted Teke to stem the tide. He struck out catcher Johnny Bench, walked first baseman Dan Driessen and forced third baseman Ray Knight to fly out to center field, ending the inning.

In the ninth, Teke struck out center fielder César Gerónimo before giving up consecutive doubles to Héctor Cruz and Dave Collins. Cruz scored, leading to a 2–2 tie. Tanner brought in Dave Roberts, who walked Joe Morgan. With few relievers left on the bench, Tanner turned to Don Robinson, who shut down Concepción and Foster to close out the ninth inning. With the game still in doubt, Candelaria donned a Baltimore Orioles cap as a joke. Even during such serious situations, the team hung loose, and Tanner condoned the foolishness.

In the tenth, Moreno opened with a single, and Foli sacrificed him to second. Parker singled Moreno home for the lead. Robinson set down the Reds in order to seal the deal. A combination of lucky calls, timely hitting, strong relief and a very effective Don Robinson created a tenth-inning 3–2 win and a commanding 2-0 lead, with the third game returning to the friendly confines of Three Rivers Stadium in Pittsburgh.

A light drizzle slowed the Thursday, October 4 scheduled workout, but the rains stopped well before the four o'clock start the following day. A chilly fall breeze remained as a reminder of the cold Pittsburgh winter ahead. Pirates banners covered the field reading "Madlock's Maniacs," "Omar's Amigos," "Garner's Gang" and "Chuck's Bucs." The critical third game on October 5 would be played in front of a strong local fan base. Mayor Richard Caliguiri threw out the ceremonial first pitch prior to the umpire's ceremonial shout of "Play ball!" An electrified crowd some 42,240 strong cheered wildly as the home team jogged onto the field.

The skipper penciled in Dutch-born curveball specialist and future Hall of Fame member Bert Blyleven as his starter. Although Bert could be a handful, Tanner recognized that the talented Dutchman possessed a wildly competitive spirit and always gave 100 percent in everything he did.

Blyleven rewarded Tanner with a firm command of the ball throughout his complete game. He struck out nine and won by a 7–1 score against the overmatched lanky Mike LaCross, a fourteen-game winner during the regular season. Omar Moreno started the team off with a walk in the first, a stolen base to second and a trip to third on a fielder's choice. He scored on a Parker sacrifice fly. In the second, Garner punched a ball past outfielder Dave Collins, resulting in a triple. He scored on a Foli sacrifice fly. Third-inning home runs by Stargell and Madlock made the score 4–1 and supplied Burt Blyleven with all the support he needed.

Light-hitting Bert Blyleven singled in the fourth. Moreno sacrificed him to second; Parker walked, and Stargell lined a double over first to score both runners. Blyleven lost his shutout in the sixth when Johnny Bench homered. In the seventh, with Pittsburgh leading 6–1, Pam Nicosia, Steve Nicosia's wife, led a chorus of fans to sing "We Are Family" atop the Pirates dugout. The Pirates added another insurance run in the eighth on a rare error by gold-glove center fielder César Gerónimo.

Blyleven retired the last nine batters to lock up his victory and a complete game. Chuck took only one trip to the mound all afternoon, a rarity for him. Bert had asked him to stay in the dugout. Assistant sports editor Marino

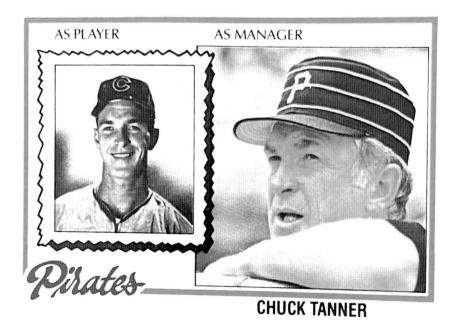

Chuck Tanner card. *Pittsburgh Pirates.*

Parascenzo of the *Post-Gazette* called Blyleven's fastball "zippy, and his curve ball bent like a five-cent cigar."[60]

The fans went berserk, singing and dancing with raucous abandon. The team had upset John McNamara's vaunted Cincinnati Reds in three straight games. The clubhouse exploded in a champagne-popping frenzy. Manager Chuck Tanner kissed Blyleven on the cheek. Thirty-nine-year-old "Pops" Willie Stargell, the team's crutch, had ignored his spreading girth and arthritic knees to hit two doubles and two home runs in three games. His combination of brute power enhanced by a phenomenal .455 batting average earned him the well-deserved series Most Valuable Player award.

"We were a dirty-shirt ball club. We weren't afraid to try anything. We were a blue-collar team in a blue-collar town," the Pirates manager gleefully told the press.[61]

Willie Stargell symbolized the heart and soul of the team. As he had done all season, Pittsburgh's elder statesman rewarded deserving players with Stargell stars to sport on their caps. Chuck considered Willie the glue that held the team together and the closest thing to an assistant manager that he had. "He deserved that MVP award," Chuck said.

When asked to describe the key attributes required for managerial success, Tanner enumerated, "The first secret is to have patience. The second is to be patient. And the third most important secret I'd say was patience." He also added, "Baseball isn't a week or a month, but a season—and a season is a long time."[62]

CHAPTER 10

THE 1979 WORLD SERIES

Nothing succeeds like success.
—Alexandre Dumas

Tanner's mother, Anna, had suffered a stroke the week before the Cincinnati series and remained in serious condition at the Greenville Hospital. Chuck called frequently as her health teetered. When Chuck spoke to her, she knew that the Pirates had made the World Series. Chuck kidded her that she had better watch, and she promised to view every game on the television.

With little time to relish the euphoria of the playoffs, Tanner now faced the American League's Baltimore Orioles and its chain-smoking, umpire-baiting manager, Earl Weaver. The opposition had won 102 games during the regular season, the highest total in the majors. Weaver bragged to the Maryland press that he intended to send his low-ball hitters to sink the six-foot-four beanpole, low-ball reliever Kent Tekulve, the "Human Drainpipe."

Chuck laughed off Weaver's boast. He countered with his intention to steal bases on Baltimore catcher Rick Dempsey using his fleet-footed runners like league leader Omar Moreno. Dempsey recognized the strategy and countered by calling for a steady dose of fastballs, a sure remedy to end the base-running threat. The Pirates stole no bases during the entire series. However, the Pirates fastball sluggers would feast on Oriole pitching.

The Pittsburgh manager recognized that a battle lay ahead, but he aimed for nothing less than a World Series victory. In New Castle, signs filled store windows and hung on light poles along North Jefferson Street, goading the Pirates to win. A giant banner hanging near the square on Washington Street read, "Hometown of Chuck Tanner. Go Bucs!" A *New Castle News* October headline proclaimed, "Hometown Takes Pride in Tanner."

When *Baltimore Sun* sportswriter John Steadman mocked the "We Are Family" theme song as a cheap grandstand play, the jibe cemented the resolve of the Pittsburgh players. The Pirates considered themselves family. They thought of their theme song as no joke. Rather, it served as a symbol of their team togetherness, and such ridicule only served to solidify their determination.

A mix of rain and snow canceled game one, scheduled on Tuesday at Baltimore's Memorial Stadium. Although a tarp covered the infield, rains left the outfield a soggy mess. Both teams remained anxious to play, but nature nixed the contest. In fact, commissioner Bowie Kuhn worried that Wednesday's game also might become a washout. Tanner philosophized, "We're disappointed, but we didn't want anybody hurt on either side. The World Series is supposed to be fun."[63]

Chuck remained low-key and calm, refusing to be thrown off-kilter by the weather, even though Baltimore claimed to have won sixteen out of seventeen games in the rain during the season. The experts considered Pittsburgh a distinct underdog. Detroit Tigers manager Sparky Anderson and Hall of Fame member Bob Lemon believed that the Orioles held the superior pitching, and maybe they knew what they were saying.

The Baltimore staff included Tippy Martinez, a pitcher who had won ten games during the season and posted a 2.88 ERA. Scott McGregor, a future 20-game winner, put up a 13-6 record in '79 and would produce 138 victories over his career. Mike Flanagan led the American league in wins during the season and would produce a total of 167 over eighteen years. Steve Stone had won 11 games during '79 and would earn the Cy Young Award for his 25 wins the following year. He would amass a total of 107 victories during his eleven-year stay in the majors. Ace Jim Palmer already had posted 20 or more wins eight times and accumulated three Cy Young Awards. This future Hall of Fame member would win 268 games over nineteen years. Dennis Martinez started thirty-nine games, the most in the National League, and would win 245 over a twenty-three-year career. Reliever Don Stanhouse, a highly competent closer, led the team with twenty-one saves and maintained a strong 2.85 ERA through the season. In short, Baltimore possessed a very strong set of arms.

Tanner refused to let the weather, strong competition or outside opinions rattle him. He knew something the experts forgot. Possibly the Orioles' blue-ribbon staff of starters, who led the American League with a sterling 3.28 earned run average, might be a tad better than those of Pittsburgh. Smart money pointed out that the Orioles indeed possessed a strong starting pitching staff. However, Chuck disagreed. He argued that aces Blyleven and Candelaria could hold their own against any starter in either league—and Bibby and Kison performed ably as backups—but regardless, he would stack his crew of relievers against any team in the majors; he had a ton of faith in the "Lumber and Lightning Crew's" ability to produce runs.

The bookies established Baltimore, which had finished eight and a half games ahead of the Milwaukee Brewers during the regular season, as a solid favorite to win the series. They liked Weaver's "Oriole Magic," and how the team had bested the California Angels in four games to win the American League pennant.

Although the Pirates chorus sang their "We Are Family" theme song to encourage the team, the Orioles countered with their own gimmick. "Wild" Bill Hagy, a bearded cab driver and super fan, dressed in his orange T-shirt, leaped from his seat, stood in front of his section and twisted his arms and body to spell out the word O-R-I-O-L-E-S, propelling the entire Baltimore fan base to rise to their feet and follow his lead to "awaken" the Baltimore offense.

Pre-game, Tanner sat at his desk chewing on Red Man tobacco and spitting into a paper cup as he formed his lineup for game one. Portable stereo equipment boomed with rock music emanating from the locker room. Some of the quieter members of the team watched television in a corner away from the noise. Others played cards or just relaxed. Chuck wanted his guys to feel loose. Practical jokes among the team proved the norm rather than the exception. Jim Rooker found a roasted pig's head hanging in his locker as a prank. Rook took the gag in stride and laughed. He had seen worse. Matt Alexander trimmed Bill Madlock's hair with a pair of scissors. Although the fellows might act like a bunch of teenagers in the locker room, they performed like professionals on the field.

Rain and sleet pelted the stadium the following Wednesday morning, October 10. The swirling wind guaranteed a chilly afternoon. Although a tarp kept the infield in good shape, the outfield contained several soft and slippery spots. The temperature teetered at a wintry forty-one degree mark and dropped even farther by game time. Catcher Rick Dempsey later told the sportswriters, "It wasn't a game. It was an endurance contest."

Baltimore mayor William Schaefer protected himself from the cold beneath a knit cap and woolen gloves, and Maryland senator Paul Sarbanes wore a winter parka. Sunny's Surplus on Greenmount Avenue sold out its inventory of thermal underwear to lucky spectators. An excited crowd of 53,735, including a large and vociferous Pirates section, ignored the frigid weather and awaited a great game ahead.

Forty-two-year-old future Hall of Fame infielder Brooks Robinson tossed out the ceremonial first pitch to third baseman Doug DeCinces. Pirates starter Bruce Kison, a slender, six-foot-four, 178-pound righty, faced Orioles ace and twenty-three-game winner Mike Flanagan, an athlete who would receive the American League's Cy Young Award as the outstanding pitcher for 1979.

Kison got off to a rocky start in the first inning, giving up a looping single to Al Bumbry and a walk to Mark Belanger before throwing out Ken Singleton on a grounder. He next walked Eddie Murray. With the bases loaded and one out, Kison forced left fielder John Lowenstein to hit a potential double-play grounder to Phil Garner. The cold had played havoc with the second baseman's fingers. The wet ground had made the ball slippery, and Phil overthrew shortstop Tim Foli at second base. The ball rolled into left field, scoring two runs on the error. Garner later told the press, "My feet were cold, and I was shivering."

A wild pitch brought in another run. "I had a hard time gripping the ball. It slipped out of my hand, and I couldn't get the feel of things," Kison explained. A deep home run into the stands by DeCinces with Lowenstein on base led to a five-run hole. The cold weather had numbed Kison's fingers, forcing Tanner to pull him. Temporary nerve damage would incapacitate Bruce for the balance of the series.

Tanner replaced Kison with spot-starter Jim Rooker, who shut out the Orioles for three and one-third innings. Romo, Robinson and Jackson continued the scoreless streak. Although Parker delivered four hits, Garner three and Stargell produced a two-run homer, the damage had been done. The Bucs produced eleven hits to only six by the Orioles, but the visiting team fell by a 5–4 margin. Each team committed three errors due to the unseasonably cold weather conditions. Baltimore's winning pitcher Mike Flanagan had stranded ten Pirate runners in a respectable outing. Reliever Tekulve parroted his manager's positivity and announced to "Pops" Stargell, "We lost, but we showed that we can play with them."

Earl Weaver put his own spin on the game. "Nobody likes playing baseball when it's thirty degrees, but when you win it doesn't bother you so much."[64]

Dave Parker tried to cheer the guys up with a pep talk in the locker room. "We may be down, but we're not out by any means." The squad opted to forget the loss and feasted on Maryland's famous steamed crabs and a few cans of beer as if they had won the game. Chuck and his crew recognized that a series involved seven games, not just one. The players believed in their ability to win the next one.

After showering in the locker room and licking his wounds following the loss at Memorial Park, Willie Stargell returned to his hotel room at the Hilton to discover that a burglar had stolen $2,000 in cash, some checks and his stereo equipment—a bad omen for the Bucs captain. Luckily, the thief attempted to cash the checks at a hotel down the street. He showed the clerk his driver's license containing his actual name and address. The Baltimore police had little difficulty in arresting one of America's dumbest crooks.

Tanner, always upbeat, told the guys, "Good game. We'll get them tomorrow. We have the tools to make a comeback," and he proved correct. Two future baseball immortals met in a classic duel. Bert Blyleven would defeat Jim Palmer that day. The Bucs outhit the Orioles eleven to six in game two, the same as the previous day, but resulting in a better outcome for the Pirates.

Pittsburgh opened the second inning with Stargell and Milner singles. Then Madlock drove Stargell home for the Pirates' first run. Milner landed on third. Ed Ott brought Milner home with a sacrifice fly for the Pirates' second run. The inning ended with Madlock caught stealing and Garner grounding out, short to first.

Baltimore rallied with two runs of their own. First, they cut the lead to 2–1, courtesy of a towering Murray lead-off home run to right in their half of the second. The Orioles struck again in the sixth. Ken Singleton singled. Then Murray drove Singleton home with a long double to left.

Starter Bert Blyleven had thrown six strong innings, giving up just two runs. Tanner brought in Don Robinson for the seventh. Orioles starter Jim Palmer lasted through seven full innings, also giving up just two runs.

In the eighth, against righty reliever Don Robinson, manager Earl Weaver called on left fielder John Lowenstein to hit away rather than sacrifice with Eddie Murray and Doug DeCinces on base. The strategy backfired, and the Oriole outfielder grounded into a double play. Weaver later shook his head and philosophized, "When you shoot craps, sometimes you lose."[65]

Reliever Robinson pitched a scoreless seventh and eighth to hold the line. In the bottom of the ninth, pinch hitter Bill Robinson singled sharply to left off Baltimore reliever Tippy Martinez. Earl Weaver brought in Don Stanhouse. Pinch runner Matt Alexander replaced Robinson on first, but Rick Dempsey cut him down when he tried to steal second, a Tanner gamble that backfired.

After Madlock flied out to center, Ed Ott singled on a hard grounder that bounced off second baseman Billy Smith's chest. A timely walk by Phil Garner moved Ott to second. With two outs and two on, Chuck called on "bad-ball hitter" Manny Sanguillén to pinch-hit for Don Robinson. Manny had produced only seventeen hits and four RBIs during the entire season. However, the Panamanian catcher responded by lobbing a single to right off Stanhouse, the Orioles' top reliever and team-saves leader during the regular season. Manny's hit drove Ott home for the eventual game-winning third run.

Kent Tekulve picked up the save with a no-hit ninth to preserve a tightly fought 3–2 victory at Baltimore. He struck out Kiko Garcia on a curve, froze Rick Dempsey with a fastball and forced Al Bumbry to ground out short to first. When sportscaster Vin Scully watched Teke's jerky motion, he announced, "Tekulve wheeled like a unicycle on a seesaw when he struck out those first two batters."[66] The Pirates had prevailed against eight-time twenty-game winner Jim Palmer. A split against an ace of his stature in the opponent's home park proved an acceptable outcome to Chuck.

On Friday, October 12, game three returned to the friendly confines of the Steel City's Three Rivers Stadium. However, the weather again refused to cooperate. Rain followed the night flight home from Baltimore. The ground crew had siphoned gallon after gallon of water off the synthetic turf. The temperature for the evening game barely hit fifty degrees and sank to a low of just forty-two.

One sign in the stands read, "#8 Stargell for President" and another "Ain't No Stopping Us Now." The fans craved a victory and expected to get one. Pittsburgh-born governor Dick Thornburgh handed a baseball to ex-manager Danny Murtaugh's widow, Kate, to toss out the ceremonial first pitch. The sold-out attendance of 50,848 chilly souls faced an ugly evening, but the crowd in the stands appeared more than ready to meet the challenge of a frosty night.

For those unable to get a seat in the stadium, ABC sports commentator Howard Cosell announced the game on television in his inimitable fashion. In the background, the sound of "We Are Family" roared through the stadium, and the Pittsburgh fan base teemed with excitement.

Tanner penciled in his usually reliable lefty John Candelaria, a former twenty-game winner with a no-hitter on his résumé, to start against Scott McGregor, another talented lefty. Although Candy's back ached, he ignored the pain to give his all.

The game kicked off on a positive note in the first inning with an Omar Moreno double and his advance to third on a balk. He scored on a Dave

Parker sacrifice fly to center, giving the Bucs a 1–0 lead. The Cobra had struck. In the second, Garner doubled, scoring Stargell and Nicosia for a 3–0 lead. Disregarding the chill in the air, the Pirates started strongly.

In the Orioles third, the American League champs rallied. Kiko Garcia walked, and Benny Ayala smacked a two-run homer to cut the lead to 3–2.

Candelaria's back stiffened after a sixty-seven-minute rain delay following the third inning. All hell broke loose in the fourth. Rich Dauer doubled to center. Rick Dempsey singled to right putting Dauer on third. Sloppy play on the wet field then nullified Pittsburgh's chances. Scott McGregor reached first on an error by the Pittsburgh shortstop to load the bases. A Garcia triple scored all three Orioles resulting in a 5–3 score.

Tanner had seen enough of Candy, who appeared to be hurting. He replaced the ailing pitcher with righty Enrique Romo, who fared little better. Romo beaned Al Bumbry, sending him to first. Ken Singleton singled, scoring Garcia from third for a sixth run and sending Bumbry to third. After a Murray fly out, Bumbry scored on a DeCinces sacrifice fly to secure a 7–3 Orioles lead.

In the sixth, Madlock drove Stargell home for a run to cut the deficit by one, but the game had ended for all practical reasons in the fourth. Romo gave up a double to Dempsey and a single by Garcia in the seventh to bring the score back to a four-run edge for the visiting team.

Grant Jackson replaced the faltering Romo to end the inning. Kent Tekulve mopped up with two final scoreless innings, but the Pirates had dug too deep a hole. The game closed with the Pirates on the losing end of a 8–4 score. Poor pitching, a crucial error and a missed double play proved the Pirates' undoing. The Orioles now held a 2-1 lead. McGregor had won his second game in a row, this one a complete game. "We played bad," Stargell and Parker told the press.

Candelaria's father had traveled to Pittsburgh from Puerto Rico to watch his son pitch. He had never seen him throw a major-league game. To relieve the tension, he joked, "Do you mean I came this far to see something like this?"[67]

Chuck looked at the loss with his typical rose-colored glasses: "I don't think we played that bad. The pitcher just didn't always get the ball where he wanted to, and there were a couple plays where we didn't execute. It's not over. We'll be back tomorrow."

Various team members relied on superstitions and charms to end a losing streak. Teke often wore a yellow T-shirt under his uniform. Pitcher Don Robinson sported his lucky shoes. Executive vice-president Harding Peterson carried his red pen given to him by Pirates scout Cecil Cole. Hopefully, the amulets would lead to a win in game four.

A Catholic priest prayed for the Pirates to prevail. The stadium rocked with "We Are Family" for Saturday, October 13's wintry game. Tanner penciled in six-foot-five righty Jim Bibby to face Nicaraguan star Dennis Martinez. In a slugfest, the Pirates opened with a big second inning. Stargell led off with a deep home run over the center field wall. John Milner singled to right, and Bill Madlock hit a ground-rule double to left, driving Milner to third. Both runners scored on an Ed Ott ground-rule double. Phil Garner singled and reached second when the Orioles caught Ott in a rundown. Manager Weaver yanked Martinez and inserted long-reliever Sammy Stewart to stem the tide. Moreno singled Garner home before being picked off at first, ending the inning with the Pirates ahead 4–0.

The Orioles answered quickly in the third, opening with catcher Dave Skaggs on first due to a Madlock throwing error. A single by Al Bumbry followed by doubles to Kiko Garcia and Ken Singleton brought the game to a tight 4–3 score.

In the fifth, Milner drove Parker home with a key hit off reliever Steve Stone to give the Pirates a 5–3 lead. In the sixth, Foli scored on a Parker double to up the score to 6–3. The Pirates appeared on the verge of victory with a three-run lead, but fate presented Tanner's team with an unpleasant surprise.

The Orioles stormed back with a vengeance in the eighth. Garcia and Singleton singled off Don Robinson. DeCinces walked. Tanner summoned ace reliever Kent Tekulve, one of the best in the league, to face pinch hitter John Lowenstein, who promptly doubled. Tekulve intentionally walked Billy Smith in order to face Terry Crowley, a .317 hitter during the regular season. Crowley smacked a double to right, scoring DeCinces and Lowenstein. As icing on the cake, light-hitting pitcher Tim Stoddard, the eventual game winner, stroked a single to score Smith from third. Then Bumbry, a pinch runner for Crowley, came home on a force out. Garcia, who had started the onslaught with a single, mercifully struck out to end the inning. The Pirate relievers had yielded two doubles, three singles, two walks and six runs in a single inning. Although Pittsburgh outhit Baltimore seventeen to twelve, the final score showed Baltimore with nine runs to Pittsburgh's six. The Orioles had tagged Pittsburgh's star reliever, Kent Tekulve, with three earned runs and an ugly loss.

Willie Stargell, Phil Garner and Dave Parker consoled the losing pitcher in the clubhouse. Teke apologized over a beer for letting the team down.

"Pops" Stargell put his hand on Teke's shoulder and said, "We might lose this thing, but before we do, let's just show the world one time how the Bucs really play baseball."[68] The vaunted Pittsburgh relievers had failed to save the victory that Saturday. In fact, the team had fallen in their last two home outings. Down 3-1 in games, Pittsburgh needed a victory at home and two more on the road. One confident bookie posted 100-1 odds against such a comeback victory. Another loss meant elimination.

The Pittsburgh veterans refused to yield to negativity. "Turn up the volume on the music," Stargell yelled. "Our backs are against the wall, but we're not done yet."

Tanner supported his losing reliever, telling the newscasters, "Teke brought us to the World Series. He threw a couple of pitches that didn't sink. You know, I would bring him in again under the same circumstances. He's the best reliever in baseball."

Unfortunately, the bad news for Chuck multiplied. The stroke that had landed his mother in the Greenville Hospital had proved extremely nasty. The outlook for seventy-year-old Anna Marie Baka Tanner's recovery appeared questionable at best. Concerned family members checked on her or visited daily. The Tanner family prayed for the best but recognized the precarious nature of Anna's health.

Chuck dialed his mother's room Sunday morning, October 14, prior to game five to see how she was doing and perhaps receive a friendly word or two of encouragement. When a nurse picked up the phone in his mother's room, he asked, "Can I speak to Anna Tanner? This is her son."

"I am sorry. Mrs. Tanner died at 7:40 this morning," came back the voice on the telephone. The news crushed Chuck. The previous Sunday, his mother had experienced a rally and seemed full of life. With her eyes glued to the television, she shouted from her bed, "Come on Bradshaw!" as she cheered on her beloved Steelers while they defeated the rival Browns at Cleveland Memorial Stadium in a 51–35 offensive slugfest. Franco Harris racked up 153 yards rushing, including a first-quarter 71-yard score. Rocky Bleier added a 70-yard touchdown of his own, the longest run in his entire professional career. Quarterback Terry Bradshaw connected for three touchdowns to receivers Bennie Cunningham, Sidney Thornton and Jim Smith. Anna loved sports, especially her Steelers and Pirates, and this game had put her in good spirits.

Chuck's family had tried to reach him to give him the sad news. Once they located him, both Babs and his father, Chuck Sr., told him, "Mom would have wanted you to put on the Pirate uniform as if nothing happened. Go get 'em!" With the Pirates down 3-1 to the Orioles, Chuck gritted his teeth and prepared to do battle in the Pittsburgh stadium he knew so well. "I honestly think Mom is in heaven. I will try to concentrate on the upcoming game, but I miss her so much." Even at a low point in his life, Chuck chose optimism. Pessimism was for the other guy.

The team had latched on to the Sister Sledge hit "We Are Family" as their theme song during the season, and they hung on to it during these tough times. Although the possibility of a World Series victory appeared remote at best, Chuck hoped for a "family" miracle: "My mother was a great Pirates fan. She knew we were in trouble, so she went upstairs to get some help." His inner strength during this time of sadness motivated his teammates to battle at his side against the odds. Even during the most difficult times, Chuck held on to his ability to pick a daisy or two from a field of weeds.

Chuck sat at his desk and pondered how to write his mother's obituary. Words failed to capture his depth of emotions. Anna Marie Baka Tanner had been a wonderful mother to him and his two brothers and a loyal wife to his father. An obituary merely recited organizational memberships, names of the spouse and children plus a hodgepodge of extraneous facts but failed to capture the true essence of the departed. How could one crystallize a mother's importance to her family and friends in a handful of sentences? The paper might list the names of her three sons—Charles, William and Robert—but it missed how Anna had supported her husband, Chuck Sr., and raised those three boys through the worst days of the Depression. "I never would have been a baseball player and manager without her support." Chuck knew that his mother had molded him into the person he now had become.

"I retained wonderful memories of my mother. She called me 'Junior' when I was a boy since I was named for my father. I remember the sandwiches she delivered to the ball field at Gaston Park around lunch time so I could continue playing. She was a terrific mother. Now, that she is gone, I miss her very much."

Anna Tanner had been a loyal member of St. Michael Church and belonged to the Mable Wilson Lodge 576 of Railroad Trainmen. Chuck recalled how she enjoyed the railroader's picnics at Cascade Park. The obituary told little about the care she bestowed on her family, the meals she cooked or her interest in sports. When a loved one passes, those left behind suffer from a hole in their heart, an emptiness in their soul and a soreness and void in their gut. Only time can ease but never erase that pain.

Chuck's mother had been a strong woman who would have wanted her son to continue with his work. She understood that his destiny revolved around baseball. How could he lose both his mother and the World Series in the same week? Chuck set his sadness aside and concentrated on the upcoming game. That is what his mother would have wanted him to do. He would mourn for her privately in his own time and way, but for now, he had a team to manage, a job to finish.

Willie told his skipper that he could handle things if he wanted to stay with his father. "I know the guys will understand." Chuck thanked his first baseman but declined.

When sportscaster Lanny Frattare walked into Chuck's office to offer his condolences, he asked the manager if he would be able to oversee the club with so much on his mind. "Lanny, I know that I am capable of leading the team and concentrating on winning this thing. I'm not ready to give up." He wiped a tear from his eye and continued, "My mother would want us to charge on, and I intend to do so." Ed Ott explained, "In essence, that is what Chuck was all about."[69]

When the press asked if Chuck thought he could come back from a 3-1 deficit, Chuck looked the reporter in the eye, smiled and echoed a Phil Garner comment, "We've got them just where we want them."

With his back against the wall, Tanner called on an often-injured twelve-year veteran: thirty-seven-year-old control-pitcher Jim Rooker. Rook sported a mediocre 4-7 record and an unspectacular 4.60 earned run average during the regular season, but he had steel in his heart. He would face Baltimore ace Mike Flanagan. The experts assumed that Chuck would select Bruce Kison for the start, but a forearm and hand injury had eliminated him from contention.

Tanner could have moved Blyleven up to start, but he opted to go with Rooker. Although his pitching selection looked crazy on paper, Chuck recognized that Rook offered one of his freshest and most rested arms. Chuck played a hunch that the vet would step up and perform well. "All we want is five," Tanner told his starter. About Rook, Chuck said, "I don't care what other people think. I have confidence in Rooker. When he's healthy, he can beat anybody."

The squad recognized Rook as a crafty, gutsy guy. Chuck and Rook intended to stifle the Oriole bats with a steady dose of inside fastball pitches and sliders, even though the scouting reports suggested a different tack.[70]

Jim Rooker. *Pittsburgh Pirates.*

When Rook learned that he would start, he went home and packed his gear for an elk hunting trip with former Pirate Goose Gossage after the series. After Tanner announced his selection to the guys in the locker room, twenty-three-year-old rookie catcher Steve Nicosia glibly joked, "Oh shit, everyone pack your hunting gear. The season's over. Rooker has packed his stuff." Since the Pirates were a loose group, the guys busted their asses after Steve's wisecrack in the face of such difficult odds.

"The Pirates possessed the knack to laugh at the ridiculous and the impossible. We worked hard but had fun," Teke said. As Jim Snow and so many others who knew him well said, "If you can't play for Chuck, you can't play for anybody."

Rook returned a call to me from Jacksonville with his remembrances. "The team trusted Chuck. He always had our backs. We were a bunch of goofballs. Bert Blyleven and Candelaria were off the charts, and Ed Ott was right behind them. Chuck possessed a knack of taking all the pieces of this strange puzzle of personalities and completing it."

Rook said, "With Chuck, you knew where you stood. However, he was not a starting pitcher's manager. He had good relievers and liked to use them. If you got in five good innings as a starter, it was no surprise if he took you out. I recalled a game against the Mets where the Bucs were ahead by two in the eighth. He yanked me with one out. I wanted to stay and finish the game, but I handed him the ball without an argument. Then the relievers blew the game. Chuck could see I was sore. He wanted to explain his strategy, but I said, 'You are the manager. You don't have to explain anything.' Chuck looked at me, patted me on the shoulder and said, 'I wish I had ten more like you.' That was his way of apologizing."

"Anything else you might want to add?" I asked.

"Yes, I miss him," Jim Rooker responded.

Reliever Kent Tekulve shared Chuck's enthusiasm. His upbeat attitude spread through the entire team for the next game like the sun's rays heating a bright summer afternoon.

Chuck truly believed that his team could come back and win. Other teams had done it, and so could his Pirates. In fact, he offered his friends the Snows free tickets to game seven in Baltimore. With Pittsburgh facing an uphill climb, Pitt student Gary Snow announced, "Not too likely we'll get to use them. We have to win today in Pittsburgh and then again Tuesday in Baltimore, and I have a test to study for on Friday."

"Let's hope for the best. Gary, you can study in the car on the way to Baltimore," his dad suggested.

"You're right. This would be a once-in-a-lifetime opportunity. I'll do it if we get the chance to go," but Gary believed the chances fell somewhere between slim and none.

At Three Rivers for do-or-die game five, the loudspeaker led the fans in a hearty rendition of "The Star-Spangled Banner." The stadium rocked with excitement. A volley from New Castle's Zambelli fireworks exploded in perfect timing with the words "the bombs bursting in air."

Former 1960 World Series home run hero and future Hall of Fame second baseman Bill Mazeroski tossed the ceremonial first pitch on to the field, while 50,920 fans cheered before the start of the game. The crowd rose for a moment of silence to honor Anna Tanner, Chuck's mom. Three Rivers Stadium banners reading "Never Say Die" echoed Tanner's and Pittsburgh's positivism. One sign promised to pluck the Orioles' feathers, cook the birds in the oven and eat them for dinner. Only three teams had taken the series after a three-to-one-game deficit, but Grant Jackson urged the team to win one for Chuck's mom. The umpire's cry of "Play ball!" set the crowd roaring.

Pirates fans, who had come en masse to support their team, refused to concede defeat. The stands boomed with approval as the home team took the field. Looking down on the stadium, the resulting picture resembled a black-and-gold abstract painting as the seats filled with Pirate hats, jerseys, T-shirts and other paraphernalia. Banners throughout Three Rivers lauded "Chuck's Bucs," "There's no quit in Pittsburgh" and "Don't Give In." Pittsburgh fans had made it through some bad times, including the closing of its steel mills. They certainly could cheer their team on to overcome this deficit. The Pirate team dedicated game five to Chuck's mother. "Let's win one for Anna."

Baseball writer Kenneth Shouler, the author of *The Real 100 Best Baseball Players of All Time…And Why*, offered a dim view of potential success for the Pirates: "With the Orioles up three games to one, I remember my father telling me the birds can't lose, especially with pitchers such as Palmer, McGregor and Flanagan available to pitch."[71] "Bah! Humbug!" the Pirates fans countered.

Prior to game time, the Pittsburgh players caught a *Baltimore Sun* article highlighting Mayor William Donald Schaefer's call for a 11:30 a.m. parade to honor the "World Champion Orioles" once they wrapped up their fourth and final victory. The Pirates intended to rain all over the mayor's celebration. Teke summed up the team's psyche: "When we saw the *Sun* we knew we wanted not only to win the next game, but we had to stop that parade."

Someone pinned a press clipping on the Pirates' locker room wall of catcher Rick Dempsey discussing how he planned to spend his "winner's share" of the World Series. This dismissal of Pittsburgh's chances stirred their combative spirit to the boiling point. Their opponent's bravado stoked rather than intimidated the Bucs. Garner told the team that there was no way now they could lose. Teke reiterated Phil and Chuck's pronouncement: "We got them just where we want them."

The selection of Jim Rooker as the starter to face Mike Flanigan made Tanner look like a genius. He pitched four hitless and scoreless innings in a pitcher's duel. His slider snapped across the plate, nibbling on the corners with precise accuracy. After flying out against Rook, Orioles slugger Eddie Murray returned to the dugout, dropped his bat and said about the Pirates pitcher, "Sore arm, my ass." In the fifth, Oriole Gary Roenicke led off with a double to center and landed on third after Doug DeCinces singled to right. Rich Dauer grounded into a double play but managed to score Roenicke and eke out a 1–0 Orioles lead.

During the Pirates fifth, Chuck pinch-hit Lee Lacy for Rook, who had done everything expected of him and more. Tanner brought in ace Bert Blyleven, who tossed a strong sixth inning. When the Bucs came to bat in their half of the inning, Flanagan's domination over Pittsburgh's bats faltered, Foli walked and Parker followed with a single to center. Robinson bunted to advance Foli to third and Parker to second. A Stargell sacrifice fly permitted Foli to scamper home. Madlock followed with a single to score Parker, providing a 2–1 razor-thin Pirates lead.

Blyleven shut out the Orioles in the seventh. Garner opened the Pirates half with a single, but a Moreno fielders-choice erased him at second. However, the play inserted the speedy Panamanian outfielder on first in his place. A timely triple by Foli off reliever Tim Stoddard scored Moreno. Parker followed through with a double to score Foli, pushing the Pittsburgh lead to 4–1.

Pittsburgh tacked on three more runs in the eighth. Stargell opened with a single against Tippy Martinez. Manager Weaver pulled Martinez and summoned reliever Don Stanhouse. Madlock singled, and Garner followed suit with a hit, scoring Stargell. After an intentional walk to Moreno, Foli singled to center scoring both Madlock and Garner, providing Pittsburgh with a 7–1 edge. The Bucs had pounded out thirteen hits against only six for the opposition. Parker called the Pittsburgh hitting "contagious." "When one of us hits, we all hit," he continued.

Blyleven continued his shutout pitching to close out the victory. His overhand-drop curveball, one of the best in the majors, worked like a charm that Sunday. He held Baltimore to just two singles and a double in four innings. The scoreboard flashed "Unbelievable!" The crowded shouted and sang to the beat of Sister Sledge's "We Are Family."

The win produced plenty of heroes. Madlock went four for four, and Foli drove in three runs with a double and a triple and participated in two double plays. Parker had two hits, including a double to score Foli. Rooker had held the Orioles in check and taken pressure off the pitching staff, and Blyleven won in relief, only his sixth such appearance. Rooker summed up the feelings of the Pirates: "They had a good team; we had a better team."

When asked if he planned to go to Baltimore after game five, Chuck answered from his maple desk in his clubhouse office, "I don't know yet. The team is going to work out here tomorrow at eleven and then take a charter flight at three in the afternoon, but I don't know what I'm going to do yet. I'm going to talk to my dad tonight. If it's okay with him, then I'll go with the team. If he wants me to stay another day, I'll stay."

Chuck explained, "Mom loved sports. All her kids loved sports, me and my two brothers, and my dad loved sports, too. It was our life, so it was her life and my dad's life."

Pirates owner John Galbreath came to Chuck's office to extend his condolences. Dozens of sportswriters, friends, players and coaches followed suit and stopped to offer their own thoughts and prayers. The outpouring of sympathy fortified the manager's resiliency. "I needed and appreciated the support," said Chuck.

When a reporter asked what he remembered about his mom, he said, "I never wanted to do any work around the house. I never wanted to wash dishes. She poked me in the shoulder and said, 'All you want to do is play ball.' And that's all I did when I could. There was a playground over the hill from our house in New Castle. The first eighteen guys who showed up every morning got to play in the game. So I made sure I got there early, and I'd stay all day. I was only eight or nine, and the other kids were fourteen or fifteen. They stuck me in right field, but I played. At lunchtime, my mother would make a peanut butter sandwich and bring it to the playground for me."

A reporter asked if the loss of his mother crossed his mind and motivated him during game five. "The time Dave Parker was up in the seventh, I remembered how he had phoned her for her seventieth birthday last May, and how she was so happy about that. He was her favorite player, and she had told everyone how she had talked to Superman. And when he was up, I said to myself, 'Hit one for Grandma,' and he lined that double to left to put us ahead 4–1."

Parker told the press that he and Chuck were more than manager and player, "We were friends. Anything that I do the rest of the series, I'd like to dedicate to Chuck and his mother."

Chuck remembered when his grandmother passed. "I was a kid outfielder with the Atlanta Crackers in the Southern League, but when my grandmother died, my mother and my dad told me that I didn't have to come home for the funeral—that my grandmother would understand. That's the way my mother and father always were. When I left home to play ball in the minors at seventeen, my mother told me, 'Do what you want to. It's your life.' Later on I was playing in Owensboro, Kentucky, when I had to go to the hospital with bleeding ulcers. My parents came down to see me then, and another time they came to Denver. My mom was great. My mother and father didn't have many rules for my two brothers and me. We just had to do what was right."

"Was she always optimistic like you?" came the question.

"Both she and my dad were. I'm sad now. I'm sad as I ever have been in my life, but I'm strong, too. I know everybody here is supposed to hit the deck sooner or later. It's not hard for me to accept that, because I have faith in God. I know my mother's in heaven now."[72]

When the press asked his final thoughts about his mom, he said, "Of course I've been thinking about her a lot ever since it happened. She would understand and know that I have a lot going on. I know mom would want me on the field."

Chuck continued, "You've got to be strong mentally. You have sadness in your heart, but you have to understand that is going to happen to all of us some day. So let's enjoy our time here and give it our best. I can be strong because the people around me are strong."

The fifth-game win closed the gap, but Tanner faced a herculean task ahead of him. The "Lumber and Lightning Crew" now battled the Orioles on their home turf, still needing to win two games.

Chuck skipped the scheduled workout before heading to Baltimore in order to meet with his father and finalize the funeral arrangements at Noga's Funeral Home in New Castle. The family set calling hours from 7:00 p.m. to 9:00 p.m. on Tuesday and Wednesday evenings. They agreed to postpone the funeral ceremony until Thursday and the end of the series. After the details had been completed, Chuck went to the airport to catch the 3:00 p.m. charter flight to Maryland with the team.

The disco group Sister Sledge had sent a giant bouquet of flowers to their Pirates family as a sign of good luck. Teke handed flowers to his teammates and their wives as they boarded the plane. Lightness and joviality filled the flight. This team intended to return with a World Series victory and have fun doing it despite the odds being stacked against them.

John Candelaria sported an Orioles cap. Tanner ignored it but smiled. Chuck believed that a porous defense and cold weather had hurt the team. They needed to tighten play, but the team exuded confidence and Chuck liked their fighting spirit. Chuck recognized the importance of talent, but courage and attitude proved equally essential for a winning series.

When equipment manager John Hallahan reminded the team to bring their luggage downstairs at the hotel in case the team would have to leave Baltimore that evening, Candelaria refused. "I'm pitching tonight. Why should I bring my luggage downstairs? We're going to be here at least one more night."[73]

Earl Weaver started eight-time, twenty-game winner Jim Palmer in game six, probably his best. The Baltimore public address system belted out the Jim Croce song "You Don't Mess Around with Jim," while he tossed his warmups.

Tanner had penciled in the six-foot-seven John Candelaria, one of his two top aces. Regardless of his aches and pains, Candy always gave his all. The stars on both teams threw goose eggs through the first six innings in a classic pitcher's duel between two of the top pitchers in baseball.

In the seventh, Moreno scooted a single through a hole to right following a Lacy strikeout. Foli singled Moreno to second on a hit and run. Dave Parker came through to advance Foli and drive Moreno home with a bad hop single past second. A Willie Stargell sacrifice fly scored Foli from third. The Bucs led 2–0. Things looked up for Pittsburgh.

Candelaria had been magnificent, but his back locked up on him again. Prior to the game, he could not even bend over to tie his own shoes. Still, he pitched without complaint, and very well indeed. Tanner sent Kent Tekulve to relieve Candelaria in the seventh. Kent gave up a meaningless single and then ended the inning uneventfully.

In the eighth, Ott singled, and Garner hit a ground-rule double after a long Madlock fly out. Bill Robinson scored Ott from third with a sacrifice fly, and Moreno singled Garner home for a 4–0 lead. A Tim Foli pop-up to the catcher ended the inning.

Teke's "whirlybird sinker" quieted the Baltimore bats over the next two innings. Slugger Ken Singleton led off the ninth. With a one-ball, two-strike count, catcher Ed Ott grabbed his face mask, signaling an overhand slider. Teke shook his head in disbelief to signal no way. He no longer possessed that pitch in his repertoire. He hadn't used it in competition since his minor-league days. Ott repeated the signal. What the heck. Teke threw a perfect strike breaking at the belt buckle. Singleton swung for the fences and missed for the out. Eddie Murray lofted an easy fly to right, and Doug DeCinces struck out to end the game. The underdog Pirates had evened the series with the 4–0 victory. Tanner told the press that the Pirates team never gives up to adversity.

"Well, we postponed that Baltimore parade for at least one day," Teke joked.

After the game, Teke asked Ott, "How did you come up with that pitch to Singleton?"

"I just wanted to see if you had the nerve to throw it."

In the clubhouse, Chuck also asked about the pitch, "What was that?"

"He called it," Teke replied. Chuck turned his gaze to Ott.

"He threw it," Ott answered. Chuck responded with a look of total confusion. Anyhow, it worked.

"Chuck never told me what to throw. He would just hand me the ball and say, 'Go get 'em.'" Teke went on to explain, "The only exception was when I followed Grant Jackson, Grant would hand me the ball instead of Chuck. Once I told Buck, I always called him 'Buck' instead of Grant, 'Buck get me a beer. I'll be done in a minute.' Chuck would shake his head at our shenanigans, but Grant opened a can of beer for me and poured it into a thirty-two ounce stein that he kept in his locker."

Teke possessed a wonderful sense of humor. When he played at Shea Stadium against the Mets, the fans could be quite rambunctious. "A golf cart decorated with a Pirate hat delivered the reliever from the bullpen behind the left field fence. Since the cart driver tried to avoid the grass, he followed the perimeter of the outfield, and the Mets fans showered the relievers with beer. I smelled like a brewery by the time I met Chuck at the mound. They kept missing my mouth and getting my shirt," Teke complained. The Pirates manager loved his give and take with Teke, a man he felt certain had been vaccinated with a phonograph needle.

The 76th World Series came down to the Wednesday, October 17 seventh and final game. A heavily weighted crowd of 53,733 mostly Baltimore fans jammed the stands for an evening game. The front page of the *Pittsburgh Press* read, "One more time, Maestro, if you please." Each side looked for an edge to seal the deal. The Bucs already had canceled two Baltimore parades. Could they do it again? The Pittsburgh players intended to relocate that cavalcade from Maryland to Pennsylvania.

The temperature at Memorial Stadium bounced from a balmy afternoon warmup to a low of thirty-nine degrees by the 8:30 p.m. game time, but the psyched Pirates appeared oblivious to the weather. They had come this far, and they intended to win the World Series.

After Gary Snow, his brother John and his parents picked up the four tickets Chuck left for them at will call, they entered the stadium assuming that their seats would be buried in the upper stands. Imagine their surprise to learn that they had received four front-row seats in a temporary plywood box along the first base line in the owner's box. The price on each 1979 ticket read $17. As a comparison, during the 2021 World Series, Minute Maid Park's standing-room price in Houston ran $431. Field-level seats started at $1,000, and the cheapest seats sold for $707.

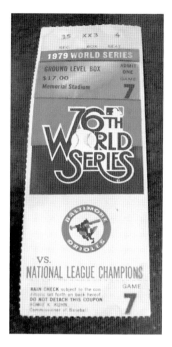

Photo of a game seven, 1979 World Series ticket. *Collection of Dr. Gary Snow.*

President Jimmy Carter, the first sitting president to open a World Series game since Dwight D. Eisenhower appeared at Ebbets Field in 1956, tossed the ceremonial first pitch from his front-row seat on the third base line to Baltimore catcher Rick Dempsey. Speaker of the House Tip O'Neill sat beside the president. He smiled and waved at the cameras snapping his picture for the television audience.

Tanner called on thirteen-game winner and power pitcher Jim Bibby to face twenty-five-year-old Scott McGregor, a lefty with finesse. "He was my only rested pitcher," Chuck explained. McGregor correctly described his opposition as a "free-swinging" team. He intended to nibble his pitches around the plate, teasing the Pirate sluggers without feeding them a pitch to drive out of the park.

Both pitchers threw scoreless ball through two innings, but second baseman Rich Dauer led off the third with a towering homer to left field in the third to give Baltimore a 1–0 lead. Tanner called in Sanguillén as a pinch hitter for Bibby in the fifth to try to generate some offense, even through his pitcher had been firing bullets for his four-inning stretch. The ploy failed. Sanguillén grounded out to the pitcher.

Tanner brought in Don Robinson for the fifth. Doug DeCinces produced a single to center, but Robinson settled down with fly-ball outs to Dempsey and Dauer. As his shoulder tightened, Robinson's control faltered, and he committed a huge no-no. He walked the pitcher Scott McGregor. The Pirates manager yanked Robinson and turned to Grant Jackson, who forced Al Bumbry to pop-up a foul ball for the third out.

McGregor had kept the Pirates at bay for five innings, but the Pirates rallied in the sixth. After Parker grounded out to second, left fielder Bill Robinson whacked a single past shortstop Kiko Garcia. "Pops" Stargell, old reliable, who already had hit a single and a double, came to bat. He drove a slider, his third home run of the series, to right field just a few feet beyond the grasp of Orioles outfielder Ken Singleton to eke out a 2–1 Pirates lead.

With Pittsburgh hanging tenuously to a one-run edge, the Baltimore eighth inning proved especially scary for the Pirates. Grant Jackson, who had yet to give up a run during the series, forced Rich Dauer to lift a lazy fly to short for out number one. Then Jackson walked Lee May and Al Bumbry. Weaver brought in the speedy Mark Belanger to pinch run for May.

Tanner could see that Jackson had tired. He called time and brought in ace reliever Kent Tekulve. After Grant handed the ball to Teke, the lanky reliever faced pinch hitter Terry Crowley, the same batter who had hit a game-winning double off him in game four in Pittsburgh. Teke's low pitches forced the batter to bounce out for the second out of the inning, but Belanger advanced to third and Bumbry to second. To create a force out at any base, Teke intentionally walked Ken Singleton, bringing up the always dangerous Eddie Murray, a slugger who had batted .295 with twenty-five home runs and ninety-nine RBIs during the regular season. The partisan Baltimore crowd screamed "Eddie! Eddie!" as he strode to bat.

With the pressure whistling at the boiling point, Stargell called, "Time!" The captain sought to ease the tension on his pitcher. He sauntered to the mound and grinned, "Hey, Teke, if you're afraid of him, I'll pitch and you can play first." Teke cracked up and told the captain he could go back to where he belonged. The pitcher aimed a sinker to Murray, who lofted a long fly ball to right fielder Dave Parker for the out.

Weaver brought in Tim Stoddard to relieve McGregor for the ninth. Phil Garner opened with a double to left field. Tekulve, a .133 hitter with just two hits in fifteen at bats during the year, failed to sacrifice bunt the runner to second. Orioles manager Weaver called in Mike Flanagan, the major league's leader in wins during the regular season, to face Omar Moreno. The center fielder singled and brought Garner home for the

Pirates' third run. Baltimore summoned their third pitcher of the inning, Don Stanhouse.

Tim Foli singled off reliever Don Stanhouse, moving the speedy Omar Moreno to third. In a Hail Mary move, Weaver brought in the fourth pitcher of the inning, Tippy Martinez, to face Dave Parker. Tippy beaned the batter, sending him to first.

Weaver yanked Tippy Martinez to bring in the fifth pitcher of the inning, a World Series record. The new pitcher, Dennis Martinez, facing a bases-loaded scenario, smacked Bill Robinson with an errant throw, bringing Foli home from third for a 4–1 lead.

The Baltimore fans in the stands screamed that the ball had struck Robinson's bat, not his hand. Trainer Tony Bartirome raced on the field to check out his player's fingers. When he looked, he could find no apparent injury. He dug his nails into Robinson's skin to draw a trickle of blood. When Dempsey complained to umpire Jerry Neudecker about the call, Bartirome and Robinson showed the ump the blood, and the call stood. Willie Stargell grounded into an inning ending double play, but the Pirate bats had done their damage.

Teke breezed through the ninth with two strikeouts on six sinkers, most of them out of the strike zone, and pinch hitter Pat Kelly's long fly to Omar Marino in center sealed the victory. Teke jumped in the air with glee as the team embraced him after his save, possibly the most memorable one in his entire career. "We did it. I knew we could," Tanner cried as he threw his hands in the air.

Pandemonium spread through the Pirates loyalists in the stands. Pitt student Gary Snow leaped from his field box and raced onto the field. Dressed in his Pirates jersey, he sped toward Willie Stargell, John Candelaria and Bill Madlock. Gary's brother John made for the mound and snatched the rosin bag, an artifact he still treasures.

Sometime later, Gary felt unsure when, Chuck gave Dr. Jim Snow his no. 7 hat. Inside it he had signed in pen, "To Jim, my friend. Chuck Tanner, World Series game seven."

A section of Pirate fans atop the dugout reverberated throughout the stadium. When Baltimore ushers warned the fans that the roof might not hold their weight, Omar Moreno's wife told the usher not to worry, "Honey, don't you worry; we got plenty of insurance."[74]

Thirty-nine-year-old Willie Stargell had recorded a home run, two doubles and a single, four hits in five at bats during game seven. Omar Moreno came through with three singles. Although the overall hitting proved strong, the four-hit pitching of Jim Bibby, Don Robinson, Grant Jackson and Kent

Left: Kent Tekulve and Steve Nicosia. *Pittsburgh Pirates.*

Below: 1979 World Series euphoria. *Pittsburgh Pirates.*

Tekulve in the final game proved exceptional. The victory became only the fourth time a team had come back from being down 3-1 to win the series. Teke tied a record with three World Series saves.[75] *Sports Illustrated* wrote, "In truth, the Pirates won the world championship more than the Orioles lost it."

The Bucs batted an amazing .323 during the series, a record for a World Series winning team. Their eighty-one hits stood second only to the 1960 New York Yankees' ninety-one hits. Five Pirates—Stargell, Garner, Moreno, Parker and Foli—produced ten or more hits, and all members of that quintet batted .333 or better. Madlock had nine hits and a .375 batting average. Foli did not strike out during the entire series in thirty-three

Chuck Tanner's hat from the 1979 World Series game seven. *Collection of Dr. Gary Snow.*

at bats, another series record. The Buccos, who stole 180 bases during the regular season, failed to steal a single base during the series, and Baltimore threw them out each time they tried.

The Orioles managed only a .232 batting average. In fact, the Pirates held them to just two runs in the final three games. Pittsburgh pitchers chalked up a 3.34 earned run average versus 4.35 for Baltimore. Willie Stargell's .400 batting average and three home runs earned him the Most Valuable Player Award (MVP), making him the oldest man ever to receive the honor. Interestingly, Stargell became the first player to score the winning run in game seven of two World Series, 1971 and 1979. Each full winner's share from the World Series amounted to $32,000. The losing Baltimore players received $27,000.

"I always give credit to my coaches for that year. They had a lot to do with our success. I had Harvey Haddix, Bob Skinner, Joe Lonnett and Al Monchak. We had a team. We made some trades—getting Bill Madlock, getting Tim Foli, getting Phil Garner. It all came together. The group that was assembled was a good team. It wasn't exceptional. There were at least three teams better than us, but we won it all," Tanner reported.

Pittsburgh sportswriters reveled that nice guys can finish first. Candelaria played for eight different managers, and he rated the Minneapolis Twins' Tom Kelly, winner of the 1987 and 1991 World Series, and Chuck at the top of his list of favorites.

1979 World Series Champions
Chuck's Bucs
We Are Fam-a-lee!

1979 World Series champions. *Pittsburgh Pirates.*

The song "We Are Family" echoed through the hallways outside the locker room, jammed with exuberant Pittsburgh fans. The pop of champagne corks, the roar of the Pirates faithful and their screams of joy made hearing nearly impossible. President Carter congratulated Chuck in the locker room, but with all the hullabaloo, the noise drowned his voice. Afterward, Chuck could not remember one word he said.

The Snow family reveled in the locker room festivities. Gary Snow and his brother John considered game seven and the celebration afterward as one of the highlights of their lives. When someone asked pitching coach Harvey Haddix if his no-hitter topped the series win, he answered without hesitation, "Oh no, this was much better. These are my guys."

President Carter and Bowie Kuhn appeared on a makeshift stage to present a championship trophy to owner John Galbreath and his son Dan. When reporters advised Stargell that he had won the MVP award, he modestly stated that the prize should be divided among the manager, coaches, clubhouse men and players. The award included a new sports car. When reporters asked Chuck to describe Stargell, Tanner said, "He is like a diamond ring on my hand."

As the festivities wound down, the Pirates departed for the airport for the short flight home. When the Pirates arrived in Pittsburgh around 3:30 a.m., nearly one thousand hardcore supporters greeted them at the airport. After a long, emotion-filled game night, a flight and little or no sleep, Chuck knew that he had yet to face his mother's funeral later that morning.

In New Castle the following day, the City Council and Mayor Francis J. Rogan voted to declare October 27 as Chuck Tanner Day. The parade, originally planned for Baltimore when the series totals sat at 3-1, now would take place on Washington Street in Chuck's hometown. The city of Pittsburgh would have its own celebration.

Although the World Series victory raised Chuck to the pinnacle of his professional success, the loss of his seventy-year-old mother now became his primary concern. Anna had been the mother of three boys—Chuck, William and Robert—and the grandmother of eleven. The bereft son suffered through the funeral with great difficultly, thankful for his mother's life and certain that she would experience joy in the next world.

The funeral procession departed Noga Funeral Home on Thursday, October 18, at 10:00 a.m. for a Christian burial at St. Michael's Church, followed by interment at SS Phillip and James Cemetery. Reverend Charles Georgevich officiated throughout the ceremony. Many members of the Pirates team came to New Castle to attend and offer their condolences.

In contrast to the Tanner family's loss, the entire town of New Castle celebrated Chuck Tanner and the Bucs' remarkable come-from-behind victory. Jimmy Vascetti, co-owner of Egidio's Restaurant on Wilmington Road along with his partner, Norm Rigotti, posted a giant canvas sign on their building congratulating "Chuck Tanner, the World's Best Manager." Chuck took notice of the sign and soon began to frequent the restaurant in the off season.

On Saturday, October 27, flush with the World Series victory, almost fifty thousand citizens turned out for the eleven o'clock Chuck Tanner Parade in downtown New Castle. Guests of honor Chuck Tanner Sr.; Babs, who usually hung back in the background; and Chuck waved to the adoring fans from the back seat of Sandy Petruso's 1935 pale-yellow LaSalle convertible. Teacher Pat Zona recalled having her art class design several signs for the celebration.

Mayor Francis Rogan, a firm supporter of Lawrence County sports, proved instrumental in making the parade happen. He rode in the second car with Pirates executive vice-president Tom Johnson, Dr. James Snow,

Chuck Tanner in the 1979 parade through downtown New Castle. *Chuck Shira.*

KDKA radio celebrity Roy Fox, Councilman Eugene DiCaprio and glass artist and designer Gene Scalia. Other cars in the caravan featured Chicago scout Fred Shaffer, the eighteen-year-old Bruce Tanner, Kent Tekulve, Ralph "Pops" Johnson and his wife, sportscaster Milo Hamilton, Bill Madlock and the Pirates Parrot. Pennsylvania state representatives Tom Fee and Ralph Pratt, U.S. Representative Eugene Atkinson and Chief of Police Williams McCallion followed in yet another vehicle.

The music of Sister Sledge's "We Are Family" reverberated through the downtown via loud speakers. Thousands of locals clad in black and gold jerseys, jackets and hats lined Washington Street. Folks waved Chuck's Bucs banners as the cars and bands passed. Bags of confetti poured like rain. KDKA celebrity Roy Fox took the microphone and led the crowd in a "Hip...Hip...Hooray" cheer. Gene Scalia presented Chuck with a glass sculpture he designed for the event.

The mayor presented a citation from the city, while state and federal House of Representatives proclamations followed. Tanner received a car from Chambers Motors. Shenango China and Fisher's Big Wheel offered their own awards. The night concluded with a massive celebratory display as the sights and sounds of rockets filled the air in the "Fireworks Capital of America."

Thousands attend New Castle's Chuck Tanner Parade. *Chuck Shira.*

Chuck pontificated about the quality of sports in the area:

> *I believe, and I'm sincere about this, that per capita Lawrence County produces as many athletes and great coaches as any place in the country.... Look at the exceptional coaches that have come from here—Phil Bridenbaugh, Lindy Lauro, Buzz Ridl, Butler Hennon, Harold Burry, Joe Fusco, Ron Galbreath, Mike Covelli and there's probably a raft of them I missed. I can't resist tossing out more names....I mean Bill McPeak who played for Pitt and the Steelers, Darrell Dess who played for Union, North Carolina State and the New York Giants and Bruce Clark who played for New Castle, Penn State and the New Orleans Saints...and Walt Mangham who played for New Castle and Marquette, a guy who set a national scholastic high-jumping record....Now who was the best basketball player to come out of Lawrence County. Most guys will tell you it was Don Hennon, who helped put Wampum on the map and was an All-American at Pitt....Dick Allen unquestionably was the greatest athlete to come out of Lawrence County....Where do I stop? I know I'm going to miss someone—Tom Brzoza, who played football at Neshannock and was an All-American at Pitt, and Harry Toscano, who played professional golf, and don't forget Dick Allen's brothers Harold and Ron, who also made it to the major leagues after they led Wampum to a state championship*

166

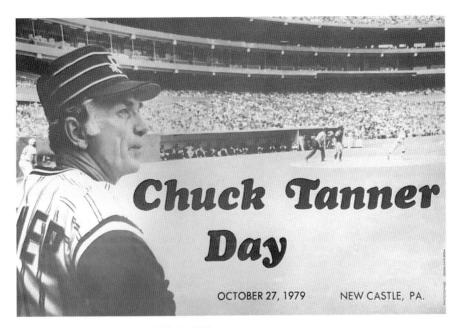

Above: Chuck Tanner Day. *New Castle Public Library.*

Left: Chuck Tanner plaque. *New Castle Public Library.*

in basketball. There was Cash Koszela, one of New Castle's basketball greats who could have been a major league baseball player if the war hadn't come along, and I've got to put in a word for Fred Shaffer, who pitched for Louisville in the '30s. He still serves as a scout.[76]

Fuzzy Fazzone recalled that Gennaro Paving presented Chuck with a tennis court in his backyard—"A nice gift, but I don't even play tennis." New Castle's most popular citizen couldn't walk down the street without being mobbed with compliments and requests for autographs and baseballs.

A week after the win, Chuck, Dave Parker, John Candelaria, Bert Blyleven, Jim Bibby and Bill Madlock joined a National League team managed by Tommy Lasorda to represent the Pirates on a baseball tour in Japan.

When Chuck returned to the States, the locals took every effort to show their appreciation for the man whose World Series victory had brought recognition to the city of New Castle. On December 17, 1979, Principal Connie Palumbo honored him at a Shenango High School assembly. On February 10, 1980, the Neshannock Kiwanis Club sponsored a Tanner roast at the Harbor Community Center emceed by Roy Fox, the host of KDKA radio's popular show the *Fox's Den*.

Once the Steelers won the Super Bowl, *Sports Illustrated* named quarterback Terry Bradshaw and Willie Stargell as its first dual "Sportsmen of the Year," making Pittsburgh truly the City of Champions.

The 1979 season indeed had ended on a high note. Chuck enjoyed the fall respite from the pressures of the major leagues, allowing him to recover from the loss of his mother and the excitement of the season, but he also faced a slew of opportunities and issues.

Chuck continued to frequent Egidio's Restaurant shortly after the series. He and owner Jim Vascetti struck up a cordial relationship that looked like it might evolve into a possible business partnership. Since businessman Norm Riggoti had considered selling his interest in Egidio's in order to concentrate on his other ventures, Vascetti pegged the popular Pirates manager as an ideal replacement.

Vascetti remembered Chuck as a teenage star athlete for the Shenango AC's in the North County Baseball League. "I usually sat on the bench," he admitted, but he became excited that the popular Pirates manager might be interested in an investment in the Wilmington Road eatery. Chuck mulled over the possibility, weighing the pros and cons of such a venture, but hesitated to take immediate action.

Ace Bert Blyleven had pitched only four complete games during the 1979 season versus eleven or more the previous three years. This rankled the high-strung athlete. He threatened to retire if the Pirates did not trade him to a team that would allow him more innings and a better shot at finishing games.

When the team initially rejected his demand, Blyleven complained to his teammates and the press. In the pitcher's defense, he pitched in twenty no-decision games, the highest total since 1908. However, Blyleven's festering dissatisfaction might seriously affect team unity during the upcoming season and required addressing by Chuck and General Manager Harding Peterson.

The fans expected another bang-up year in 1980, but Chuck also found himself wrestling with problems affecting team solidarity, as well as a host of personal financial decisions.

CHAPTER 11

PIRATES' SEASONS, 1980–1985

If things are going well, enjoy it, because it won't last forever.
—Barbara Elsborg

Baseball is a mighty uncertain game.
—Hack Wilson

Chuck's baseball success would never again reach the 1979 high point. The parades would end, but banquets and speeches stacked up for Chuck during the off season. Roasts, speaking engagements and honorariums filled his fall and winter months. On Wednesday, January 30, Chuck, Los Angeles manager Tommy Lasorda and Los Angeles third baseman Bill Russell dropped into Valentine's Restaurant prior to attending a sports affair in Bridgeville in Allegheny County. The following night, Chuck and his cohorts took part in an all-sports dinner at Sandalini's in Meadville. A photo in the *New Castle News* showed Lasorda and Tanner in a makeshift heated discussion about the upcoming baseball season. As spring training approached, Chuck shifted his attention to the upcoming 1980 competition.

Chuck maintained a firm corollary that every player who came to the Pirates deserved a clean slate. If an individual created a problem on another team, he would cut that guy some slack. The Atlanta Braves traded Eddie "Buddy" Solomon to Pittsburgh on March 28 after he shot out the lights at a hotel swimming pool in West Palm, Florida, during spring training. The Braves considered Solomon a troublemaker, but not Chuck. When he had treated Dick Allen, Tim Foli and Bill Madlock with respect, each man responded as a team member who produced outstanding statistics and minimal discipline issues.

After traveling secretary Charley Muse advised Chuck that Buddy had arrived, he welcomed the new addition warmly: "What you did in West Palm is over the wall. All I want you to do is pitch the eighth for me." Solomon responded well to his new manager and performed above expectations as a spot starter and reliever with two of the best years of his career in 1980 and '81.

An April 1–8 strike ended spring training prematurely as the players and management bickered over free agency terms. Although the disagreement festered, the 1980 season began on schedule.

The Pirates opened their regular starting game at 2:12 p.m. on Thursday, April 10, with a hard-fought match against St. Louis. Blyleven ended up on the losing end of a 1–0 three hitter against Johnstown native Pete Vuckovich. Josh Haims told a great story about that game. Josh had been at the Tanner home on Maitland playing ping-pong with his classmate and Chuck's youngest son, Bruce, during the winter break from his freshman year at Washington University in St. Louis.

Chuck popped downstairs and played a game with his son while Josh watched. Bruce was crushing his dad 19–11. In typical fashion, the elder Tanner guaranteed a comeback. He never quit even when it appeared impossible to win. He did catch a few quick points but nonetheless lost. After the game, the manager gave Josh a signed Pirates photo of the 1979 World Series winning squad.

Chuck mentioned that the Pirates would open at Busch Stadium in April during the upcoming season, and he could get Josh seats if he reminded him a few days before the game. Josh took up the offer. He called Pittsburgh and reached Chuck without much difficulty.

"Hi Josh, how can I help you?"

"When we talked last December at your house, you mentioned you might be able to get me a few tickets to the opening game."

"Sure, how many do you need?"

"Well, if it's not too much to ask, I could use four."

"No problem, they'll be at will call. How's school?"

"Fine, except for economics. I have a big test coming up."

"You'll do great. See you at the game."

The evening of April 9, the night before the game, Josh went to the posh Chase-Park Plaza Hotel, where he met several of the players. Dave Parker invited him to sit at the bar for a cocktail.

"I ordered a coke since I was underage. Parker spoke to me for nearly three quarters of an hour about baseball. People give him a bum rap. He really was a nice guy and a gentleman," Josh said.

The next morning, Josh had breakfast with Omar Moreno, who spoke minimal English, but he had a friendly smile and seemed happy to have the company.

In the afternoon, Josh picked up the tickets at will call for himself and his three college friends. They had come early and discovered that they had scored some of the best seats in the stadium. As they watched batting practice, Chuck came over and greeted the boys. "Josh aren't those great seats?" Josh beamed.

"Yes, they are terrific."

"How did you make out on that economics test? I bet you did fine?"

"No problem." Josh's friends could hardly believe that Josh knew the manager of the Pittsburgh Pirates and that he displayed an actual interest in Josh. Chuck even brought over Bill Madlock and Phil Garner to say hello. "This was one of the best days of my life," Josh recalled. "I learned a key lesson in human relations. Chuck Tanner had made a nineteen-year-old college student feel like a million dollars."

After the game, Bill Robinson and Enrique Romo asked Josh and his friends to take them to a local hangout. They ended up at the Oz Night Club, where the two players checked out the ladies. To this day, the Pirates experience remains an important memory for Josh.

Although the Pirates won the next three games against St. Louis, the Tanner magic had begun to unravel, and Chuck felt the pressure. Don Robinson's pitching had fallen off from the previous years, as had John Candelaria's and Bert Blyleven's. With his performance lagging, Don Robinson anxiously awaited his turn to start and asked pitching coach Harvey Haddix when he could expect his next mound appearance. "Probably a week from Saturday, twelve days from now," came the answer—not what Robinson hoped to hear.

"You've got to be kidding." Robinson griped, assuming that a quicker appearance might snap his slump.

"Hey, if you don't like it, you know where Chuck's office is," Haddix countered.

When Chuck learned of the ruckus, he called Don into his office and read him the riot act. "Who do you think you are, Walter Johnson? How many games have you won? Tell me!"

"Twenty-five."

"Well, Blyleven has won 150, and Candelaria close to 80. You got a long way to go before you reach their level. You pitch when I say you pitch. Do you understand?"

Humbled and embarrassed, Robinson left the meeting with his tail between his legs. Chuck might listen to complaints from long-term vets like Candelaria, Stargell or Parker, who received more latitude, but the newer guys had to toe the line until they earned their stripes.

Blyleven continued as an irritant who questioned Chuck's management style. He believed that relievers should be employed occasionally—not in almost every game. He wanted to pitch more innings on the mound and sought an opportunity to complete games. He threatened retirement and demanded to be traded to a team that knew how to use him better. He carped to the press, "I was always looking over my shoulder after the fifth inning. Tanner showed little faith in me. I am beginning to lose my competitive edge." He accused his manager of "quick-hooking" him and stifling his ability to achieve his personal goals.

Blyleven became one of the few players who had trouble getting along with Chuck Tanner, not so much personally, but strategically. On May 1, Bert quit the team and his $300,000 salary for "early retirement."

"It wasn't a snap decision. I'd been thinking about it for more than a year." The twenty-nine-year-old pitcher wanted to quit or be moved to another team. General Manager Pete Peterson agreed to make every effort to make a trade.

Dave Parker said, "I hope Bert regains his senses and returns to the greatest team in baseball." Blyleven did return on May 9, but his days with the Pirates proved numbered.

The team eked out an 83-79 third-place record during the troubled 1980 regular season. Madlock lost about a dozen games after a suspension for putting his glove in an umpire's face. Parker's knees ached, and he strained his Achilles' tendon. A horrendous 1-11 record against Bobby Cox's 81-80 Atlanta Braves virtually guaranteed the exclusion of the Pirates from the playoff picture.

Part-timers Mike Easter batted .338 and Lee Lacy .335. Speedster Omar Moreno stole ninety-six bases, just one behind National League leader Ron LeFlore. He also led the league with thirteen triples, but the team batting average slid from .272 to .266 and the team's home run count dropped from 148 to 118. Injuries held forty-year-old Willie Stargell to just 11 home runs in 202 at bats. He had blasted 32 round-trippers the previous season. The Captain's age had begun to show. Infielders

Garner, Foli and Madlock's batting averages dropped significantly from their 1979 levels.

Although starter Jim Bibby had a career-best year with nineteen wins against only six losses and led the National League with a .760 won-loss percentage, Candelaria, Tekulve, Blyleven and Robinson all racked up losing records. The team earned run average (ERA) rose from 3.34 in 1979 to 3.58 in 1980, a bad sign.

Blyleven continued his fault-finding throughout the year, complaining that Tanner yanked his pitchers too early, which sabotaged the starters. As a true competitor, Bert wanted to stay in the game as long as he threw effectively. He valued the importance of his personal statistics—strikeouts, innings pitched, wins and complete games. He groused that Tanner placed too much emphasis on pinch hitters and relievers. Bert hated how his manager handled him on the mound.

Tanner countered the criticism by stating that the managers in Minnesota and Texas had treated Blyleven like a "golden child." Chuck counted team wins far more than individual performances. As Blyleven grew increasingly vocal about his dissatisfaction, team morale sagged, a situation Tanner refused to stomach. The pitcher's 8-13 1980 record, his sore back and detrimental attitude made him an expendable commodity.

Chuck recognized three methods of upgrading win statistics:

1. Add better talent.
2. Improve team effort.
3. Cut those inhibiting team progress.

The Pirates chose the third alternative with Blyleven. At the December 9, 1980 winter trades, General Manager Harding "Pete" Peterson dumped the unhappy pitcher to the Cleveland Indians for the good of the team, tossing in retiring catcher Manny Sanguillén in exchange for catcher Gary Alexander and pitchers Victor Cruz, Bob Owchinko and Rafael Vásquez in what the experts called a fire sale.[77]

Blyleven would go on to win another 131 games in a Hall of Fame career. On the other hand, Owchinko pitched once for the Pirates and failed to score an out before being traded again. Alexander batted .213 and played in just 21 major-league games, and Cruz would earn a single win. Vásquez never reached the majors. Sportswriters considered the Blyleven trade among the worst in Pirates history, but sometimes an improvement in team spirit requires extreme measures.

The January 30, 1980 *New Castle News* carried Tanner's comments about his traded pitcher, whom he derided as "Cryleven." "I never talk about a player, but I don't appreciate the lie he told. He didn't like the way I managed. Well, I don't manage for one man. I manage for the good of the team. When he said I only pitched him every six or seven days, it just wasn't true."

A check of the records showed that in thirty-four appearances, Blyleven worked just seven times with more than four days' rest, and one of those times followed a game postponement. During the season, he quit the team for ten days, an affront to management. When he returned, he pitched every fourth or fifth day on until July 29, when back problems sidelined him.

"He maneuvered pretty good and got himself to Cleveland. I hope he wins twenty games. He works hard and takes the ball every time you give it to him, but he's not a Pirate. I don't like what he did to my ball club," Chuck explained.

A highlight of the 1980 season for Chuck involved the Tuesday, July 8 All-Star game at Dodger Stadium. As the 1979 pennant winner, Chuck received the honor of managing the National League squad, which included four Pittsburgh Pirates. The fans had elected Dave Parker as a starter. Jim Bibby posted a sparkling midterm 11-1 record, and second baseman Phil Garner put up steady if not outstanding figures.

Chuck added Kent Tekulve as a reward for his World Series performance the previous year. "He named me to the All-Star team. I sat on the bench, but I was there. Chuck took a lot of heat for picking me over guys like Rollie Fingers. I was a slow starter like most of the bigger guys on the team such as Willie and Dave, but we heated up when the weather got hot in July and August. I can't tell you how grateful I was to Chuck for naming me to that All-Star team."

Tanner, Tekulve, Garner, Parker and Bibby, along with public relations director Joe Safety, flew to Los Angeles from Chicago after a stunning game with the Cubs. Reliever Bibby had won his eleventh game of the year on July 6 by a 5–4 score in a twenty-inning pitcher's duel. The weary Pittsburgh contingent arrived late to the downtown Los Angeles Biltmore, and Chuck asked Joe Safety what he planned to do the following Monday morning. "I'm free," Joe told him. "Well, you and I are going to have some fun. Meet me in the lobby at one."

The following afternoon, the two Pirates met as planned. Chuck carried a briefcase. "Okay, let's go," and the men made their way to Dodger Stadium and Los Angeles manager Tommy Lasorda's office, which also served as the National League team's temporary headquarters.

(Left to Right) **Chuck Tanner & Tommy Lasorda**

Chuck as an Atlanta Brave manager and Tommy Lasorda. *Bruce Tanner.*

"Joe, say hi to my good friend Tommy Lasorda." Tommy gave Joe his million-dollar smile and a firm handshake. He served as one of Tanner's coaches for the All-Star game the following day.

"Chuck, Joe, make yourselves at home. This is going to be your office for the next few days." Dozens of photos of Tommy and various celebrities lined the walls. A tremendous spread of Italian delicacies from Little Joe's, located in Chinatown, filled the room: veal Parmesan, rigatoni, meatballs and sausages—a virtual feast.

"Tommy, this looks great," Chuck added. Lasorda's office generally looked like an Italian restaurant buffet line.

"Guys, I got to pitch some batting practice. I promised our guys I would do it, but you stay up here and enjoy yourselves. *Mangia!* There's plenty to eat. Help yourselves, and I'll catch up with you guys a little later."

As soon as Tommy left, Chuck nudged Joe, "Now the fun starts. Help me take down every one of these pictures on the wall." In minutes, only picture hooks and nails remained. Chuck opened his briefcase and removed a single framed picture of him and Jimmy Sturr.

"Let's hang this over his desk." Chuck chuckled.

When Lasorda returned, his only comment was, "What the hell?"

"You said to make ourselves at home," Chuck answered.

"Who is that?" Lasorda asked, pointing at Chuck's picture.

"That's Jimmy Sturr, the Polka King. He's the only celebrity I know." Lasorda bellowed with laughter.

During the pregame ceremonies, a host of Disney characters welcomed the crowd of 56,088. Los Angeles's all-city band performed the Canadian and American national anthems before the umpire's cry of "Play ball!"

Chuck faced his World Series opponent Earl Weaver of Baltimore in a fun game. His National League squad prevailed by a 4–2 score. Tanner reveled at managing future Hall of Fame members Johnny Bench, Mike Schmidt, Bruce Sutter, Steve Carlton, Gary Carter and Dave Winfield. The opposing American League team sported nine future Hall of Famers of its own. Chuck received an All-Star ring, which he wore with pride. In later years, his friend David "Fuzzy" Fazzone had difficulty remembering a single day when that ring wasn't on his finger.

The Pirates players loved their manager, and he loved them. Former catcher Manny Sanguillén called Chuck a "people person." His motivational intensity pushed those around him to leave nothing on the table. His magnetism drew the iron in his players to the forefront, instilling within them the need to win as a team. He told his players to go all out, all the time, just like he used to do when he was a major leaguer. Stargell summed up Chuck Tanner: "He was at the heart of our team's craziness. All of us respected and loved him dearly."[78] Tanner shut his eyes to the Pittsburgh party atmosphere and foolishness. He believed that baseball should be fun. He allowed his players a great deal of latitude as long as they produced results on the field.

Teke described his teammates as a "pack of exquisite agitators." Teke had immense respect for all of them. Regarding Sanguillén, he complimented him as a great hitter and fielder who weighed 219 pounds as a catcher on the squad. "He still weighs 219, but his legs don't work well." Today, Sanguillén runs Manny's BBQ at the stadium and can be readily found serving ribs during games.

Chuck captained a loose and crazy ship, steering it jauntily through the waves of competition but never permitting it to sink on his watch. He frequently joined in or initiated a good joke. As an example, Joe Lonnett enjoyed playing the lottery. Tony Bartirome and Tanner decided to have some fun with the coach. The trainer peaked over Joe's shoulder and copied all the numbers from his ticket. A little later, Tony said, "Chuck, I am going into the clubhouse and check my lottery ticket. I'll be back in ten minutes. Is that okay?"

"Sure," came back the answer. "Oh, yeah, let us know what numbers came up."

Bartirome returned and read off the exact numbers on Lonnett's ticket. The coach went crazy. "I won! I won!" As Tony and Chuck roared, Lonnett realized that his pals had tricked him.

"Okay, you got me," Lonnett admitted.

The media wrote that Chuck always appeared positive even when he shouldn't be, but Chuck disciplined his players when required. However, he rarely leaked problems to the press because he chose never to embarrass his teammates. Dewey Lutz, the manager at Spencer's Paint Store and a steady diner at Valentine's, said, "Chuck never discussed his individual players with the guys." He told the press, "Every kid on my team had a mother and father, and I didn't want them thinking something bad about their boys."[79] Only Bert Blyleven appeared as an exception to Chuck's no-comment rule.

"When you wake up, everybody has a problem. The way to do it is to assess the situation. How you handle the problem is the critical thing. I want to make every day the best day of my life. There's always something good out there. I wish more writers would take that approach. I believe the key to managing a baseball team is recognizing who your key people are. I lead, but people like Stargell, Parker, Tekulve and Madlock have more freedom. I let them know they were stars. The rest of the guys took their cues from them....That's the way I did it. It worked."[80]

When Chuck displayed his World Series ring to a sportswriter, he cautioned, "I learned a long time ago that the size of your funeral is going to depend on the weather so don't get too cocky." On another occasion, Chuck philosophized, "You handle horses. You communicate with people." He indeed represented the whole package.

Chuck's office at Three Rivers sat just around the corner from the mini lockers where the players kept their valuables during the game. As each player opened his locker to recoup his possessions, the Pittsburgh manager would spout a motivational or positive comment geared to that particular individual.

In New Castle, Chuck purchased a fixer-upper home directly across the street from his Maitland Lane location. Friend Chuck Farris repaired the roof and refused to take any money for his labor, explaining, "Chuck, you never asked a penny for the tickets, jackets, hats and baseballs you gave me. Let this be my treat?" Chuck eventually rented the house to Tony Bartirome, the Pirates trainer, for several months.

Chuck Farris with jackets given to him by Chuck Tanner. *Photo by author.*

"Chuck often took care of me for dinner when I went to Tanner's after he purchased the restaurant," Farris continued. "So, I picked up an evening's dinner for Babs and him at Troggio's Restaurant as a thank-you one night."

Many a morning Chuck could be found at Valentine's talking baseball and trash with his cronies. He also worked out and took a sauna at the YMCA on his free days. Wherever he was, locals gathered around him, and he always supplied a friendly and encouraging word.

At a meeting of his investment club at the Traveler's Inn, he talked the club into buying a company that made easy-breathing athletic uniforms. That company became a huge loser. His co-investors forgave him but looked askance at his future tips. None of the guys in the club made a fortune, but they had lots of fun.

Chuck's father aged noticeably after his wife Anna's death. As his body weakened, his sons recognized that he could no longer live alone. The three Tanner brothers situated him at the Overlook Nursing Home for better attention. Chuck visited him frequently and often brought baseball souvenirs as gifts for the staff.

In 1981, a June 12–July 31 player's strike shortened the season to just 113 games. A key issue involved free-agency compensation. Supposedly the animosity between the agent for the players, Marvin Miller, and the management negotiator, Ray Grebey, grew so severe that the two men refused to pose together once a settlement had been reached.

On August 31, the Pirates traded Phil Garner to Houston for the highly rated rookie second baseman Johnny Ray and pitcher Randy Niemann. The trade worked well for Pittsburgh. Although Ray played sparingly during 1981, he would earn the *Sporting News* Rookie of the Year Award in 1982. He also would lead the National League in doubles in both 1983 and 1984, while sporting a strong batting average. Niemann, a throw-in reliever, managed just a single win with the Pirates.

The Pirates suffered a disappointing 46-56-1 fourth-place finish in strike-shortened 1981. Madlock checked in with a .341 average and his third batting championship. Rookie catcher Tony Pena came through with a .300 batting average, but the hitting of Tim Foli, Dave Parker and Jason Thompson landed below expectations. Rick Rhoden led the pitching staff with a 9-4 record, and former Atlanta Braves righty Eddie Solomon sported an 8-6 record, his best year in the majors; injuries caused John Candelaria and Don Robinson's statistics to drop off the grid.

Most people fail to recognize the pressure a big-league manager faces. The mix of late nights, constant travel, changing time zones and stress played havoc with fifty-three-year-old Chuck's body. He took garlic pills to calm his heart. Teke joked that when he was on the mound and not pitching well, he tried to stay away from his manager to avoid the dreaded garlic breath and the viselike grip on his shoulder demanding his full attention.

Chuck possessed a giving soul, and he did whatever he could to help his players. "Matt the Skat" Alexander had served as an outstanding designated runner and base stealer during the past eight years, three of them spent with the Pirates. Matt had stolen more than one hundred bases and led the majors in base-running appearances. Like Hank Allen and Chuck at the end of his own playing career, Matt needed a few more games to earn a major-league pension. Chuck made sure Matt received the necessary time before assigning him to the AAA Mexican League to finish out his career.

When the season ended, Chuck continued to serve as a frequent speaker during various sports banquets. The fall and winter of 1981–82 proved no exception. On January 30, he lauded Laurel High coach George Miles and his WPIAL Class A football championship team at a dinner for 750 guests at the Harbor Community Center. Tanner's brief remarks ended with the hope that Coach Miles would receive the college offer he so richly deserved.

During spring training in 1982 at Bradenton, Chuck proceeded to give the identical speech he had given the last several years. John Candelaria and Kent Tekulve mouthed it word for word in the back of the room, but Chuck still had the ability to motivate, and Teke and Candy never joked about that.

In 1982, the team improved dramatically. Madlock batted .319, Pena .296 and Lee Lacy .312, with forty steals, and Jason Thompson, who batted a steady .284, pounded out 31 home runs and drove in 101 RBIs. Rookie of the Year Johnny Ray batted .281 with 30 doubles.

The team finished fourth in the league behind St. Louis with an 84-78 record, a large statistical improvement over the previous year. At the end of the season, Tanner rewarded recently retired pitcher Grant Jackson with a spot as his reliever pitching coach.

In 1983, the Pirates finished second in the league to the Phillies with an 84-78 record, identical to the prior year's totals. Madlock led the team with a .323 average, good enough to win his fourth and final batting championship. Mike Easler banged the ball at a .307 clip. Lee Lacy managed a .302 average. Catcher Tony Pena batted .301, and utility infielder Jim Morrison hit the ball for a .304 average, the top figure in his career.

First baseman Jason Thompson led the team with eighteen homers and seventy-six RBIs. John Candelaria and Larry McWilliams each rang up fifteen wins. Rick Rhoden and Lee Tunnell put up eleven apiece. All four starters had even or winning seasons. Teke provided seven wins and eighteen saves, but other than Cecilio Guante and Manny Sarmiento, most of the other relievers suffered off years. Free agent Dave Parker left the team at the end of the year for greener pastures in Cincinnati, but his offensive statistics had declined significantly over the past few years.

Dewey Lutz drove Chuck to several ball games during the '80s and received premium seats and a visit to the locker room as his reward. "I loved baseball and enjoyed listening to Chuck discuss why he had made one move or another." Dewey remembered him as "loyal to his friends, loyal to his coaches and loyal to his players."

Chuck discovered another reason for optimism in 1983. His youngest son, Bruce, after leaving Florida State, where he both pitched and caught, signed with the Chicago White Sox's Eastern League Glen Falls team. The following year, Bruce put up an excellent 12-4 record and 1.96 earned run average with Appleton in the Class A Midwest League. His strong performance gained him a trip to the majors the following year, where the six-foot-three

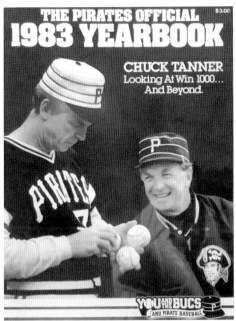

Left: 1983 Pirates yearbook. *Pittsburgh Pirates.*

Right: Bruce Tanner. *Collection of attorney Carmen Lamencusa.*

220-pound right-hander pitched in ten games with the Chicago White Sox in the big leagues.

At the end of the 1983 season, the Atlanta Braves released the injured pitcher Bob Walk, who asked his pitching coach John Sain for advice. The four-time, twenty-game winner for the Milwaukee Braves and top-notch talent spotter phoned Tanner with a tip: "Chuck, this kid Walk might help the Pirates. He's good, and you probably could pick him up for a song." Tanner listened carefully to his old Chicago White Sox pitching coach and telephoned Walk to offer him a shot.

Free agent Walk appreciated Sain and Tanner's helping hand, responding with several good years and huge popularity in Pittsburgh. The Pirates initially signed him to a minor-league contract, where he led the Pacific Coast League in earned run average and wins, gaining him a promotion back to the majors.

Chuck had told the team that that his door always remained open. "I am a player's coach. If I can help in any way, you always can come see me." Most importantly, he meant what he said.

Money proved especially tight for minor leaguers. Bob Walk required a deposit to obtain a mortgage in Pittsburgh and asked Chuck if he could speak to the brass to come up with an advance on his salary.

"How much do you need?" Chuck asked.

"I told him about $1,000," Walk recalled. "I assumed he would ask the front office, but he pulled out his check book, wrote a check and put it on the table. He said I could pay him back later when I had the money. I never forgot that kindness." Few managers would have leaned over so much for a player in need, but Chuck remembered his own minor-league tight-money days.

Chuck demonstrated a tough side when necessary. In a game against Cincinnati, Benny Distefano, no pushover himself and usually an outfielder, played first for Pittsburgh. He blocked the base with his leg when slick-fielding shortstop and speedster Dave Concepción took a big lead. The pitcher tossed the ball to first, and Distefano tagged the blocked runner for an out. An angry Concepción barked a threat that the first baseman would pay for that move. He would be fair game as target practice the next time he batted.

When the team returned to the dugout at the end of the inning, Chuck asked Benny what he and Concepción had been jawing about during what looked like a heated discussion. "Nothing, Skipper. He just said the Reds planned to throw at me when I come to bat." Chuck determined to protect his player. He ran onto the field and pointed at the Reds shortstop, "If you guys throw at my first baseman, our boys aren't coming for the pitcher. We are coming directly for you, Concepción." Needless to say, Tanner's threat squelched any thought of retribution.

Pitcher Walk mentioned that if Chuck required a pitcher's attention, he would grab that player in his viselike grip. Many a mound man winced when the manager dug his thumb into his shoulder to make sure he took in every word of Tanner's message.

Like a general on the battlefield, the Pirates manager employed his unique brand of strategy. He utilized pinch hitters, pinch runners and relievers with frequency. He parlayed the full arsenal of weapons at his disposal, including the occasional hunch. He did the same thing during practice sessions. Traditionally, starting pitchers took batting practice first. Chuck flipped the tradition on its head. He opened with the position starters batting and put the pitchers in the outfield. When Bob Walk questioned why, Chuck explained, "If the pitchers go first, the coaches end up shagging balls while the pitchers hang out in the clubhouse. This way all my players are working out for the entire practice."

In the spring of 1984, the Lawrence County Historical Society Sports Hall of Fame installed Chuck into its inaugural class, a signal honor. Chuck thanked his audience at a dinner: "I am really honored by what this town is saying to me. It was really a humbling factor when I found out I had been put in the same category as a Phil Brindenbaugh, Richie Allen and all the others."

Veteran *New Castle News* sportscaster Bob Vosburg added a special tribute to Tanner: "A good man leaves everyone he meets feeling a little better than they did before. He's a pleasure to be around, an inspiration in good times and a gift for all seasons."

Besides Chuck Tanner, the inaugural class included National Football League two-time All-Pro guard Darrell Dess, Wampum coach L. Butler Hennon, University of Pittsburgh All-American basketball guard Dr. Don Hennon, American Basketball Association basketball player and high school high-jumping record holder Walter Mangham, Pittsburgh Steeler defensive end and Washington Redskins coach Bill McPeak, Westminster College coach G. "Buzz" Riddle, Hall of Fame baseball player Lewis "Hack" Wilson (who still holds the major league RBI record of 191 set in 1930 with the Chicago Cubs), baseball All-Star Richard "Dick" Anthony Allen and legendary football coach Phil Bridenbaugh, winner of 265 games at New Castle High School.

The year 1984 also included its low points for Chuck. His seventy-five-year-old father died, and the Pirates sank to a last-place 75-87 record. Most of the heroes from the 1979 World Series winning team had aged out or departed. Second baseman Johnny Ray came through with a .312 average, his best ever with the Pirates, and he led the league with thirty-eight doubles. Lee Lacy batted .323 with seventy RBIs, but the team lacked power. Jason Thompson led the squad with just seventeen homers, and Jose Peña topped the team with only seventy-eight RBIs. In short, the Pirates failed to score runs even though the pitching proved strong. Rick Rhoden produced a 14-9 record, and John Candelaria, Larry McWilliams and John Tudor all finished with identical 12-11 winning records. However, the entire relief staff of Kent Tekulve, Don Robinson, Rod Scurry, Lee Tunnell and Cecilio Guante produced losing records and just thirty-four saves versus forty the previous year. Star hitter Bill Madlock slumped to a .253 average.

Although his Pirates had fallen on hard times and he missed his dad, Chuck felt special pride when his son Bruce pitched for the Chicago White Sox and won his major-league debut after being called up from the AAA Buffalo Bisons for a June 12, 1985 game against the Seattle Mariners at the Kingdome. In six and one-third innings, he gave up just two runs for a 6–3

1984 inaugural class of the Lawrence County Hall of Fame. *Lawrence County Historical Society.*

victory. Against Oakland in his second game at Comiskey Park, he yielded a single run in five and one-third innings, leaving the game with a 3–1 lead. Unfortunately, his relievers failed to hold the Oakland offense, and his effort resulted in a no-decision. Bruce spent his final games as a reliever. He would return to the minors in 1986 and pitched through 1989, retiring with a 37-32 minor league record. Bruce would spend several years as a minor-league pitching instructor and as a bullpen coach for the Pirates from 2001 to 2005. Since 2008, he has served as a Detroit Tigers scout.

During the 1983–84 season, the lackluster Pittsburgh Penguins hockey team finished dead last in their division with a 16-58-6 place finish—horrible news for the Steel City. However, the poor finish guaranteed them the first draft-choice selection, and they chose wisely. Mario Lemieux, later known to his fans as "Magic Mario" and "The Magnificent One," developed into one of the finest centers ever to skate on the ice. Big no. 66 would score 690 goals and bring home two Stanley Cups as a player and three more as a Penguins owner.

After a formal signing ceremony, the press and management accompanied Mario on a tour of the city, including a stop at Three Rivers Stadium. There, he met Chuck Tanner in the locker room. Although his English proved minimal, he asked Chuck if he could have a Pirates jersey. Chuck naturally agreed but requested through an interpreter a signed Mario Lemieux jersey in exchange. The two shook hands, and the trade was completed.

Several years later, Bruce Tanner and his friend Jeff Grossman were playing ping-pong at Chuck's Maitland Lane home. After the game, the guys talked about which sports star they would most want to meet. Jeff thought for a minute and announced Mario Lemieux, the man who had single-handedly saved Pittsburgh hockey and who later would deliver decades of winning seasons, both as a player and as an owner. Chuck overheard the conversation, went into another room and brought in a box. "Let me show you something special. Well, I don't have Mario here, but this is his jersey." Chuck then unwrapped the no. 66 Penguins jersey with Mario Lemieux's signature written across the front that he had received from Mario in trade. The presentation suitably impressed Jeff.

Tanner had produced six out of nine winning seasons with Pittsburgh, but in 1985, the team imploded. The magic from the 1979 "We Are Family" team had vanished. The Pirates opted to reduce high salaries and rebuild for the future.

Kent Tekulve had spent parts of twelve years with the Pirates, and his longevity gave him the ability to block a trade. He recognized that the team had aged, and Pittsburgh's minor-league system appeared poorly stocked. His 1985 season had started slowly with him only pitching in three games. To dump his high salary and declining statistics, the Pirates moved the thirty-eight-year-old Tekulve to the Phillies on April 20 in exchange for Al Holland, whose name had been connected with cocaine and who later would be called to testify at formal hearings concerning his use. On August 2, the team traded John Candelaria, Al Holland and George Hendrick to the California Angels for Pat Clements, Mike Brown and Bob Kipper. The Pirates lacked depth, breadth and youth.

Tanner's final year in Pittsburgh ended in shambles with a dismal 57-104 record. The manager had added Willie Stargell to his coaching staff to appease the unhappy fans. Only pitcher Rick Reuschel managed a winning 14-8 record, but with a sky-high 4.47 ERA. Pitcher José DeLeón suffered through a 2-19 won-loss record with a 4.70 ERA. The team ERA ballooned to 3.97 from 3.11 the prior year. The Pirates batting average slumped from .255 in 1984 to .247 with part-time center fielder Joe Orsulak topping the starters at a .300 level. Johnny Ray led the team with thirty-three doubles, seventy RBIs and sixty-seven runs scored. A team cannot win without hitting and pitching.

The fans grew restless and disappointed. Attendance figures for the year sunk from 1,646,757 in 1980, the year following the World Series victory, to just 735,900 in 1985, guaranteeing losses for the Pirates shareholders. To stem the bleeding, owner Dan Galbreath took bids for the debt-laden franchise. Rumor suggested that the team might relocate to Tampa, New Orleans or even Denver.

On an even more unfortunate note, the Federal Bureau of Investigation received a tip that drugs ran rampant throughout the Pirate clubhouse. The authorities began their questioning with pitcher Rod Scurry, who had spent a month in rehab the prior year after walking two batters on four pitches each and taking out his frustration by destroying a hotel room in a fit of paranoia. He admitted to using cocaine at least nineteen times. To cut a deal for himself, Scurry implicated other players in past and current use.

Dale Berra, another prime offender, revealed the names of key narcotic suppliers to the FBI in exchange for leniency. John Milner admitted to buying narcotics in a Three Rivers bathroom stall. Users Lee Lacy and Dave Parker provided evidence as well. All the Pirates received partial immunity from prosecution in exchange for their testimony against the dealers. Not one of the players using drugs lost a single game of playing time for their misadventures.

Rooker recalled his personal awareness of when drugs found their way to the Pirates locker room. As early as 1978, he witnessed guys with white power on their noses. He saw Dave Parker and John Milner go into an equipment room next to Tanner's office and snort cocaine. "I couldn't believe they'd do it right next to Tanner's office. They'd come out with stuff on their faces. In Chuck's defense, I really don't think he knew what was going on. Tanner always gave you credit for knowing your job, and he didn't bother you. It didn't make any sense. I think Dave Parker blew a Hall of Fame career."[81]

The Pittsburgh drug trials in September 1985 led to the conviction of seven men who sold narcotics to various team members. Pirates players Rod Scurry, Dale Berra, Lee Lacy, Lee Mazzilli, John Milner and Dave Parker appeared before a grand jury. Lacy testified to having cocaine delivered to him during the World Series. Scurry once left the stadium during a game to dig up some cocaine.

The investigation broadened from Pittsburgh throughout the major leagues to include star players like three-time twenty-game winner Vida Blue and former Most Valuable Player first baseman Keith Hernandez, a man who declared that he had difficulty remembering much of a full year in his life.

Tanner claimed to have little knowledge of the drug dealings, but user Dale Berra testified that Tanner had warned him to stay away from drug dealers. Teke stated that he had no idea fellow reliever Rod Scurry had a drug problem.

Several players implicated in the drug trials continued to suffer from their addictions. Rod Scurry would die from a cocaine-induced heart attack on November 5, 1992, in Reno, Nevada, at the age of thirty-six. Heavy-hitting first baseman Willie Mays Aikens received a sentence of up to twenty years in jail for selling fifty grams of crack cocaine to an undercover police officer in 1994. All-Star pitcher Lary Sorensen, following a sixth drunk-driving conviction, received a two-year sentence in 2005. Second baseman Alan Wiggins died in 1991 at the age of thirty-two after contracting HIV from intravenous drug use.

"It was a sad chapter for the game of baseball, a sad chapter for the city of Pittsburgh and the Pittsburgh organization," said former Pirates president Carl Barger.[82]

Baseball commissioner Peter Ueberroth handed down suspensions to eleven players on February 28, 1986, but reduced the punishment to drug testing, fines and community service in exchange for their cooperation in the investigation. The bulk of the penalties fell on the six men who procured the drugs for the players, none of whom happened to be hardened drug sellers. All of them sold or gave the drugs to the major leaguers to feel important, hang out with the players and for personal enjoyment. Dale Shiffman, a hero-worshiping freelance photographer and nickel-dime dealer seeking friendship from the players, obtained the coke. Kevin Koch, the Pittsburgh Parrot, delivered it. Philadelphia dealer Curtis Strong and six Pittsburgh men, including Dale Shiffman, received jail time.

The Pittsburgh Associates, a public-private partnership composed of local corporations including Alcoa, Westinghouse, PNC, Mellon and Carnegie-

Mellon University, among others, along with a handful of concerned citizens, stepped in to purchase the Pirates for $22 million, outbidding a rival consortium that included Chuck Tanner. Malcolm "Mac" Prine, the CEO of Ryan Homes and the newly elected Pirates president, announced his goal of finding a permanent owner who would keep the team in the city.

Within a week of the changeover, Prine took steps to change managers and clean house. The team fired Tanner following the horrendous losing season and the team's involvement in drugs. Tanner refused to offer excuses for his firing. He called the decision "mutual." "They didn't want me, and I didn't want them." He added, "I would have fired myself."[83] Jim Leyland took over for Chuck as manager. The Pirates also replaced Harding Peterson with Syd Thrift as general manager. Chicago White Sox manager Tony La Russa summarized the mercurial nature of working as a baseball manager or executive with two simple words of advice: "Always rent."

The losing season and the Pittsburgh trials presented a low point in Chuck Tanner's career. As a physical fitness adherent and manager who trusted his team, he undoubtedly had been unaware of the drug problem that permeated the Pirates during the season. He felt sad and betrayed, but he accepted the blame for a losing season and a loss of control. He was the manager, and as Harry Truman said, "The buck stops here."

Chuck ended his Pirates managerial career with 711 wins against 685 losses. Only Fred Clarke and Danny Murtaugh had racked up more Pirate victories. One secret of Chuck's success involved his love of people, and people loved him in return.

Chuck took his firing in stride and developed a close relationship with his successor, Jim Leyland, who said, "He gave me lots of advice about the city, the players and baseball in general. Later, when he managed Atlanta, we played against each other and became friendly competitors. Chuck had a wry sense of humor. Once he told me, 'I never made a bad decision. Some just didn't work out.'"

The debacle of 1985 would not end Chuck's managerial career in the majors. Within a few months, the Atlanta Braves would come knocking on Chuck Tanner's door, hoping that he possessed the magic to revive another zombie team.

CHAPTER 12

MANAGING ATLANTA, 1986–1987

Yesterday's home runs don't win today's games.
—Babe Ruth

There's no crying in baseball.
—A League of Their Own

The 1985 Atlanta Braves team lay in shambles. Owner Ted Turner fired manager Eddie Haas partway through the season after a disastrous 50-71 start and replaced him with interim manager Bobby Wine, who finished the year with an equally awful 16-25 record. Turner needed a new manager.

Chuck proved too good an option to remain unclaimed. Owner Ted Turner axed Wine and hired the former Pirate for the 1986 season, providing him with a rich $3 million three-year contract, making him the highest-paid manager in baseball. Turner also replaced General Manager John Mullen with former major-league third baseman and Toronto Blue Jays manager Bobby Cox.

The new manager looked forward to the challenge of rebuilding a 66-96 last-place team. He tempered his optimism by noting, "I don't think a manager should be judged by whether he wins the pennant, but whether he gets the most out of the twenty-five players on his team. One can only get so much out of the talent one has been given."

In 1986, the Lawrence County Sports Hall of Fame elected Chuck's close friend Fred Shaffer to its membership. Fred also joined the Braves organization as a special-assignment scout around the same time as Chuck, probably with a strong push from his New Castle crony. He remained with the Braves for several years and earned the major league's East Coast Scout of the Year Award in 1993. Many say that Chuck and Fred had been joined at the hip, two inseparable pals. Where one was found, the other usually would be nearby.

Shaffer possessed a natural talent for assessing talent. He had signed Grove City's Gary Peters, an eventual twenty-game winner, and Johnstown's Pete Vuckovich, who led the American League in win-loss percentage for 1981 and '82. He also inked Joe Carter, the 1985 American League RBI leader. After he watched young Ken Griffey Jr. play, his bosses asked what he thought. Fred advised, "Take a big checkbook with you. You're going to need it. He's that good."

Chuck made and kept friends wherever he went, whether it was Fred Shaffer, Jim Leyland, Phil Garner or so many of the men he had played with or managed. He kept in touch with many of them. Among his acquaintances, Chuck and his son Bruce maintained a special fondness for Dick Allen. Bruce described him as "extremely even tempered. I only saw him blow up one time. He was the Chicago White Sox minor league coordinator, and I pitched for the AA Buffalo team in 1985. During batting practice, the guys sputtered at the plate. Dick assumed that they were not trying hard enough. The forty-three-year-old ex–home run hitter grabbed a bat and pounded out line drive after line drive to show the players what they should be doing."

Chuck's leadership helped the Atlanta–Fulton County Stadium's "Bomb Squad" improve to a 72-89 record in 1986. Left fielder Ken Griffey Sr. hit for a solid .306 average, although injuries halved his playing time to only 292 at bats. Dale Murphy put up a good but not great year with a team-leading twenty-nine home runs, but the Atlanta pitching remained suspect. A team needed strong arms to win. Pitcher Rick Mahler led the team with fourteen wins but combined them with eighteen losses and a hefty 4.88 ERA. Zane Smith produced an 8-16 season, and only David Palmer put up a winning 11-10 record with a respectable 3.65 ERA. Overall, the team's ERA stood at the 3.97 level, far too high to generate a winning season without All-Star level bats. Further complicating the situation, the team's $17,940,286 payroll stood as the highest in both leagues, nosing out the second-place big-spending New York Yankees.

Once the baseball season ended and he returned to New Castle, Chuck agreed to a partnership in Egidio's Restaurant with Jim Vascetti. Former partner Norm Rigotti, happy to sell his half share of Egidio's, got together with Chuck's accountant, Tom "Bonesy" DeLorenzo, and established a price agreeable to both parties.

Vascetti grew ecstatic over the new arrangement. Rigotti had been a great partner and added skill in construction and operations, but Chuck provided a celebrity status guaranteed to attract customers. The three inked the final agreement in November 1986, and Chuck added a restaurateur designation to his résumé. As Jim anticipated, Chuck pulled in customers and served as a welcoming host. The new Tanner-Vascetti partnership promised to work well. Businessman Norm Rigotti turned to the other investments he controlled.

Chuck's hospitality to his friends and fans at the stadium proved amazing. Western Pennsylvania residents Jack and Carol Benninghoff had moved to the Atlanta area in 1977. He and his wife drove New Castle guests, teacher Ron Oleskyski and his wife, Susan, on a tour of the city in 1987. As they approached Fulton County Stadium, Jack asked Ron if he might like to visit Chuck. "Sure," Ron answered. He had taught Chuck's sons at Neshannock High School, and the idea sounded fun.

The two couples drove to the stadium entry, where a guard promptly stopped them. Jack explained that they knew Chuck and wanted to visit him. After some further explaining, the guard allowed them to pass. Since they only planned to stay a few minutes, Jack parked in owner Ted Turner's private space. When a female employee told them to move, Jack told her that they only wanted to say hello and would be gone in ten or fifteen minutes. The woman agreed to allow them to stay. As they made their way toward the locker room area, trainer Tony Bartirome blocked their path and announced, "Hey, you can't go in the locker room." After they explained that they knew Chuck, Tony agreed to go to the locker room and check if Chuck wanted to see them.

Within minutes, the Atlanta manager appeared. Even though he had a game about to start, he gave his guests his usual warm welcome because that is the kind of man he was. "Of course, you probably would like some tickets to the game?" Chuck asked. Ron blurted, "Thanks, Chuck, but we have plans to go to the Stone Mountain laser light show." After a courteous farewell, the group departed, still to this day regretting their refusal to accept what probably would have been some of the best seats in the house.

The Braves dropped to a dismal 66-92 record in 1987 due to a talent gap. The offense put up strong numbers. Dale Murphy smacked forty-four home runs and drove in 105 RBIs. Ken Griffey Sr. batted .286, Dion James hit .312 and substitute outfielder Albert Hall produced a .284 average. Even catcher Ozzie Virgil hit a career-high twenty-seven home runs.

However, the pitching proved pathetic. Zane Smith started thirty-six games and produced a 15-10 record but with a 4.09 ERA. The entire staff accumulated a horrendous 4.63 ERA. Starters Rick Mahler, David Palmer and Doyle Alexander combined for a 21-34 record with an ERA north of 4.70. The relief staff performed equally poorly. Closer Jim Acker's 4-9 record and 4.16 ERA landed him toward the bottom of the National League. Bobby Cox, the general manager, placed the blame on poor field management. Quite frankly, Chuck lacked the horses to bring home a winner.

On May 22, 1988, the Braves beat Pittsburgh 6–4 but found themselves eleven and a half games behind league leader Houston. With a 12-27 record, Cox axed Chuck along with coaches Willie Stargell, Bob Skinner, Al Monchak and trainer Tony Bartirome during a painful three-hour meeting at the team hotel on May 23.

"This is the first time I've ever been fired in my life during the middle of a season," a stunned Tanner told the press. "We were improving. We had a lot of young players on this team." He was in the third year of an extended five-year contract. His replacement, Russ Nixon, manager for the AA Southern League Greenville team, took the high road and reported to the press, "Chuck had them playing hard. He is a great guy and had a tough day yesterday. Knowing Chuck, he'll land on his feet."

Chuck felt that Cox treated him unfairly, even though his 153-208 losing record signaled the need for a change at the top. "It's tough to win without top-level pitching," Tanner explained. The Braves arms proved subpar. Chuck believed that Cox and Turner had sabotaged him. The dismissal ended his major-league managerial career at 1,352 wins, twentieth on the all-time list. He had spent the last nineteen seasons of his career as a manager in the bigs, the longest term at that time among active skippers.

Once he took the time to reconsider his abrupt ending with the Braves, he told a friend, "Well, it's not so terrible when I pick up my $33,000 check on my way to the golf course."

Chuck indeed had acted as Mr. Sunshine throughout his years in baseball. Although he considered his firing a "raw deal," he sucked up his pride and accepted things as they were. Chuck spotted the best in even the worst of circumstances. His contract guaranteed him more than enough money, and

Babs and Chuck. *Bruce Tanner.*

he realized that he would find work in the industry. He summarized the ups and downs of baseball with his usual positivity: "The greatest feeling in the world is to win a major-league baseball game. The second greatest feeling is to lose a major-league baseball game."[84]

"I've been in baseball for forty-seven years. My wife, Barbara, made it possible. I never cooked a meal for the kids. I went away for six years as a manager in the minors. We didn't have any money. She told me, 'I'll take care of the kids. You want to be a manager, go ahead.'"[85] Chuck recognized that a new time in his life had arrived, but he would come out on his feet with his numerous connections throughout the baseball world.

Throughout his career, Chuck had maintained a friendship with Milwaukee Brewers owner and president Allan Huber "Bud" Selig. The relationship payed dividends when Selig offered him a job as a major-league scout.

When the *New Castle News* interviewed the fifty-nine-year-old ex-manager following his firing, he explained, "I've been busy. It's hard for me to believe so much time has passed." The restaurant Egidio's, which he co-owned with Jim Vascetti; his scouting duties with Milwaukee; and a growing interest in race horses occupied his time. Chuck's one-time boss, John Galbreath, a champion horse breeder and the majority owner of the Pittsburgh Pirates, had piqued his interest in raising and training race horses several years ago, and now he owned a few quality prospects. Life continued to be good to him. He had lots of possibilities and a full schedule ahead of him.

CHAPTER 13

THE REST OF THE STORY

A true hero is a hero forever.
—Michelle Gish

I must be the luckiest man in the world ever to wear a baseball uniform. Here I am a native of the Greater Pittsburgh area, who had an opportunity to become a major-league baseball player, but also who enjoyed the satisfaction of serving as manager of the Pittsburgh Pirates, a team I followed ever since I was a boy growing up in New Castle. As a big bonus, I had the opportunity to bring back to my hometown a World Series championship in 1979.
—Chuck Tanner[86]

With his managing career behind him, Chuck concentrated much of his interest on horses. He first caught the racing bug when he and Hall of Fame pitcher Jim Kaat put up a few thousand dollars to purchase a small claims horse named Pork Filet. Chuck encouraged his friend, Boston Red Sox manager Don Zimmer, to bet on the nag, and each time he lost. "The one time I didn't bet on the horse, Pork Filet won and paid 28-1 odds," Zimmer carped.

In 1988, Tanner became the controlling partner in a two-year-old colt, foaled on February 28, 1986, named Majesty's Imp, one of three horses he housed in Lexington, Kentucky, and at the Fairgrounds in Louisiana.

As a Pirate, Chuck earned about $150,000 in salary, but he took many bonuses and raises in breeding rights from the Galbreath family's Darby

Dan Farm's stable of Thoroughbred horses. Majesty's Imp came from racing royalty—namely D.J.'s Imp and Stonewalk, the winner of fourteen races and more than $500,000 in purses.

"I want to be the first person to win a World Series and the Kentucky Derby," Chuck told a reporter with his usual confidence. Ex-pitcher Rick Rhoden, ex-outfielder Bob Skinner, attorney Carmen Lamencusa and friends James Vascetti, Sandy Petruso, Dr. Ray Travaglini and Dr. Frank Raynak also bought into a piece of the action. In its first year, the horse started with a strong record, producing one win and one place in three races. The following year, Majesty's Imp collected two wins, one place and two shows in seven races, a promise of future financial success. The horse had opened its second season by earning $60,406, with several key races yet to follow.

In fact, Majesty's Imp had qualified to race at the Kentucky Derby, a huge step forward. In May 1989, Tanner received some unfortunate news. An "X-ray found bone chips in the horse's knee, which would incapacitate the steed from competition at the Derby," as reported in a *Los Angeles Times* article.

"We're going to put him on a van and take him to Keeneland in Lexington, Kentucky, to do arthroscopic surgery on the knee.…We have to do what's best for the horse," Tanner advised the press.[87]

Majesty's Imp recovered from the surgery and produced his best year in 1990 with three wins, three places and two shows in sixteen races to earn $148,477. In 1991, the horse produced two more wins in five starts and $44,054 in prize money at the Fairgrounds in New Orleans during the Louisiana and the Diplomat Way Handicaps.

Unfortunately, the horse crashed into a railing in Kentucky, severely injuring himself. Following a full physical recovery, Majesty's Imp lost his competitive edge and dropped his interest in running. The horse's final appearance on the track ended on March 16, 1991, in a disappointing fourth-place finish at the Tampa Bay track in Oldsmar, Florida, during the Sunshine Budweiser Breeder's Cup.

All in all, Majesty's Imp produced $260,056 in career earnings with eight wins, five places and four shows in thirty-one starts. The investors failed to recover anything in the way of profits. Horse racing proved an expensive luxury. Trainer Sturges J. Ducoing (a pro who had earned more than $15 million in lifetime purse money), top professionals like jockey Ricardo Lopez (a winner of 2,500 races), bales of hay, buckets of oats and boarding fees at the Batarasan Stables proved a costly enterprise.

Even though Majesty's Imp delivered major victories at the Diplomat Way Handicap in New Orleans, the Morton City Handicap in Detroit and the 1 1/16-mile Budweiser Breeders Cup in Tampa Bay, the horse failed to produce dividends for its own owners. Restaurant partner Egidio James Vascetti had invested $16,000 for a share in the horse. The ninety-six-year-old retiree stated, "I never saw a dime from that animal, but we had lots of fun on our trips to Kentucky. On one occasion, I took my twenty-one-year-old granddaughter to the track. We stayed in a motel along with several other investors from places like Meadville and Youngstown."

Chuck ended up with eight horses, but only Majesty's Imp proved a winner. Stud fees paid for most of the costs, but the racing bug proved a costly hobby.

Chuck still received a big salary from the Atlanta Braves under his contract through 1991. "To be honest," he told a reporter, "the only thing I have cooking right now is the food at Egidio's. Baseball's been good to me and life in general. I feel like no matter what happens from here on out, my life is complete."

Chuck continued to be in demand as a keynote speaker for local groups. His folksy style, upbeat personality and keen sense of timing made his sports stories a hit with every audience. Kids lined up in droves following his speeches to get an autograph at events such as the North Hill Boosters All-Sports Banquet.

May 1989 proved a rough month for Chuck. Not only had Majesty's Imp been scratched from the Kentucky Derby due to bone chips, but on Saturday, May 6, around 8:30 in the evening, more ill luck followed. A fire spread through a basement storage room, enveloping the entire lower floor of Egidio's Restaurant. The smoke forced nearly 150 staff members and dining patrons to evacuate the building as the fire department doused the flames. Authorities estimated the loss at $750,000. Chuck vowed to rebuild.

The restaurant reopened as Tanner's in October with a renovated kitchen and an enlarged seating area. Vascetti converted the motel behind the restaurant into a professional building for small offices and stores called Egidio's II.

With the restaurant back in business, hungry locals, friends and fans received a warm smile, a firm handshake and even an autograph from Chuck at the newly updated Wilmington Road establishment. "If people come in to see me, they can usually find me."

Shortly after the fire, Tanner and Vascetti mutually decided to end their partnership, and Chuck took over as the sole owner. Vascetti moved on

Tanner's Restaurant. *Photo by Michele Perelman.*

to the Villa in Shenango Township. Chuck and his family managed the rebranded Tanner's Restaurant, the name by which it still is known today. Chuck generally could be found seated on the second stool in the bar on the left-hand side when in town, either welcoming customers or "discussing" baseball strategy with his friends. Pictures of local athletes lined the walls, enhancing the hometown-sports feel of the restaurant.

Players and managers from Chuck's past periodically dropped in to Tanner's to visit, sometimes with a question or maybe a favor to ask, but usually just to gab about sports. John Candelaria remembered stopping into Tanner's Restaurant for a chat about baseball and just to say hello, but he made it a point to complete the trip with a couple of New Castle's famous Coney Island chili dogs. Candelaria admitted, "I never had the disposition to coach or manage. Chuck possessed that unique ability to handle twenty-five different personalities and make them better men than they had been before they had met him."

Chuck worked for General Manager Sal Bando of Milwaukee as a professional scout. Former Pirate player "Scrap-Iron" Phil Garner had replaced Tom Trebelhorn as the team manager following the 1991 season. Continuing in baseball with men he enjoyed, Chuck felt like he belonged.

Bando called Chuck "the most positive person I've ever seen. He was my mentor and friend."

Phil Garner had played for managers Tommy Lasorda and Bill Virdon during his major-league career. "You learn from all of them. Virdon, my manager at Houston, had been very quiet, but after being fired, he told me, 'I always appreciated the way you played.'" Garner added, "But Chuck was special."

When newly hired manager Garner asked Chuck for advice, Chuck counseled him to stock up on pitching. "And after you get pitching, get more pitching." He emphasized the importance of a strong relief staff. He explained his reasoning: "Starters were only openers, and you need strong arms to finish the game."

Sal Bando invited Chuck into the locker room to pump up the team prior to the opening of the season as only he could do. Chuck spent eleven years with the Milwaukee organization followed by five with Cleveland, where he frequently wore a Pirates cap while scouting for the Indians.

Phil Garner summed up Chuck's great attitude: "He never had a day he didn't like. He taught me the importance of uplifting the team. When I played for him and missed a sign, he would call me out, but I considered this a badge of honor, since he knew I would just play harder.…You know, he traded for me when I was in Oakland, and that made me feel good. The umpire never said, 'Work ball!' He always started the game with 'Play ball!' Chuck loved his job and the game."

In 1992, Chuck's son Bruce worked as a pitching coach for San Diego's Class A South Carolina farm club, the Charleston Rainbows of the South Atlantic League. Chuck had come to Charleston, West Virginia, to visit his son and scout the talent. As he sat in the stadium talking to Bruce, manager Dave Trembley approached and asked Chuck if he would mind giving a pep talk in the locker room to his players. Chuck agreed to speak.

During his ten-minute speech, all twenty-five players listened intently as he talked about the importance of positivity. "Never give up. When things appear the most difficult, that is the chance for you to work the hardest—to demonstrate your inner strength. I started like you in A ball, and it wasn't always easy, but you have a great opportunity here. Take advantage of it, and most of all, dream big! Only you can make it happen. You wouldn't be here if you didn't have a chance to get to the bigs."

The nineteen- and twenty-year-olds clapped after the talk. The message resonated with the players, but even more so with manager Trembley. "Chuck also motivated me to keep plugging away. I had labored for thirteen years as a high school, small college and minor-league manager. I would remain stuck in the minors until I was fifty-five-years-old, but I took Chuck's message personally, as if he were talking only to me. I refused to quit until I got to where I wanted to be."

Trembley had worked hard and earned three Minor League Manager of the Year awards. Like Chuck, he persevered. He refused to remain buried in the minor leagues. After managing nearly three thousand games, his tenacity and resolve eventually won him the job as the manager of the Baltimore Orioles. In 2007, his dream job at last came true, and Trembley believed that Tanner's message played an important part in sustaining his "never give up" attitude. Players Joey Hamilton, Homer Bush, Bryce Florie, Charlie Greene and Rich Loiselle from that 1992 Charleston Rainbows team also dreamed big and eventually earned a spot in the major leagues, pretty good statistics for a Class A team.

Another honor came to Chuck in 1993. The Western Chapter of the Pennsylvania Sports Hall of Fame elected him to membership along with Steelers halfback Dick Hoak and sports personality Myron Cope among its class of twelve.

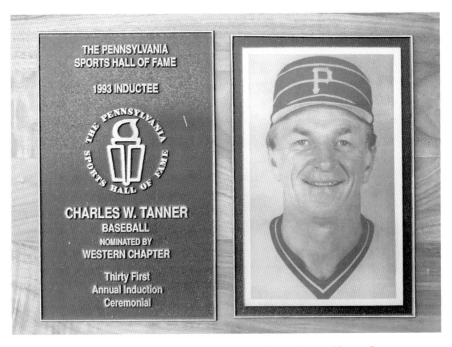

Chuck Tanner, inductee into the Pennsylvania Sports Hall of Fame. *Tanner's Restaurant.*

In New Castle, the restaurant required much of Chuck's time and effort while providing minimal financial rewards. Chuck considered selling. "Gus" Papazekos, who owned a small eatery on Washington Street in downtown New Castle, learned through the grapevine that Chuck might be open to a deal. From their first meeting, Chuck liked Gus and recognized that he would be the right man to take care of the restaurant with his name on it. Gus agreed to run the restaurant as an owner/operator/cook, and Chuck recognized that this was exactly what Tanner's required. "I know I could have gotten more money, but I wanted Gus to have it. I know it will be in good hands," he confided to his spiritual adviser Reverend John Yergan.

Gus and Chuck shook hands and reached an agreement after a minimum of discussion, and the final sale went without the slightest hitch. Gus closed his downtown location and relocated to Wilmington Road in January 1996. Although Gus lacked all the ready funds required, the two men set up a mutually acceptable payment plan. What began as a business arrangement quickly turned into a close personal friendship.

With his name still on the sign, Chuck wanted Gus to succeed. He continued to sit at the counter in his usual seat to greet friends and fans as they entered the restaurant just as he had done prior to the sale. The Tanner family dined at the restaurant quite frequently, and Babs developed a special fondness for Gus's Chicken Française. Gus expanded the menu from primarily Italian specialties by adding a selection of typical Mediterranean and comfort food items. Anyone ordering Gus's Greek Omelet for breakfast knew they were in for a treat.

The new owner admired Chuck's down-to-earth kindness. Gus described one especially busy Christmas Eve: "We were jammed. Chuck asked if he could help, and he did. He seated people and even bussed tables. That's the kind of friend Chuck was."

"During a sold-out New York Mets game at Three Rivers, Chuck spotted me, my cousin and two nephews in the crowd," Gus continued. "He waved to us and called out, 'Hey Gus, you and your crew, come over here.' The four of us enjoyed the rest of the game sitting in the VIP enclosed area."

Chuck considered Tanner's Restaurant as his New Castle home field, especially after the closing of Valentine's during the late 1980s. A crowd of Chuck's pals gathered every Wednesday morning at eight to reminisce over old times and share baseball tall tales. Sometimes as many as thirty or thirty-five ex-jocks and sports aficionados showed up to discuss sports. Over the years, the group dwindled as its members passed on or moved until only Bob Jackson, Lew Grell, Mike Saginak and Louis Carkitto remained as the final four attendees. They also aged out or died, ending the breakfasts.

When given a few free hours, Chuck and his pal Dr. Frank Raynak might be found on the Greenville Country Club golf course, where both belonged. Professional golfer Harry Toscano described Chuck's style of play as aggressive. "He never played half way. You could count on him almost never laying up to go the safe route. With Chuck, it was all or none. He was a decent golfer—shot in the low eighties most of the time, occasionally in the high seventies, but he hit the ball a long way, but where it went could be a question."

With his four boys now adults and with children of their own, Babs and Chuck found themselves with eleven grandchildren, and they enjoyed spending time with them. Holidays in the Tanner home at 34 East Maitland proved a hoot. "Lots of love," grandson Mat remembered, "but we were a noisy crew. The house filled with uncles, aunts and cousins. There was high volume intensity, but our family liked being together. Some of us played board games, others watched football on television or just talked. We enjoyed being a family and spending time together."

Mat continued, "Gus usually catered a turkey for Thanksgiving and a ham for Christmas at the house. Grandma Babs used an extra stove in the basement to heat up the food, and we all sat around a giant table with a plastic tablecloth. I still can see the red corduroy couch and chair in the basement."

Chuck loved those rowdy family gatherings. As he leaned back in his chair, he closed his eyes for a moment to thank the Almighty for the joyous holiday season and the gifts baseball had bestowed on him. Grateful for his past successes, he felt a tinge of regret ooze through his veins for all the weeks he had spent away from home as a player and minor-league manager. He had sacrificed time with his wife and sons in order to further his own career and those of the players he mentored. His success on the field had come at a high cost. He had missed much of the pleasure in watching his four children grow from toddlers to boys and then into men. He rued his absence from the Maitland Lane dinner table over the years and the athletic events of his sons that he failed to attend. Now, senior-citizen status allowed him more time to enjoy his children, grandchildren and, most of all, his beloved wife, Babs. That provided a wonderful plus for him.

In 1995, the Pittsburgh ball club presented Chuck with the Pride of the Pirates Award. Upon accepting the honor, he stood and thanked those present. "I played for the Braves, Cubs, Indians and Angels, but this is my home—my backyard. Once a Pirate, always a Pirate....I'm proud of the fact that we were able to accomplish the top of the mountain while I was here.…I hope it goes that way again."[88]

Chuck remained as celebrity number one in New Castle. Police arrested Rodney King during a visit to Lawrence County for allegedly driving while intoxicated in May 1995. King previously had won a $3.8 million judgement against the City of Los Angeles after four white policemen beat him unmercifully, bringing him immediate name recognition and notoriety. Tanner's attorney, Carmen Lamencusa, represented King against the charge. When the press clamored around Carmen for a statement, one reporter asked, "How do you feel about defending a celebrity?" Without skipping a beat, attorney Lamencusa shot back, "Do you mean Chuck Tanner?" King later would be acquitted in a jury trial.

Prior to a July game against the Houston Astros at Three Rivers, Chuck told writer Jim O'Brien, "I could work in baseball another fifty years, and I couldn't pay back what I've gotten out of it." He recognized how lucky he had been to play and manage for more than half a century.

Grandson Mat Tanner described his trips to Bradenton during his student years. "I drove with the family for three weeks of spring training. The teachers gave us our homework, which I did, but I had lots of fun in Florida. I lacked the interest to play baseball like Chuck, my father and my younger twin brothers, Trent and Jordan. Instead, I ran cross country and enjoyed art. Chuck didn't care as long as I worked hard at whatever I was doing, and Grandma Babs bought me paints and art supplies."

On February 17, 1998, Babs Tanner suffered a massive heart attack, stroke and two separate falls while in Bradenton. She underwent surgery for a quadruple bypass and a pacemaker. Mat remembered his shock at visiting his grandmother at Sarasota Memorial Hospital, where he saw her rigged with wires and tubes. "I was twelve and never had encountered a critically ill person, much less a close family member."

Although Babs never fully recovered and her body declined, her mind remained sharp. Chuck tended to her every need as she struggled to recuperate. He took a leave of absence from his scouting duties and stayed close to her side, returning the love and support she had provided him during their forty-eight years of marriage. Babs told a solicitous reporter, "Chuck is a good man, and I am lucky to have him."

Therapists treated Babs at home, while her husband rarely left her. He drove her to the Jameson Care Center for rehab appointments. One specialist described her as "an excellent patient who remained upbeat throughout difficult times."

Bab continued rehab treatments, but her body refused to cooperate. She needed assistance with everything, and that helplessness became difficult for her to accept. Her loss of dignity frustrated her to the core. She hated being a burden, and she struggled with the reality of declining health. Nonetheless, she rarely complained. Daughter-in-law Kimberly, Bruce's wife, and other family members tended to her when Chuck was unavailable. Mat recalled his grandmother "as a witty lady, and I adored her. We all did."

Babs's frail health plummeted after she fell to her knees and landed on her back, tearing the muscles and ligaments in her legs, further aggravating her handicap. Although Chuck and the entire Tanner brood provided her with amazing care, she suffered through intolerable pain on a daily basis.

Baseball executive Jack Zduriencik never golfed with his friend Chuck. "Once, I played in a foursome behind him, but never together. I asked him if he would like to play, and he told me, 'Jack, I really don't golf anymore. For all the years that I played and managed, Babs raised our four boys and took care of the house. It wouldn't be fair to leave her alone when she needs me. I may go to the Pittsburgh games in the evenings, but I have to sit with Babs during the day.'"

Even during the most difficult of times, Chuck held on to his marvelous sense of humor. Perennial All-Star Jim Fregosi had held down the shortstop position for the California Angels for the decade of 1961–71, ending a long and illustrious career in 1977–78 as a utility infielder with the Tanner-led Pirates. Chuck had played a few games with the Angels in the twilight of his own career in 1961–62 with at best mediocre results. Chuck wore no. 11 on his Angels uniform, but Fregosi switched from no. 16 to 11 after the team bounced Chuck to the minors. In 1998, the Angels retired Fregosi's no. 11, a signal honor. When Chuck ran into his former teammate, the two shook hands. Chuck grinned and joked, "I guess it's about time they retired our number."

With the twentieth anniversary of the 1979 World Series victory approaching, *New Castle News* reporter Kayleen Cubbal asked Chuck if he ever heard from the fans. He lifted a stack of autograph requests from the top of the refrigerator. "These came today." He laid them on the kitchen table. There appeared to be about thirty letters. Chuck modestly added, "I don't get this many every day."

"And he answers every one of them," Babs piped up to the reporter. "Sometimes I see the light burning at two o'clock in the morning, and I ask him what he's doing, and I realize he's answering mail."

Chuck served as the commissioner for a fantasy camp in Bradenton in 1999. Ten members of the World Series–winning 1979 Pirates team joined their old manager. On one rainy day, the group found themselves in the clubhouse. Fifty-two-year-old Kent Tekulve looked around and remarked, "Chuck, look at this. Twenty years have passed and not one thing has changed. You had these same guys playing cards and those guys over there yelling at each other."[89]

Dr. Lou Zona, the director of the Butler Art Museum in Youngstown, Ohio, and an ardent baseball fan, attended fantasy camp in Florida, one of his fondest memories although a painful one. A rogue fastball thrown by a camper struck Lou on the hand. The umpire shouted, "Take your base." The batter grimaced in pain but took his base like a trooper. Ex-Pirate Dave Giusti, who manned first, shook his head in sympathy.

"Bet that hurts."

"Sure does," Lou answered. He had broken his hand, eliminating him from further playing time.

Chuck tried to make a kind comment about each player's strengths. Lou remembered Chuck's observation after watching him toil on the field. "Lou, you do a wonderful job carrying that glove." Both had a good laugh, and despite his injury, Lou treasured his week at fantasy camp. Teke recalled a surgeon attending for several years, risking his hands and his livelihood all for the love of the game.

Chuck appreciated and enjoyed his opportunity to act as a professional scout for Milwaukee, where he worked directly under Sal Bando, the general manager. When the team hired fellow New Castle native Jack Zduriencik as the head amateur scout, Chuck greeted him warmly with a "Hi, boss," even though Jack technically was not his boss.

During the 2001 winter meetings at the Embassy Suites in Phoenix, scouts Chuck Tanner, Harold "Hank" Allen and Jack Zduriencik sat in the lobby around a fire at the end of the day sipping a drink or two and swapping war stories about Western Pennsylvania athletics. All three men had starred in high school sports—Chuck at Shenango, Hank at Wampum and Jack at New Castle. Jack, a former minor-league second baseman who had played on his 1967 high school WPIAL championship football team, joked, "What do Terry Hanratty, Joe Namath, Joe Montana and Jack Zduriencik all have in common?" No one hazarded a guess. "They were all famous Western Pennsylvania quarterbacks." Chuck and Hank roared with laughter, kicking off a talkfest.

The younger scouts gathered around the veterans as they rehashed their accomplishments from bygone days. Chuck touted his football days and strength routine. Hank, an All-State basketball player, told how his legendary coach Butler Hennon made his players practice for games in clodhoppers rather than tennis shoes. One younger guy seemed totally confused and blurted out, "What the heck is a clodhopper?" The older scouts roared, and the stories continued until late in the evening.

April 9, 2001, proved a sad day for Pittsburgh and Chuck Tanner. Sixty-one-year-old Willie Stargell, who had suffered from kidney problems, died from complications of a stroke in Wilmington, Delaware. "Pops" Stargell, the "Captain," had earned a place in the Hall of Fame in 1988, his first year of eligibility. Chuck considered him an outstanding human being and one of the most talented players he had ever managed. Forty-four-year-old Don Robinson, who ran an instructional facility in Bradenton, could recall the need for very few formal team meetings when Chuck managed in Pittsburgh. "Willie took care of almost everything himself."

Chuck's youngest son, Bruce, recalled, "Some of my best times with Chuck came when I coached the bullpen for Pittsburgh, and he scouted for Milwaukee after his managing days had ended. The older I got, the smarter he became. He always kept notes, and he knew more about strategy than anyone I knew."

Shortly after grandson Mat received his driver's license, his parents allowed him to drive to the ballpark, but his mother told him to check in with his dad to notify him that he had arrived safely. "Well I arrived during the second inning, dad was in the bullpen. As I tried to cross the bridge that security closed during active innings to reach dad, a guard stopped me cold in my tracks. I told him my dad was a Pirates coach, and I needed to speak to him, but the guard didn't believe me. Since I was more afraid of disobeying my parents than the guard, I zipped past him and called out to my dad, 'Hey, Bruce,' although I always called him Dad at home. He looked up at me with that what's-going-on look, but everything worked out okay."

Mat continued, "Later, I saw Chuck sitting in the front row. He always wanted us to call him Chuck instead of Grandpa. You could spot him one hundred yards away in his bucket hat and with a noticeable gold tooth. He was keeping notes, but looked up at me and smiled. He asked if I wanted a hot dog or a coke. Since he appeared preoccupied in his work, I thanked him and declined the offer, and he told me to enjoy the game."

Former East Maitland Lane resident Dan DeFerio, the manager of the local downtown Pizza Hut, remembered Chuck as a down-to-earth neighbor. "Always a smile, liked a cigar once in a while and even an occasional vodka. He always looked you in the eye and made you feel important. He lit up the room when he walked through the door. From time to time, he visited us on our deck to be friendly. He was a great guy to have next door."

Dan remembered an accident on Maitland, a busy thoroughfare. "Chuck appeared like Johnny on the spot, taking charge, making sure everyone was okay, calming frayed nerves and suggesting the damaged car be taken to McConnells on Wilmington Road for repair." When Dan's son visited Bradenton on spring break while attending Ohio State, "Chuck brought him on the field to meet the players, something my boy always remembered and appreciated."

Shortly after Mark Shapiro became president of the Cleveland Indians in 2001, he offered Chuck a job as a scout. Although Chuck liked his time with Milwaukee, the lure of the 102-mile proximity to New Castle made the offer irresistible. However, Cleveland scout Tanner often could be found in a Pittsburgh ball cap as a reminder of his past association with his beloved Pirates.

Chuck remained a physical specimen as he aged. During a routine checkup at the clinic, his doctor told him he had the body of a fifty-year-old. Unfortunately, tests also discovered prostate cancer. He received treatments at Shadyside Hospital in Pittsburgh. The doctors told him that a full recovery rate ran north of 90 percent. Luckily for Chuck, the forty radiation treatments proved effective. The doctors credited Chuck's upbeat attitude and physical fitness as critical to his cure.

Pittsburgh sportscasters frequently called on Chuck for a comment or two on some current controversy, and his opinion sometimes added fire to the ruckus. When the 2002 All-Star Game at Miller Park in Milwaukee ended in the eleventh with a 7–7 tie after the opposing managers opted to save the wear and tear on the players rather than go more innings, Chuck expressed his dissatisfaction with the decision.

"Not one person thought a tie was a good idea. It took something away from the game….I don't like a tie. In baseball you play until someone wins. I would have kept playing," Tanner explained. "In 1980, when I managed the National League team I kept Kent Tekulve and Jose Cruz on the bench in case the game went to extra innings."

American League manager Joe Torre and National Leaguer Bob Brenly naturally disagreed with Chuck. They opted to allow as many players as possible in the game and not overwork any of the pitchers in what they termed "just an exhibition." Their strategy allowed everyone to play but risked the chance of an extra-inning tie, which was exactly what happened.

Jim Leyland became a St. Louis Cardinals special scout in 1999, tasked with reviewing talent playing in Cleveland's Jacobs Field and Pittsburgh's Three Rivers Stadium.[90] He frequently sat with Chuck, and the two men, already cordial colleagues, quickly bonded into even closer pals. Leyland described Chuck as "a softy with a stern exterior. He never met a stranger. Everyone was his friend, and he always maintained an 'everything-will-be-okay' attitude."

In 2004, reliever Jose Mesa produced an unbelievable season with Pittsburgh racking up forty-three saves. "He became as close to unbeatable as any pitcher in the league. When Mesa came into the game in the ninth at PNC, Chuck and I knew the game was over for all practical purposes, and we would leave. Whenever anyone asked how scouts could skip out before the final out, we always answered, 'We're on a pitch count.' Then, we walked away to avoid additional questions," Leyland explained.

On July 31, 2004, at 11:30 a.m., seventy-six-year-old Chuck Tanner received a significant honor. A year earlier, Mike Banko, Mike DeRosa and Frank Augustine had formed a committee to rename the Shenango High School ball field after Chuck Tanner. A group approached Superintendent Dr. Larry Connelly, who approved of the idea and volunteered to act as treasurer for the project.[91] The executive committee added Bill Brown, a baseball enthusiast, as secretary. Bill remembered a visit to Chuck's Maitland Lane home, where his host showed him his collection of trophies and offered him a Chuck Tanner bobble head and a signed ball. "His generosity and hospitality proved unbelievable."

At the formal dedication, former Pirates pitcher and television commentator Nellie Briles introduced Chuck to the crowd of guests. The Rainer Devido Stone Company had carved a slab of hand-polished South African granite weighing 4,200 pounds and standing five feet tall into a monument placed on the field reading:

"The most important thing one must do in order to be successful is never quit! The second most important thing one must do is never quit. But the most important thing of all is...Never Quit!"

Chuck Tanner

Pitcher John Candelaria, who rarely attended such functions, remained the entire day for the ceremony. Chuck always had said of Candy, "If I had to pick one pitcher to win a big game, he'd be my choice." Dave Giusti,

Manny Sanguillén and Kent Tekulve joined the former Pirates who came to honor their former manager.

Teke roasted his former boss about the monument. "If you asked me, they should show Chuck with his right hand on my shoulder ordering me back onto the mound to pitch." Most of the crowd remembered Chuck had called on Tekulve to appear in ninety-four regular-season games in 1979 plus seven more during the playoffs and the World Series.

State Representative Frank LaGrotta had obtained a grant to purchase a scoreboard, bleachers, flagpole and fencing for the newly named Tanner Field. "I was thrilled with the honor," Chuck, almost speechless for once in his life, told the crowd. "I understand the most meaningful recognition one can earn is that received in your own backyard."

Although Chuck rarely bragged about his accomplishments, he possessed a dry sense of humor. After attending a plaque-hanging ceremony at Miller Field honoring the 1955 Milwaukee Braves, family friend Mike Saginak told him, "Oh, you get your name along that of Hall of Fame member Hank Aaron."

"No, he gets his name with mine," Chuck smirked without cracking a smile or skipping a beat.

"THE MOST IMPORTANT THING ONE MUST DO IN ORDER TO BE SUCCESSFUL IS NEVER QUIT!

THE SECOND MOST IMPORTANT THING ONE MUST DO TO BE SUCCESSFUL IS NEVER QUIT

BUT THE MOST IMPORTANT THING OF ALL IS... NEVER QUIT!"

CHUCK TANNER

Chuck Tanner monument at Shenango High School. *Author's collection.*

Steve Blass vividly remembered his experience at the January 23–30, 2005 fantasy baseball camp. Nellie Briles acted as the camp director, and Hall of Fame second baseman Bill Mazeroski, outfielder Bill Virdon and pitchers Elroy Face, Bob Friend, Cy Young winner Vernon Law, Steve Blass and Bob Walk attended. Chuck Tanner served as the camp commissioner.

At one time, Steve Blass had been one of the finest pitchers in baseball. In 1972, he won nineteen games and played on the National League All-Star team. The next year, he had trouble getting the ball over the home plate. Chuck sympathized with Steve Blass's mysterious loss of control

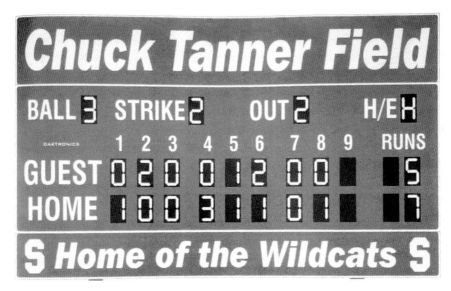

Sign at Shenango's Tanner Field. *Author's collection.*

after a sterling career in which he won more than one hundred games. A camper had been agitating Steve all week, and Chuck politely asked, "Do you want to pitch to this guy or not? You don't have to." Blass refused the out and pitched. He threw a wild fastball, which soared high above the plate for ball four.

Chuck worried about how this might affect his pitcher and friend. He walked to the mound and said, "Steve, do you want out of here?"

"No, Chuck, let me try the next guy."

Blass completed the game at McKechnie Field without giving up a run. Chuck came up to him after the game and said. "Hey, great game. That was fun, wasn't it?"

Chuck brought Blass in for another game for three more shut-out innings. Sixty-three-year-old Steve Blass threw eight and two-thirds innings without giving up a run. Chuck's encouragement certainly helped. Steve still had it, but so did Chuck.[92]

During the regular season, Chuck made an effort to attend the home games at PNC Park, often accompanied by New Castle friends who drove. Chuck's loyalty to his hometown and love of his beloved Pirates rarely waned, even when he scouted for another team.

In 2006, former Pirate and Houston Astro's manager Phil Garner named Chuck as honorary captain at PNC Park for the July 11 National League All-

Star game. Chuck also received the honor of tossing out the ceremonial first pitch. Reappearing in the stadium meant the world to him, and he treasured the National League All-Star ring given to him. Chuck truly appreciated Phil's remembrance of his old manager and friend.

As Babs's health declined, Chuck spent more time with her at the Jameson Care Center. She could no longer take care of herself. Don Daugherty remembered his own mother sitting beside Babs. Chuck fed both women with a spoon while offering encouragement. His kindness appeared evident to anyone who witnessed his actions.

Less than a month later, on August 9, his best friend, seventy-eight-year-old Barbara "Babs" Joann Weiss Tanner, died at the Jameson Hospital. She had been confined to a wheelchair for much of the time since she suffered a heart attack and a stroke in 1998. Phil Garner described Babs as "a wonderful lady. We were all blessed to be part of her life." Chuck could only say, "She is in a better place now. I like to think that she has gone to that big baseball diamond in the sky." New Castle folks remembered Babs as the family boss who raised her four boys during Chuck's baseball career, a sustaining mother and loyal wife with an angelic soul.

Bruce said he had not known Chuck as well as he would have liked growing up. "He was gone so much. We bonded with baseball as I got older. As I pitched and coached, I learned to respect him for his knowledge of the game, managerial skills and ability to create teamwork, but when mom grew ill and he took such good care of her, I learned to admire him for the fine human being he was. He had a good heart, and when mom was at the Jameson Care Center, I saw him feeding a woman who had no one there to care for her. If a man demonstrates kindness when he thinks no one is watching, then you know this is a special person."

Babs had allowed Chuck to follow his dream from minor-league player to a major-league player, manager and later a scout. She had watched over the family, provided guidance for her children and kept Chuck and the Tanner brood firmly grounded. If Chuck stood out as a public hero, Babs's persona reminded everyone who knew her of the immortal words of the poet John Milton in *Paradise Lost*: "They also serve who stand and wait." She, too, was a hero.

Reverend Andrew Jillison of Northminster Presbyterian Church officiated over a private family service and interment at the Castle View Memorial Garden. Fuzzy Fazzone believed that Chuck buried his World Series ring with Babs as a sign of his love and with the certitude that he would be reunited with his beloved wife and his ring in the next life.

Reverend John Yergen had known Chuck "face to face" since the time Babs had first required hospitalization. He now acted as an even more important support for the grieving husband. Chuck became a different guy after losing Babs. She had served as his rock, a grounding force who had been the love of his life since high school. He carried on, but he faced a huge void.

Chuck returned to scouting to keep busy and soothe his sadness. He recognized that death stood as a part of the human existence and that he and his wife would meet in the afterlife, but he missed Babs. He ate dinner at Tanner's five nights a week and maintained his usual upbeat exterior, but inside he hurt.

On April 21, 2007, the community honored former Pirates All-Star pitcher and color commentator Steve Blass and Chuck at an affair held at New Castle's Scottish Rite Cathedral. After Chuck received a proclamation, he showed stage manager Bob McKibben the gift certificate he received. "Would you look at this, I just received a gift card for Tanner's Restaurant," but Chuck took it in stride, laughing off the gaff.

The Pittsburgh Rotary Club initiated the Chuck Tanner Manager of the Year Award in November of that year in which it honored manager Joe Torre of the Los Angeles Dodgers. Three years later, Rotary added a Chuck Tanner Baseball Collegiate Manager of the Year Award, with the University of Pittsburgh's Joe Jordano as its first recipient.

Chuck's health slowly deteriorated following the loss of Babs. He ended up at Jameson Hospital in 2007 with a loss of blood from a bleeding ulcer. He went to bed on April 30 after the Pirates-Chicago Cubs game and woke up around five o'clock in the morning. When he went to the bathroom, he saw the bowl filled with blood. He called his son Gary, who took him to the hospital. A blood transfusion and surgery followed. Jim Leyland sent flowers, and Dave Parker, Bill Madlock, Al Monchak and Tony Bartirome all called to wish him a speedy recovery. After two weeks, Chuck returned home. The nurses told him they never had a better patient. "In fact, they told me I picked them up."[93]

Whether sick or healthy, Chuck remained in touch with his fan base, creating new ones every day. He visited the third-grade class at the Kennedy School after his release from the hospital, where he told baseball stories to the kids, who ate up his enthusiasm.

When Frank Coonelly became president of the Pirates in late 2007 and Neil Huntington the general manager, the team determined to remedy a terrible oversight. The new executives hired Chuck as a senior advisor.

Chuck attended team meetings and spring training at Bradenton, Florida, where he roamed the field and assessed talent. He loved being back with Pittsburgh and relished the honor.

However, Chuck's physical endurance had eroded, and the family did not want Chuck to drive the more than one thousand miles to Florida on his own for spring training. Fuzzy Fazzone, a former New Castle native, volunteered to fly from his home in Bradenton, where he worked as a probation officer, to Pittsburgh and then drive Chuck's car to Pirate City in late February for the preseason. Since Fuzzy's twin brother and other family members still lived in the area and he worked on salary, the trip worked well for Fuzzy. The drive to Florida allowed him to spend a few days with Chuck while they discussed baseball along the way.

Fuzzy met Chuck at Tanner's Restaurant around nine o'clock in the morning as prearranged. Chuck offered to pay him for his missed time at work and air expenses. Fuzzy at first declined. Chuck took out his wallet—he always carried a lot of cash—and began to count out hundreds. "You tell me when to stop."

"You don't have to pay me. I enjoy the trip."

Chuck ignored the answer. "Let's see, one, two, you tell me when to stop, three, four…." Chuck hesitated.

"I didn't tell you to stop." Chuck gave Fuzzy a look but counted another $100.

"You don't have to do this." Chuck handed him the $500, but Fuzzy would have done it for free and been happy.

Tanner played an active role with the Pirates for two years until his fragile health nosedived. Even then, he remained in close touch with the team. Chuck often could be found bantering baseball with good friend and former manager Jim Leland at the Pirate games. He and Leland held another trait in common. Both made it a point personally to answer all their fan mail and phone calls. As Dave Trembley so aptly described Chuck, "You don't have to be a big leaguer to be in the big leagues."

Once they reached Bradenton, Fuzzy frequently joined the team in the locker room as a guest. "I stayed until Chuck announced a clubhouse meeting, a signal for me to make myself scarce."

Chuck and Fuzzy ate out together from time to time in Bradenton. On one chilly and rainy day, Fuzzy ordered pasta fagioli soup at the Michelangelo Pizzeria and announced, "This is the best pasta fagioli I ever had."

"Is it as good as Gus's?" Chuck referred to Gus at Tanner's Restaurant.

"I think it is."

David "Fuzzy" Fazzone. *David Fazzone.*

"Are you sure?"

The debate continued. Fuzzy remembered Chuck loving to hash and rehash minor details *ad infinitum* but all in good fun.

In August 2008, with Chuck's strength ebbing, Dick Allen picked him up, and the two drove the 422 miles from New Castle to Cooperstown, New York, to surprise Rich Gossage during his induction ceremony into the Baseball Hall of Fame. Goose thanked a host of his supporters but forgot to mention Chuck. As soon as the ceremony ended, Gossage rushed to Tanner to apologize for the omission. Although the lack of recognition stung, Chuck rarely held grudges. He understood that the star reliever had gotten caught up in the excitement of the moment and accidentally missed thanking the manager who had converted him to a reliever. Chuck forgave and forgot. As usual, Mr. Tanner proved the consummate gentleman.

In December 2008, Chuck ended up back in the Jameson Hospital with blood in his bladder. The day before the required surgery, he woke to find that someone had slipped a ring off his pinky finger and stolen it. Chuck told the press that he was far more interested in the return of the item than prosecuting the thief. "If they return it, that's good enough for me. I don't want to put anyone in a bad situation, especially right before Christmas."

Chicago White Sox owner Allyn had given him that ring as a gift after his second-place finish in the American League West in 1972 following a string of losing seasons. His boss had made the one-of-a-kind, yellow gold and black onyx ring with an embossed pitcher on one side and a batter on the other. Chuck estimated its value at $10,000. Chuck recovered from his surgery, but the thief never returned the ring.

In March 2009, Chuck's health issues required surgery. Doctors implanted seven wire-mesh stents to open the arteries in his heart. He had trouble breathing before the operation, but the stents helped. He exercised on a treadmill at the house to rehab. However, the years of baseball and travel had taken their toll. He never fully regained his strength.

He continued with the Pirates on special assignment. On Saturday, August 22, he took his grandsons Jordan and Trent to PNC Park to watch the Pirates rout the Cincinnati Reds by a 12–2 score and enjoy a thirty-year reunion of the 1979 veterans. Due to the stents, Chuck had to sit in a wheelchair. The boys were thrilled, and Jordan said, "Hey Chuck, I didn't know so many people knew you. Anywhere we go, we can hardly move." Although four of his former players had died—Willie Stargell, Bill Robinson, Dave Roberts and John Milner—twenty-two attended the reunion.

Chuck loved both strategizing and arguing. He asked Fuzzy to check a 2010 pamphlet and pick his squad of twenty-five players. Fuzzy took the obvious picks and added a few to his squad. Chuck looked over the list and pronounced, "Not bad, but where is your left-handed reliever?"

Fuzzy explained, "I chose the best relievers available."

"You forgot a lefty," came back the quick retort.

"Even if the righty is better?"

Chuck offered a coy half smile. "Fuzzy, there you go again, always arguing when you should be listening." Fuzzy relished those exchanges, although he never seemed to come out on top.

Chuck's illnesses accumulated and weakened him with each passing year. He found himself in Manatee Hospital in Bradenton after passing blood again. The staff treated him like a VIP and released him after a short stay.

"Fuzzy," Chuck asked, "would you take these baseballs to the hospital for the nurses?" Chuck handed him a sock filled with a dozen signed balls as a thank-you. He never forgot a courtesy and always reciprocated. Signed Chuck Tanner baseballs became a common souvenir in Florida, as he gave out scores as thank-you gifts.

Chuck continued as an adviser to General Manager Neil Huntington after his surgery, but he only offered suggestions. Some trades he agreed with, others not. "We needed pitching. We didn't have anybody in the farm system. Nobody threw in the high nineties.…We have a kid named Andrew McCutchen who is going to be an outstanding center fielder. We have some ones that we traded for, but it doesn't mean they are going to be superstars. We traded some good players away to get these guys. It's not for me to say, 'Get this guy or get that guy.' I make suggestions. I don't know if they listen. That's up to them."

On Saturday, June 13, 2009, Chuck and Kent Tekulve jointly threw out the first pitch in a game against Detroit and thoroughly enjoyed watching Zach Duke earn a 9–3 victory. Chuck rarely missed a home game, but his body had begun to disappoint him. That iron grip and the excess physical energy had disappeared.

To the question "How are you doing living alone?" he answered a reporter, "I miss Babs. Of course I do after all these years. But I know she's in a better place because she was really hurting. We used to have a hospital bed right here. (He pointed next to his living room couch.) Poor thing, we had to have a lift to get her out of bed and put her in the chair and put the lift back and put her in bed. She had a miserable time. My kids have been really good: Bruce and his wife, Kim; Gary and his wife, Jane. They were great with her. Without their help it wouldn't have been that nice for her."

Life had closed in on Chuck. He rarely went downstairs and stuck to just four or five rooms in the house. Grandson Mat frequently visited, and Chuck appreciated the companionship and conversation. When Mat found two boxes of old records, he asked Chuck, "What are you going to do with these?"

"Probably throw them out."

"Can I take them?"

"Sure, they're yours."

Mat, a budding musician, took them home and tossed out all the soft music and gospels, picking the heavy metal and hard rock groups like AC/DC to keep for his own use. Eventually, he discovered a seventy-eight in a plain white wrapper marked "WEMP Milwaukee." Neatly written in pen beside the word *program* were the words "First time up in the majors." Mat instantly knew what the record contained. Although his phono didn't have a seventy-eight speed, he twirled it with his fingers to listen to the announcer describe Chuck's home run on the first pitch of his initial appearance in the major leagues in 1955.

Mat recorded his personal version of "The Star-Spangled Banner" with his guitar on a CD, followed by the description of the historic home run, which included the words, "This is something Chuck Tanner will one day tell his grandchildren."

Mat took the CD to Chuck's Maitland Lane home for his birthday. Chuck beamed with pride as Mat played his rendition of the national anthem, a song he had heard thousands of times in dozens of minor- and major-league ball parks.

"Mat, that was terrific."

When Chuck heard the CD echo the excitement of his first at bat with Milwaukee, he thought this might be his best birthday present ever.

WEMP phonograph record of Chuck Tanner's first home run. *Mat Tanner.*

Even as Chuck's body faltered, his spirit held firm. "I've had the greatest life in the world. How many guys can say they won a World Series in their own backyard? How can that happen to a kid from Shenango?"

Mat, his tattooed grandson, had worn long-sleeve shirts when he visited Chuck. "I worried that my tattoos might freak out my grandfather if I stayed at the house to help." When the family mentioned Mat's concern to Chuck, he answered, "I don't care about his tattoos. I just want him around."

Mat noticed that his grandfather had not been eating well, but Chuck would beg off with "I'm just not hungry." Mat went to Coney Island, grabbed a few hot dogs and told Chuck, "Hey, I had a couple extras. Why don't you take them." Chuck accepted because they were "extras."

Mat sometimes picked up Chuck's mail as his grandfather's legs began to fail him. Almost every day, Chuck received requests for an autograph, and Chuck tried to answer every letter. Chuck knew that Mat had artistic skills, and on occasions when he felt particularly weak, he asked Mat to sign for him. "Sometimes I could copy his signature exactly; other times, not so convincingly," Mat confessed.

One day, Mat's father, Bruce, advised him about an obvious fake being listed on eBay. The two replaced that fake with a genuine signature, but they recognized that a few fakes still might be floating around here and there.

Eventually, the family recognized that Chuck no longer could live alone in his Maitland Lane home. He needed help and support. Chuck would spend his final months in hospice at the Jameson Care Center.

John Yergan of First Baptist Church visited him frequently while he remained at the Jameson. "I saw him often, and we discussed spiritual matters. He always remained open to prayer and the reading of God's word." Baseball friends and acquaintances called in droves to wish him well. Fuzzy Fazzone recalled Hall of Fame player and manager Frank Robinson telephoning to cheer up Chuck while he visited.

In October, Chuck faced a twenty-one-and-a-half-hour surgery to scoop out the lining of his lungs to enrich his breathing capacity. In early January, Chuck ended up at the Jameson Hospital fighting a bacterial stomach infection as a result of the operation.

Son Bruce reported that during the first few days, "He was doing lousy, but Frank Coonelly, the Pittsburgh Pirates president, came up to see him, and it seemed to light a spark in him. He told Frank he wasn't giving up....We talked to his doctor, Dr. Thomas Malvar, and he gave us an improved report."[94]

The staff hoped that a course of antibiotics might kill the infection. Daughter-in-law Kimberly said, "He made me watch the Steelers game, so

I know he is feeling better....When he's asleep, you can tell he's dreaming because he's putting out two fingers, giving signs. Even when he's battling something like he is right now, he literally eats, sleeps and dreams baseball." Unfortunately, Chuck's rally proved short-lived.

Jack Zduriencik visited Chuck right before Christmas at the Jameson Care Center. "I made a point of visiting with Chuck at least once a year. We spoke for several minutes, but he looked worn out. He told me 'Jack, you know Babs and I will be together again soon.' Then, he looked up at me and said, 'You should go now and be with your family for the holidays.' That was the last time we ever saw each other."

Car dealer Bill Fitz, who had gone to school with one of his sons, visited Chuck at the Jameson Care to say hello. "Chuck, did you hear Andy Pettitte just retired?"

"No, but he was a great pitcher and a nice guy." Chuck appeared to still have his wits about him, especially when it came to baseball.[95]

A few days before Chuck's passing, former Cy Young–winning pitcher and Johnstown native Pete Vuckovich sat quietly by Chuck's bed at the Jameson Care facility on Wilmington Road when Jim Leyland entered the room to visit his old friend. "He could not even lift his head. Chuck had been a powerful man, and it was sad to see him so weak and helpless. I knew this would be our final visit together," Leyland said.

Chuck Tanner died on Friday, February 11, 2011, one day before his and Babs's anniversary, at the Jameson Care center at age eighty-two of prostate cancer and a weak heart, shortly before the start of spring training, what he called "the best time of the year."[96] His son Bruce said, "He was just worn out."

Chuck died with his daughter-in-law Kimberly holding his hand. His last words, according to Mat, were, "I had a good life." Chuck never complained, but his medicine cabinet—filled with Tylenol, Advil and prescription drugs—told the story of a body decimated by his years of sports. A heating pad and assorted knee braces lay beside him in the bedroom.

When advised of his friend's death, Tommy Lasorda said, "Rest in peace. I loved you like a brother." When asked for a comment, Manny Sanguillén, owner of Manny's Bar-B-Q at PNC Park, repeated Lasorda's tribute in heavily accented English, "He was my brother."

Kimberly Tanner, Bruce's wife, drove her car behind the Tuscany Restaurant, where Mat worked. Mat knew that Chuck had been rapidly failing in hospice. "He's gone," Kim told her son, but Mat realized why his mom had come without her telling him.

"Do you want to come home?" his mother asked.

Mat knew how much his grandfather admired hard work—how he reacted when he had a World Series to win in 1979 after his own mother's death. He ran the question through his mind. Would Chuck have wanted me to go home or finish the day's work? When he returned to the kitchen, his boss excused him for the day, but Mat remained. "I finished the day just like I thought Chuck would have done, just like he would have wanted me to do."

Hundreds filled the Cunningham Funeral home on February 15, lining up to pay their respects. The family requested that in lieu of flowers memorial donations be sent to the Chuck Tanner "We Are Family" Fund, care of Pirate Charities. Any gifts would provide an award for the minor-league employee who best exemplified Chuck's enthusiasm.

In Chuck's honor, the entire Pirates team wore a black-and-gold no. 7 patch inside a Stargell star on their right sleeves throughout the 2012 baseball season.

Reporter Kayleen Cubbal wrote, "Chuck Tanner worked with kings, yet he was everyman, living everyman's life in everyman's hometown. He did his own shopping, pumped his own gas, did his own banking and ate low-cost meals at Chuck Tanner's restaurant, the New Castle eatery that continued to bear his name even after he sold it years ago. The home in which he lived for decades, while quite nice, no doubt was beneath his means. Perhaps the only thing that set New Castle's favorite son apart from the crowd would be the signature floppy hat, an item that became so popular that the Pirates produced one for a fan giveaway several years back."

Chuck's old friend, former Pirate player and later manager Phil Garner, put the moment in perspective: "It's a sad day but we've got to keep with Chuck's spirit. He would tell us to be sad for about thirty seconds, then to celebrate his life. Yes, the sun will come out tomorrow." Garner added for effect, "I have no doubt in my mind that Chuck Tanner patted God on the back and said, 'You'll have a good day tomorrow.'"

New Castle native and baseball executive Jack Zduriencik of the Seattle Mariners eulogized his compatriot: "To the baseball world he created his legacy as a manager, but to those who knew him, his legacy was as a great person."

Quite fittingly, Chuck wore a suit with a Pirates tie during the viewing. His Pirates cap and no. 7 game jersey lay at his side. Team president Frank Coonelly, John Candelaria, Kent Tekulve, Grant Jackson, Steve Blass, Bob Walk, Dave Giusti, Ken Macha, Al Monchak, Steve Blass, Pete Vuckovich,

Dave Littlefield and announcer Rob King, among others, stood among the baseball royalty who paid homage to Chuck "Lefty" Tanner.

Teke wore a blue tie with four stars since Chuck had been born on the Fourth of July. All the team attendees wore a lapel pin with Chuck's no. 7. Bob Walk stated that he kept his Stargell star with the seven on a bathroom mirror of his Wexford home as a reminder of his friend and former manager.

Many who could not attend, like Manny Sanguillén and Franco Harris, sent floral tributes. Chuck became the eighth member of the 1979 championship team to die, preceded by pitching coach Harvey Haddix in 1994 and players John Milner in 2000, Willie Stargell in 2001, Bill Robinson in 2007, Dock Ellis in 2008, Dave Roberts in 2009 and Jim Bibby in 2010.

The Cunningham Funeral Home received 165 letters of condolences from friends and fans throughout the country. Betsy Melman Carney, daughter of a co-founder of the Pennsylvania Sports Hall of Fame, wrote, "Chuck chose to honor us with his presence at our annual induction dinners. He was never too busy to take a few minutes to speak with a fan or sign an autograph. He was more than a great manager. He was a kind, caring and terrific man who will be missed, not just by Pirates fans, but by everyone whose life he touched."

Mat Tanner, Bruce Tanner's eldest son and Chuck's grandson, described a moment when most of the people had left Cunningham's at the end of calling hours. As the family prepared to leave, a stranger in a plaid jacket entered the room.

"I apologize for my lateness," he said. "I had to drive from out of town. I want to explain why I had to come to pay my respects. One night I sat at a bar in total depression. Life had not worked out well for me. I even considered ending it all. I found myself at the end of my rope with nowhere to go. A man I never had met sat on the stool next to me, and over a beer I described each negative that went through my mind. Depression had crushed me. With each problem I presented, the man countered with a positive. He sat quietly and listened like he really cared, although we were strangers. Somehow, the darkness that clouded my thoughts disappeared, and I drank in less of my beer and more of his positivity. By the time he had gotten up to leave, I had regained hope. After nearly an hour of conversation, we shook hands, and he departed without telling me much about himself other than his first name, Chuck."

The man continued his story, "A few minutes later, someone came up to me and prodded, 'Do you know who you were talking to?' I told him I had no idea. He then explained who Chuck was and what he did. In a single hour, that man changed my outlook on life. How could I not come tonight and pay my respects?"

"The stranger shook our hands, thanked us for listening to his story, offered his condolences and departed." The family never learned his name or exactly what Chuck had said to him, but Mat recognized that Chuck Tanner indeed had changed another man for the better.

As Ron Cook said, "Chuck Tanner lived life as we all should, always looking for the best in everybody and every situation." Everyone joked, "You can take Chuck Tanner out of New Castle, but you can't take New Castle out of Chuck Tanner."

When it came time to clean out Chuck's house after he had died, grandson Mat picked out a photo of Chuck in a Los Angeles Angels uniform at the tail end of his major-league playing career from either 1961 or 1962, signing an autograph on a program for two obviously thrilled youngsters. This would be exactly how Chuck would have wanted to be remembered—as a purveyor of joy to fans of all ages.

Chuck Tanner with two admiring fans. "How I most like to remember him." *Mat Tanner.*

Chuck Tanner. *Collection of attorney Carmen Lamencusa.*

Even today, Chuck Tanner is not forgotten. Reverend John Yergen told me that he visits the cemetery on holidays to place flowers on Chuck and Babs's graves, something he does for others as well. "Chuck has brought pride to New Castle with his many accomplishments, but more than that, he has taught us all the creed of positivity and hard work." He treated every moment of his life as a time to be celebrated.

Stories abound of his good deeds. Jean Mill appreciated Chuck's visit to granddaughter Patti-Lynn Mill, who had been diagnosed with a brain tumor. The child treasured the signed baseball Chuck gave her. Although Chuck was a star, he treated everyone he knew like a star.

There are heroes for the minutes, heroes for the day, heroes for the year and heroes for a lifetime. Chuck Tanner falls into that select group of New Castle heroes for the ages. Thank you, Chuck Tanner, for being Chuck Tanner.

TIMELINE

July 1, 1928
Charles Wilson Tanner Jr. is born to Charles and Anna Baka Tanner.

June of 1946
Graduates from Shenango High School.

June of 1946
Signs a minor-league contact with the Boston Braves organization.

February 12, 1950
Chuck and Barbara "Babs" Weiss marry.

1954 Season
Bats .323 with twenty home runs for the AAA Atlanta Crackers.

April 12, 1955
Hits home run on the first pitch of his first at bat in the major leagues for Milwaukee.

June 8, 1957
Picked up on waivers by the Chicago Cubs.

1957
Bats .286 with seven homers and forty-two RBIs for Chicago, his best year in the major leagues.

March 9, 1959
Traded by the Chicago Cubs to the Boston Red Sox for Bob Smith.

September 9, 1959
Traded to the Cleveland Indians by the Red Sox.

September 8, 1961
Traded to the Los Angeles Angels by Cleveland.

1963 Season
Retires as player to manage the Class A Quad City Braves in Davenport, Iowa.

1968
Wins Minor League Manager of the Year at El Paso.

1970 Season
Shares Minor League Manager of the Year at Hawaii with Tommy Lasorda.

September, 1970
Promoted to manage the Chicago White Sox.

1972
Receives American League Manager of the Year Award with the White Sox.

1976
Manages the Oakland Athletics.

1977
Hired to manage the Pittsburgh Pirates.

1979
Wins World Series in seven games over the Baltimore Orioles.

1980
Manages National League All-Star team to a 4–2 victory.

1985
Fired from the Pittsburgh Pirates due to the drug trials and a losing record.

1986–87
Manages the Atlanta Braves.

1988
Fired by Atlanta and becomes managing partner in Majesty's Imp, a racing horse.

1991
Special assistant to the general manager of the Milwaukee Brewers as a professional scout.

2003–7
Scouts for the Cleveland Indians.

July 31, 2004
Shenango High School Field is renamed Chuck Tanner Field.

2008
Named senior advisor for the Pittsburgh Pirates.

2010
Rotary Club of Pittsburgh announces Chuck Tanner Collegiate Manager of the Year Award.

February 11, 2011
Chuck Tanner dies at eighty-two years old.

CHUCK TANNER STATS

HITTING STATISTICS, MINOR LEAGUES

Year	Team	Games	Bats	Hits	2B	3B	HR	RBI	BA
1946	Owensboro (D)	23	80	20	3	1	0	7	.250
1947	Owensboro (D)	25	104	35	9	3	0		.337
1947	Eau Claire (C)	40	151	49	6	3	7	27	.325
1948	Eau Claire (C)	67	263	95	22	5	7		.361
1948	Pawtucket (B)	46	171	47	1	6	2		.275
1949	Denver (A)	124	467	146	32	5	5	53	.313
1950	Denver (A)	154	619	195	34	9	7		.315
1951	Atlanta (AA)	134	506	161	28	6	4	44	.318
1952	Atlanta (AA)	117	440	152	18	11	2		.345
1952	Milwaukee (AAA)	11	27	4	1	1	0	4	.148
1953	Atlanta (AA)	126	465	148	29	11	6	57	.318
1953	Toledo (AAA)	17	52	10	3	0	2	5	.192
1954	Atlanta (AA)	155	594	192	35	12	20	101	.323
1959	Minneapolis (AAA)	152	549	175	41*	10	12	78	.319
1960	Toronto (AAA)	28	92	27	5	2	4	14	.293
1961	Toronto (AAA)	70	218	49	5	3	6	22	.225

Year	Team	Games	Bats	Hits	2B	3B	HR	RBI	BA
1961	Dallas (AA2)	48	170	51	12	5	1	18	.300
1962	Dallas (AA2)	114	359	113	28	2	5	41	.315
1968	El Paso (AA)	1	1	0	0	0	0	0	.000
14-Year Totals		**1,452**	**5,328**	**1,669**	**312**	**95**	**90**	**471***	**.313**

Note: Minor League statistics for RBIs are incomplete.
*Led American Association in doubles.

HITTING STATISTICS, MAJOR LEAGUES

Year	Age	Team	Games	Bats	Runs	Hits	2B	3B	HR	RBI	BA
1955	27	Braves	97	243	27	60	9	3	6	27	.247
1956	28	Braves	60	63	6	15	2	0	1	4	.238
1957	29	Braves	22	69	5	17	3	0	2	6	.246
1957	29	Cubs	95	318	42	91	16	2	7	42	.286
1958	30	Cubs	73	103	10	27	6	0	4	17	.262
1959	31	Indians	14	48	6	12	2	0	1	5	.250
1960	32	Indians	21	25	2	7	1	0	0	4	.280
1961	33	Angels	7	8	0	1	0	0	0	0	.125
1962	34	Angels	7	8	0	1	0	0	0	0	.125
8-Year Totals			**396**	**885**	**98**	**231**	**39**	**5**	**21**	**105**	**.261**

MANAGING RECORD, MINOR LEAGUES

Year	Age	Team	Wins	Losses
1963	34	Quad City (A)	66	57
1964	35	Quad City (A)	62	56
1965	36	El Paso (AA)	53	87
1966	37	El Paso (AA)	62	78
1967	38	Seattle (AAA)	69	79
1968	39	El Paso (AA)	77*	60
1969	40	Hawaii (AAA)	74	72
1970	41	Hawaii (AAA)	98*	48
8-Year Totals			**561**	**537**

*Won division title.

MANAGING STATISTICS, MAJOR LEAGUES

Year	Age	Team	Wins	Losses
1970	41	White Sox	3	13
1971	42	White Sox	79	83
1972	43	White Sox	87	67
1973	44	White Sox	77	85
1974	45	White Sox	80	80
1975	46	White Sox	75	86
1976	47	Oakland A's	87	74
1977	48	Pirates	96	66
1978	49	Pirates	88	73
1979	50	Pirates	98*	64
1980	51	Pirates	83	79
1981	52	Pirates	46	56
1982	53	Pirates	84	78
1983	54	Pirates	84	78
1984	55	Pirates	75	87
1985	56	Pirates	57	104
1986	57	Atlanta	72	89
1987	58	Atlanta	69	92
1988	59	Atlanta	12	27
19-Year Totals			**1,352**	**1,381**

*Won division, pennant and World Series.

NOTES

Chapter 2

1. Newspaperman and neighbor Bob Melder mentioned that a man named Fall once owned the tract of land that he subdivided and sold for residential parcels.
2. O'Brien, *We Had 'Em All the Way*, 109.

Chapter 3

3. Future major leaguers Bill Ayers, slick-fielding first baseman Frank Torre (the elder brother of Hall of Fame member Joe Torre), Bob Trowbridge, Roy Jarvis, Virgil Jester, Earl Hersh, Leo Cristante, George Estock, Dick Donovan (a twenty-game winner for the Cleveland Indians), Bob Giggie, Gary Gearhart, Nat Peeples, Pete Whisenant, Junior Wooten, Don McMahon (an eighteen-year major leaguer who finished his career with 152 saves, 90 wins and an ERA of 2.96) and Chuck Tanner all played on the 1954 Atlanta Crackers.
4. See Vosburg, *Scooter's Days*.
5. O'Brien, *We Had 'Em All the Way*, 105.
6. Condon, "In the Wake of the News."

Chapter 4

7. Gene Lamont, a Detroit catcher with only four home runs in his career, would duplicate Tanner's feat in 1970. Like Chuck, Lamont would manage the Pirates between the years 1997 and 2000, accumulating a 553-562 record.

8. Sahadi, *Pirates*, 4.

9. Lew Grell and his wife, Pam, both earned election to the Lawrence County Hall of Fame—Pam in 2006 based on her scores of equestrian ribbons and trophies and Lew in 2008 through a long and successful baseball playing and officiating career.

10. Second baseman Chet Boak would play ten games in the majors for Kansas City. Gary Peters would become a 20-game winner for the Chicago White Sox in 1964 and would win 124 games over a fourteen-year career.

11. Early Wynn, a mean one on the mound, won that game by a 4–2 score for his twenty-first victory. He went on to earn a total of twenty-two games and lead the American League with victories in 1959.

Chapter 5

12. O'Brien, *We Had 'Em All the Way*, 392.

13. Ibid., 106.

14. Liptak, "Conversation with Chuck Tanner."

15. Chuck eventually left this position after his promotion to the majors as a manager. Joe Castiglione, a broadcasting talent fresh out of Syracuse and Colgate Universities, would replace him and advance to a long and successful career as a Boston Red Sox announcer.

Chapter 6

16. McCollister, *Tales from the 1979 Pittsburgh Pirates*, 105–6.

17. Society for Baseball Research website.

18. Abrams, "Sidelights on Sports."

19. Condon, "In the Wake of the News."

20. Jack Zduriencik never may have made it to the big leagues as a player, but he excelled as an executive. The New Castle native worked as a scout, general manager of the Seattle Mariners and commentator for the Pittsburgh Pirates.

21. Kashatus, *Dick Allen*, 141.
22. Ibid., 145.
23. O'Brien, *We Had 'Em All the Way*, 104.
24. Wikipedia, "Dick Allen."
25. O'Brien, *We Had 'Em All the Way*, 103.
26. McCollister, *Tales from the 1979 Pittsburgh Pirates*, 98.
27. Jimmy Dykes spent twenty-two years in the majors between 1918 and 1939 as an outstanding second and third baseman and twenty-one years as the manager of the Chicago White Sox and five other teams.
28. *New Castle News*, December 28, 1971.
29. See Kashatus, *Dick Allen*.
30. Steinberg, "Harry Caray Obituary."

Chapter 7

31. Brown, "Retracing Tanner's Path to the Pirates."
32. Holmes, "When the Pirates Traded."
33. Valentine's sat on a postage stamp–sized lot on the corner of East Washington Street and Croton Avenue by a bridge. The parcel contained six separate businesses: Henry the Barber, Clooney's Bar, Tisch's Jewelry, Paula Stefano's Beauty Shop, Valentine's Restaurant and Kwolek's Photography, which was located upstairs. At some point, Clooney's closed, and Paula Stefano moved her beauty shop to an upstairs location in the building. Toward the end of the '80s, the Redevelopment Authority demolished the building and created a very tiny park.

Chapter 8

34. The New York Mets acquired manager Gil Hodges on November 27, 1967, from the Washington Senators for $100,000 and a player to be named later—Bill Denehy, a none-too-successful pitcher who amassed a 1-12 major-league record.
35. Brown, "Retracing Tanner's Path to the Pirates."
36. Fields, "Chuck Tanner."
37. In 2017, McKecknie became Lecom Field after Lake Erie College of Osteopathic Medicine purchased the naming rights.
38. Weber, "Chuck Tanner."

39. Sahadi, *Pirates*, 6–7.
40. The Texas Rangers traded Bert Blyleven to the Pirates after a television recording showed him giving a "finger" to the viewers. Pittsburgh gave up All-Star .300 hitter Al Oliver and shortstop prospect Nelson Norman in the deal.
41. Fields, "Chuck Tanner."
42. O'Brien, *We Had 'Em All the Way*, 107.

Chapter 9

43. On December 5, 1978, the Pirates traded pitchers Odell Jones and Rafael Vasquez along with slick-fielding, weak-hitting Mario Mendoza to the Seattle Mariners for reliever Enrique Romo, Rick Jones and Tom McMillan. Both Jones and McMillan never played for the Pirates and had little impact in the majors. However, Romo proved a key asset for the 1979 season, producing ten wins, five saves and a 2.99 ERA.
44. Sahadi, *Pirates*, 7–8.
45. Ibid., 9.
46. Weber, "Chuck Tanner."
47. McCollister, *Tales from the 1979 Pittsburgh Pirates*, 56.
48. Ibid., 76.
49. Ibid., 77.
50. After being fired by the San Francisco Giants and replaced by Dave Bristol in 1979, Joe Altobelli would return to the major leagues in 1983 to lead the Baltimore Orioles to a pennant and World Series victory.
51. "Chuck Tanner Tribute," YouTube.
52. Sahadi, *Pirates*, 56.
53. McCollister, *Tales from the 1979 Pittsburgh Pirates*, 39.
54. Ibid., 10.
55. Cous Little Italy, a mob hangout, gained additional notoriety in March 1981 after "business" rivals shot-gunned and killed Angelo Bruno outside the restaurant.
56. Interestingly, the Yankees' string of losses in 1964 continued for two more games against the Boston Red Sox before a 30-7 run delivered a pennant-cinching tear. After New York lost the World Series in seven games against the St. Louis Cardinals, the Yankees fired Yogi Berra as manager and replaced him with the winning Cardinals manager, Johnny Keane.

57. One-time Pittsburgh public relations director Joe Safety stated that John Candelaria had the neatest handwriting he had ever seen. John always wrote his last name first and then added his first name in front.
58. Willie Stargell still holds Pittsburgh's RBI record with a total of 1,540.
59. John Candelaria would suffer a lifetime of back pain and endure at least one surgery.
60. McCollister, *Tales from the 1979 Pittsburgh Pirates*, 132.
61. Schott, "October 5, 1979."
62. McCollister, *Tales from the 1979 Pittsburgh Pirates*, 104.

Chapter 10

63. Sahadi, *Pirates*, 10.
64. Klingaman, "79 Orioles Recall."
65. McCollister, *Tales from the 1979 Pittsburgh Pirates*, 141.
66. Ibid., 142.
67. Ibid., 146.
68. Ibid., 35.
69. Ibid., 110.
70. The 1925 Pittsburgh Pirates, the 1958 New York Yankees and the 1968 Detroit Tigers all had turned the tables to win the World Series after being down 3–1. Pirates manager Tanner added his name to the list, which through the year 2021 now includes six teams.
71. McCollister, *Tales from the 1979 Pittsburgh Pirates*, 150.
72. Anderson, "Your Mother Died."
73. McCollister, *Tales from the 1979 Pittsburgh Pirates*, 153.
74. Ibid., 174. Kent Tekulve questioned if this event actually happened.
75. Vernon Law recorded three saves in 1960. However, prior to 1969, saves were not considered an official statistic.
76. See Vosburg, *Scooter's Days*.

Chapter 11

77. The Cleveland Indians released Manny Sanguillén in February, probably due to the fact that the catcher had chosen to retire anyhow.
78. O'Brien, *We Had 'Em All the Way*, 108.

79. Ibid., 110.

80. Ibid.

81. Ibid., 354.

82. Cook, "Eighties."

83. Kovacevic, *Pittsburgh Post Gazette*, February 12, 2012.

Chapter 12

84. Fields, "Chuck Tanner."

85. O'Brien, *We Had 'Em All the Way*, 113.

Chapter 13

86. McCollister, *Tales from the 1979 Pittsburgh Pirates*, foreword.

87. *Los Angeles Times*, "Majesty's Imp."

88. O'Brien, *We Had 'Em All the Way*, 107.

89. Starkey, "1979 Pirates."

90. Garland, *Willie Stargell.*

91. The Committee also included a who's who of locals, including Greg Alexander, Jim Book, Jay Bruce, Jan Budai, Bill Carnahan, Tony Cialella, Jerry Gillette, Bob Hilton, Don Kirkwood, Walt Kustra, Frank LaGrotta, Carmen Lamancusa, Bob Montanari, Gus Konstantinos, Jim Snow Jr., Brad Stroia, Brian Tanner, Andrew J. Tommelleo, Butch Wehr, Archie Zarone and Jeff Ziegler.

92. Blass and Sherman, *Pirate for Life*, 220–21.

93. Cook, "Tanner Has a Lot of Life Left."

94. Cubbal, "Family Optimistic."

95. New York Yankee Andy Pettitte retired from baseball on February 4, 2011. The two-time twenty-game winner would sit out the 2011 season but return to play again in 2012 and 2013 and retire with a 256-153 record.

96. Kovacevic, *Pittsburgh Post Gazette*, February 12, 2012.

BIBLIOGRAPHY

Abrams, Al. "Sidelights on Sports." *Pittsburgh Post Gazette*, March 1971.

Anderson, Dave. "Your Mother Died at 7:40." *New York Times*, October 15, 1979.

AP News. "Rodney King Charged with Drunk Driving in Pennsylvania." May 22, 1995.

Blass, Steve, and Erik Sherman. *A Pirate for Life*. Chicago: Triumph Books, 2012.

Brown, Craig. "Retracing Tanner's Path to the Pirates." ESPN, February 13, 2011.

Bush, Frederick C. *SABR Virtual*. October 17, 1979.

"Chuck Tanner Tribute." YouTube, 2011. https://www.youtube.com/watch?v=uRpbusvnuxw.

Condon, David. "In the Wake of the News." *Chicago Tribune*, March 20, 1972.

Cook, Ron. "The Eighties: A Terrible Time of Trial and Error." *Pittsburgh Post Gazette*, September 29, 2000.

———. "Tanner Has a Lot of Life Left." *Pittsburgh Post Gazette*, May 28, 2007.

———. "Willie Stargell Memories Come Flooding In." *Pittsburgh Post Gazette*, March 27, 2020.

Cubbal, Kayleen. "Family Optimistic as Chuck Tanner's Health Improves." *New Castle News*, January 18, 2011.

———. "Love Everlasting: The Babs and Chuck Tanner Story." *New Castle News*, November 12, 2015.

Decourcy, Mike. "Why Game Five of the 1979 World Series Still Means So Much to Pittsburgh." *Sporting News*, October 14, 2019.

Dvorchak, Robert. "Chuck Tanner." *Pittsburgh Post Gazette*, July 11, 2002.

ESPN. "Pittsburgh Drug Trials." *30 for 30 Shorts*.

Feeney, Charley. "Blyleven Walks Out, Wants Trade." *Pittsburgh Post Gazette*, May 1, 1980.

Fendley, Scott. "The Most Disappointing Season for the Chicago White Sox." The Spitter, March 31, 2016.

Fields, Dan. "Chuck Tanner." Society for American Baseball Research.

Fimrite, Ron. "The Big Wind in Chicago." Sports Illustrated Vault, September 18, 1978. sportsillustratedvault.com.

Fredland, John. "Pennant Race Flashback—August 11, 1979." *Bucs Dugout*, August 11, 2015.

Garland, Frank. *Willie Stargell: A Life in Baseball*. Jefferson, NC: McFarland & Company, 2013.

Hasch, Michael. "Chuck Tanner Reports Ring Stolen While Hospital Patient." *Trib Live*, December 5, 2008.

HBO Sports. "Pittsburgh Drug Trials." August 7, 2015.

Holmes, Dan. "When the Pirates Traded for Baseball's Most Innovative Manager." Baseball EGG, July 19, 2020.

Kashatus, William C. *Dick Allen: The Life and Times of a Baseball Immortal*. Atglen, PA: Schiffer Publishing, 2017.

Klingaman, Mike. "79 Orioles Recall One of the Coldest World Series Games." *Baltimore Sun*, October 26, 2012.

Kovacevic, Dejan. "Chuck Tanner Obituary." *Pittsburgh Post Gazette*, February 12, 2011.

Kruse, Todd. "An Interview with Chuck Tanner." *New Castle News*, October, 2009.

Liptak, Mark. "A Conversation with Chuck Tanner." WSI Forum, November 11, 2021.

———. "This Day in White Sox History: Stu Holcomb Blows Up the Team." Soxnet, July, 27, 2016.

Los Angeles Times. "Majesty's Imp, a Potential Kentucky Derby Horse Was Withdrawn." May 3, 1989.

Margalus, Jim. "Tanner's Sox Fell Short, but His Stay Was Significant." SB Nation, February 11, 2011.

Markusen, Bruce. *The Team that Changed Baseball: Roberto Clemente and the 1971 Pittsburgh Pirates*. Yardley, PA: Westholme Publishing, 2006.

McCollister, John. *Tales from the 1979 Pittsburgh Pirates: Remembering "The Fam-a-Lee."* Champaign, IL: Sports Publishing, 2005.

McLennan, Jim. "Baseball's Greatest Scandals, the Pittsburgh Drug Scandals." SB Nation, April 26, 2012.

Milbert, Neil. "Tanner Goes from Dugout to Paddock in Derby Quest." *Chicago Tribune*, April 21, 1989.

Muder, Craig. "Chuck Tanner and the Pittsburgh Pirates." *Inside Pitch*, n.d.

Nathanson, Mitchell. *God Almighty Hisself: The Life and Legacy of Dick Allen.* Philadelphia: University of Pennsylvania Press, 2016.

O'Brien, Jim. *We Had 'Em All the Way.* Pittsburgh, PA: James P. O'Brien Publishing, 1998.

Parker, Dave, and Dave Jordan. *Cobra: A Life of Baseball and Brotherhood.* Lincoln: University of Nebraska Press, 2021.

Sahadi, Lou. *The Pirates: We Are Family.* New York: NYT Books, 1980.

Schott, Thomas. "October 5, 1979, a 'Family' Celebration as Pirates Sweep NLCS." SABR, 2016.

Staples, Gracie Bonds. "Atlanta Crackers Baseball History: A Celebration of the 1954 Championship Team." *Atlanta Journal-Constitution*, May 12, 2016.

Starkey, Joe. "The 1979 Pirates: A Testament to Teamwork." *Tribune-Review*, August 16, 2009.

Stefano, Paul. "Oral History Project—Baseball in Pennsylvania: Fred Shaffer." Interview, September 8, 1994.

Steinberg, Neil. "Harry Caray Obituary." *Chicago Sun Times*, February 19, 1998.

Stole, Lawrence. "Chuck Tanner's Winning Spirit Infecting White Sox." *Youngstown Vindicator*, March 1971.

Tanner, Chuck, and Jim Enright, eds. *The Official Major League Baseball Playbook.* New York: Prentice-Hall, 1974.

The Tomahawk. Shenango High School yearbook, 1945 and 1946.

Vosburg, Bob. "Chuck Tanner." In *Scooter's Days—1922–1971: A History of Sports in Lawrence County.* New Wilmington, PA: New Horizon's Publishing, 1997.

Weber, Bruce. "Chuck Tanner, Who Managed 1979 Pirates to World Title, Dies." *New York Times*, February 11, 2011.

West, Rob. "The World Is on Fire with Kevin Koch." *Cigar Store Idiots*, podcast, Episode 186, May 23, 2022.

Wikipedia. "Dick Allen." https://en.wikipedia.org/wiki/Dick_Allen.

————. "Pittsburgh Drug Trials." https://en.wikipedia.org/wiki/Pittsburgh_drug_trials.

ABOUT THE AUTHOR

Dale Richard Perelman—a native of New Castle, Pennsylvania, and retired president of the King's Jewelry retail chain—has written *Mountain of Light: The Story of the Koh-I-Noor Diamond*; *The Regent: The Story of the Regent Diamond*; *Centenarians: One Hundred 100-Year-Olds Who Made a Difference*; *Steel: The History of Pittsburgh's Iron and Steel Industry 1852–1902*; *Road to Rust: The Disintegration of the Steel Industry in Western Pennsylvania and Eastern Ohio*; *Lessons My Father Taught Me*; *The Scottish Rite Cathedral* (coauthored with Rob Cummings); *New Castle's Kadunce Murders: Mystery and the Devil in Northwest Pennsylvania*; and *Death at the Cecil Hotel in Los Angeles*. Perelman holds a Bachelor of Arts degree from Brown University in English Literature, an MBA from the Wharton School of the University of Pennsylvania, a Graduate Gemologist's designation from the Gemological Institute of America and a certificate of completion from the Yale University summer writer's program.